Personal Relations Theory

Personal relationships concern us all, they are essential to our becoming who we are and constitute our most vital experience of what it is like to be alive and human. This book proposes a new approach to understanding who we are based on the work of Ronald Fairbairn, John Macmurray and Ian Suttie, whose ideas provide a positive perspective on our future collective possibilities.

Personal Relations Theory presents a new and comprehensive account of Fairbairn's mature theory. Part I provides a thorough overview of Fairbairn's work and its ramifications for our understanding of creativity and the nature of inner reality. Part II covers Fairbairn's relationship to Macmurray and Suttie, and their relevance to realist philosophy, the scientific status of psychoanalysis, attachment theory and the politics of the personal relations viewpoint. Subjects discussed in depth include:

- Internal objects and inner reality: Fairbairn and Klein.
- Fairbairn's theory of art in the light of his mature model of mind.
- The preconscious and psychic change in Fairbairn's model of mind.
- The politics of attachment theory and personal relations theory: Fairbairn, Suttie and Bowlby.

The combination of Fairbairn, Macmurray and Suttie presented here forms an original strand of object relations theory, which has implications and consequences for a wide spectrum of concerns. This book will be of value to anyone interested in psychoanalysis, especially in relation to politics, society and the arts.

Graham S. Clarke originally studied architecture at the Bartlett School of Architecture, UCL. He then moved into computing and worked at City University, Anglia Polytechnic University and, for the past 20 years, the University of Essex where he is a Visiting Fellow in the Centre for Psychoanalytic Studies.

Personal Relations Theory

Fairbairn, Macmurray and Suttie

Graham S. Clarke

Routledge
Taylor & Francis Group
LONDON AND NEW YORK

First published 2006
by Routledge
27 Church Road, Hove, East Sussex BN3 2FA

Simultaneously published in the USA and Canada
by Routledge
270 Madison Ave, New York, NY 10016

Routledge is an imprint of the Taylor & Francis Group, an informa business

Copyright © 2006 Graham S. Clarke

Typeset in Times by RefineCatch Ltd, Bungay, Suffolk
Printed and bound in Great Britain by
TJ International Ltd, Padstow, Cornwall
Paperback cover design by Lisa Dynan

All rights reserved. No part of this book may be reprinted or
reproduced or utilised in any form or by any electronic,
mechanical, or other means, now known or hereafter
invented, including photocopying and recording, or in any
information storage or retrieval system, without permission in
writing from the publishers.

This publication has been produced with paper manufactured to
strict environmental standards and with pulp derived from
sustainable forests.

British Library Cataloguing-in-Publication Data
A catalogue record for this book is available from the British Library

Library of Congress Cataloging in Publication Data
Clarke, Graham S.
  Personal relations theory : Fairbairn, Macmurray, and Suttie /
Graham S. Clarke. – 1st ed.
    p. cm.
  Includes bibliographical references and index.
ISBN 1-58391-781-0 (hbk) – ISBN 0-415-39352-3 (pbk) 1. Object
relations (Psychoanalysis) 2. Psychoanalysis. 3. Fairbairn, W. Ronald D.
(William Ronald Dodds) 4. Macmurray, John, 1891– 5. Suttie, Ian D.
(Ian Dishart), 1889–1935. I. Title.
  BF175.5.O24C57 2006
  150.19′5 – dc22   2005034791

ISBN13: 978-1-58391-781-7 (hbk)
ISBN13: 978-0-415-39352-2 (pbk)

ISBN10: 1-58391-781-0 (hbk)
ISBN10: 0-415-39352-3 (pbk)

Contents

List of figures and tables	vii
Acknowledgements	ix
Permissions	xi
Introduction	1

PART I   7

1	Why Fairbairn?	9
2	Fairbairn's model of mind	23
3	Fairbairn's theory and some philosophical interpretations of Freud	56
4	Internal objects and inner reality: Fairbairn and Klein	67
5	Fairbairn's theory of art in the light of his mature model of mind	91
6	The preconscious and psychic change in Fairbairn's model of mind	115

PART II   133

7	Fairbairn, Macmurray and Suttie: towards a personal relations theory	135
8	Fairbairn and Macmurray: psychoanalytic studies and critical realism	143

9 The politics of attachment theory and
   personal relations theory: Fairbairn,
   Suttie and Bowlby   169

   Notes   190
   Bibliography   193
   Index   201

List of figures and tables

Key used in all figures

→ Aggressive relationship (pushing things apart). [There is one exception to this where the aggressive links are two-way in Figure 6.2.]

↔ Libidinal relationship (holding/drawing things together)

○↔○ Object relationship

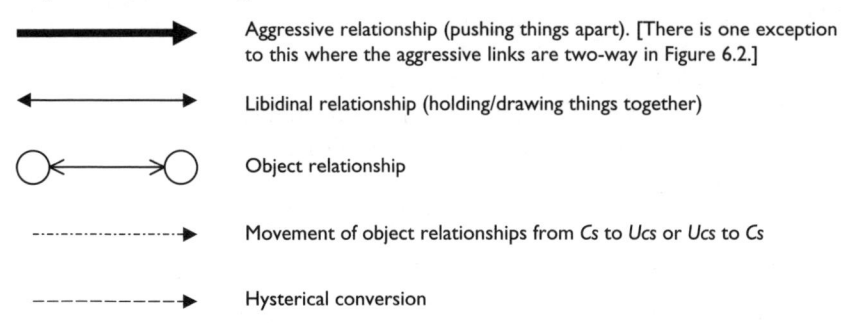

⇢ Movement of object relationships from *Cs* to *Ucs* or *Ucs* to *Cs*

⇢ Hysterical conversion

Abbreviations used in all figures

CE the central ego
EI the ego ideal
IO the ideal object
LE the libidinal ego
LO the libidinal object
AE the anti-libidinal ego
AO the anti-libidinal object
RO the rejecting object
IS the internal saboteur
EO the exciting object
OR object relationship
Cs conscious
Pcs preconscious
Ucs unconscious

Figures

2.1 Diagram of endopsychic structure based on Fairbairn's diagram ... 26

2.2	The original object relationship	27
2.3	The movement from fusion to separation	28
2.4	Physical processing of a real incorporated object	30
2.5	Psychological incorporation: the original object is incorporated into the original ego	30
2.6	Splitting of the original object based upon the infant's experience	30
2.7	The object relations origins of the basic endopsychic structure	31
2.8	Splitting of the ego	31
2.9	An alternative diagram of Fairbairn's basic endopsychic structure based on diagram in Scharff (1982)	32
2.10	The Freudian superego and Fairbairn's ego-ideal	33
2.11	The basic endopsychic structure	33
2.12	A Kleinian model based upon 'positions'	34
2.13	A 'fuzzy' diagram of the internal world	35
2.14	Possible dynamics of internalised object relationships	36
2.15	Object relations crossing the repression barrier and becoming conscious	37
2.16	Sorting the internal world during sleep	41
2.17	Psychic growth	42
2.18	Dreams as 'shorts' of internal reality	42
2.19	Hysterical conversion symptoms	43
2.20	Creativity	45
2.21	The process of psychic growth	45
2.22	Basic endopsychic structure (prior to the Oedipus situation)	48
2.23	Conflict in the Oedipus situation	49
2.24	Oedipus situation resolved in a specific way (one of many)	50
2.25	Basic endopsychic structure with similar strength sub-selves	50
2.26	Basic endopsychic structure with central ego firmly in control	51
2.27	Mature dependence	51
4.1	Kleinian and Fairbairnian models compared	68
6.1	Fairbairn's original diagram	119
6.2	A new model of inner reality	129
9.1	Bretherton's (1987) model modified to emulate Fairbairn's model of inner reality	173

Tables

2.1	Fusion and layering	47
2.2	Distribution of internal objects within the transitional techniques	54
8.1	Psychoanalytic thinking and scientific activity	146

Acknowledgements

I would like to thank Ellinor Fairbairn Birtles for her unfailing generosity and help when I was carrying out the original research upon which this book is based; I would also like to thank the late John Padel posthumously for his comments on some earlier versions of a section of my research and thank both for their vital contribution to Fairbairn scholarship.

I would like to thank the following people for reading and commenting upon some part of my original research: Karl Figlio, Barry Richards, Michael Podro, Bob Hinshelwood, (the late) Ian Craib, Roderick Main, Elvin Aydin, Allan Muir, Peter Meikle, Ross Clarke, Zoe Clarke and Sandra Davies. I would also like to thank David and Jill Scharff, and the anonymous reviewers from the British Association of Psychotherapists, the *International Journal of Psychoanalysis* and the *Journal of Critical Realism* for their comments on papers that form part of some chapters.

In particular I would like to thank Professor Joan Raphael-Leff for her generous support, enthusiasm, knowledge and encouragement throughout the original research and for the many useful and productive discussions and suggestions which she contributed towards it.

I would also like to thank Susan Forsyth for her excellent work in preparing the manuscript.

Lastly I would like to thank Sandra Davies for helping to provide a secure base from which I could carry out this work.

As usual all of the shortcomings of the book are my responsibility.

Permissions

Acknowledgements are due to the following sources for their kind permission to draw on previously published material as the basis for some of the chapters of this book:

Chapter 2: Fairbairn material first published as, Fairbairn, W.R.D. (1954) 'Observations on the nature of hysterical states', *Psychology and Psychotherapy: Theory, Research and Practice*, 27: 105–25. Copyright © The British Psychological Society.

Chapter 3: Rorty material first published as, Rorty, R. (1986) 'Freud and moral reflection', in J.H. Smith and W. Kerrigan (eds) *Pragmatism's Freud: The Moral Disposition of Psychoanalysis*, Baltimore: Johns Hopkins University Press. Copyright © Johns Hopkins University Press, reprinted with permission.

Chapter 5: material first published as, 'An object-relations theory of creativity: Fairbairn's theory of art in the light of his mature model of mind', *Journal of the British Association of Psychotherapists*, 42: 128–43, 2004.

Chapter 6: material first published as, 'The preconscious and psychic change in Fairbairn's model of mind', *International Journal of Psychoanalysis*, 86(1): 61–77, 2005. Copyright © International Journal of Psychoanalysis.

Chapter 7: material first published as, 'Personal Relations Theory', in J.S. Scharff and D.E. Scharff (eds) (2005) *The Legacy of Fairbairn and Sutherland*, London: Routledge.

Chapter 8: material first published as, 'Fairbairn and Macmurray: psychoanalytic studies and critical realism', *Journal of Critical Realism*, 2:1, 2003.

Chapter 8: Macmurray material first published as, Macmurray, J. (1995) *Persons in Relation*, vol. II of *The Form of the Personal*. Reprinted with permission from the Estate of the late John Macmurray c/o Pinter & Martin Publishers Ltd.

Introduction

When the terrorist attack on the Twin Towers took place on 11 September 2001 in New York, one of the most striking and poignant aspects of that tragedy was that, as a final act, people used their mobile phones to contact their loved ones to tell them they loved them.

At the same time by far the largest percentage of murders are committed by and on significant others – spouses, children, parents, lovers. Home Office statistics for the year 2003/2004 show that 40 per cent of male victims and 63 per cent of female victims knew their assailants. Perhaps more shockingly, 60 per cent of female victims were killed by a partner, ex-partner or lover while only 12 per cent of male victims were killed by partner or ex-partner. Of the children under 16 who were killed, 43 per cent were killed by their parents and a further 16 per cent by someone known to them. 'Where the suspect (or suspects) was known to the victim, over half the homicides resulted from a quarrel, an act of revenge or a loss of temper' (Povey 2005: 5). In short it is a breakdown in our most intimate personal relations that contributes directly to the rate at which we kill each other.

According to a recent news item on BBC Radio 4, research shows that personal happiness is directly related to the quality of our personal relationships.

All of this goes to confirm what we take for granted, that our personal relationships are the most significant of all our relationships with the world. More than that, however, in the absence of personal relationships we as human beings would not exist. The evidence of the consequences of care without human content are most dramatically illustrated in children abandoned or lost at an early age – feral children, who survive but without human care – since they never become fully functioning human beings.

Winnicott famously said 'there is no such thing as a baby' (Winnicott 1965: 39n[1]) meaning that the nursing couple is the smallest viable unit of human relationship and that it is this dyad that needs to be studied. I am arguing here that without personal relationships during infancy there is no such thing as a human being. It is one thing for an adult Robinson Crusoe to be shipwrecked on an island and to continue to live as if the social world by which he was constituted exists on the island; it is another thing entirely to imagine that an infant being washed ashore on a desert island and surviving would have any meaningful future.

Our lives are communal and without others we would languish and die. Personal relations are the essence of our existence, indeed constitute our existence as personal beings. Without personal relations there would be no person, which sounds somewhat paradoxical unless we realise that we are adapted to looking for and sustaining just such personal relationships from birth, initially through our mother or primary caregiver and later with other members of our family and friends. Later, of course, we have a relationship with the society and culture of our village, town, city, region and country which can develop into a relationship with a wider community but which is predicated upon our having become a personal being first. Our lives are lives in common despite our sometimes desperate need to believe in the complete authorship of our own individuality. Our individuality only makes sense in a specific social and cultural context.

This book looks at the work of three Scots who developed independent but related ideas of the person and their relation to society, culture and history and to the workings of the personality. They were psychoanalyst Ronald Fairbairn (1952a), philosopher John Macmurray (1995a and 1995b) and psychiatrist Ian Suttie (1960). For an introduction to the work of these men see Colin Kirkwood's (2005) paper on what he calls the 'persons-in-relation' perspective, a viewpoint which in terms of overall aims has much in common with this book. I think that Fairbairn's, Macmurray's and Suttie's work can be read together to form a coherent view of the person, their origins and the way they operate, and that this viewpoint is best described by the term 'personal relations theory' (Clarke 2005). This term also usefully separates it from the term 'object relations' with which it bears a close affinity, if only because Fairbairn is regarded as one of the originators of object relations theory. This is important since the term 'object relations' has become synonymous with Klein, in the UK at least.

Gregory Bateson, observing a captive dolphin being taught to perform new tricks, commented that, 'severe pain and maladjustment can be induced by putting a mammal in the wrong regarding its rules for making sense of an important relationship with another mammal ... if this pathology can be warded off or resisted, the total experience may promote *creativity*' (1973: 248–9). In this context I would like to rewrite that in the following way: 'If you put a person in the wrong regarding his or her personal relations that person will either grow and create or become ill, even unto death.'

Part I of this book looks in detail at Fairbairn's work and produces a complete account of his mature theory and some of its ramifications for our understanding of creativity and the nature of inner reality. In Part II Fairbairn's relationship to Macmurray is investigated in relation to a realist philosophy and the scientific status of psychoanalysis, and his relationship to

Suttie is used to explore the relevance of attachment theory and the politics of the personal relations viewpoint.

W.R.D. (Ronald) Fairbairn was born in Edinburgh in 1889 and lived and worked in Edinburgh for most of his life. He took an MA with Honours in Philosophy in 1911 and devoted the next three years to a study of Divinity and Hellenistic Greek (Scharff and Fairbairn Birtles 1994, vol. II: 462). He served in the First World War and spent some part of it in Egypt and Palestine. In 1915 Fairbairn had the opportunity to visit Craiglockhart, the hospital in Edinburgh run by W.H. Rivers (Scharff and Fairbairn Birtles 1994, vol. II: xviii) treating 'shell-shocked' soldiers and later decided to go into medicine with a view to specialising in psychotherapy (Scharff and Fairbairn Birtles 1994, vol. II: 463). He began psychoanalytic practice in 1925 but also held various other appointments:

> Thus from 1926 to 1931 I was Assistant Physician at the Longmore Hospital, Edinburgh; and from 1927 to 1935 I was Lecturer in Psychology at Edinburgh University. I was also Lecturer in Psychiatry from 1931 to 1932. At the same time I was Medical Psychologist at Jordanburn Nerve Hospital, Edinburgh and at the Edinburgh University Psychological Clinic for Children from 1927 to 1935.
> (Scharff and Fairbairn Birtles 1994, vol. II: 463–4)

He became an associate member of the British Psycho-Analytic Society (BPaS) in 1931 and a few years later was elected to full membership.

Fairbairn only published one book in his lifetime – *Psychoanalytic Studies of the Personality* (1952a) – a collection of papers published during the period 1927 to 1951, the most important of which were published between 1940 and 1951, after Freud's death in 1938. In 1994 Fairbairn's daughter, Ellinor Fairbairn Birtles, and David E. Scharff assembled all his previously uncollected papers and some other material from his estate and published them in a two-volume work called *From Instinct to Self* (1994). As Stephen Mitchell comments on the dust jacket, 'These extraordinary two volumes of material by and about Fairbairn are a virtual treasure trove for anyone at all interested in the history of psychoanalytic ideas . . . Fairbairn's contribution has been only belatedly and insufficiently recognised.' It is from this new source of material that we can see that the roots of Fairbairn's attempts to rethink and refashion Freud's theories go back to the late 1920s, when he completed his MD thesis on 'Dissociation and Repression', and was lecturing on the superego and on libido theory. These notes show that Fairbairn's mature theory, which started to appear in 1940 with the publication of his paper on the schizoid personality, was a product of over a decade of careful thought about the theoretical underpinnings of Freud's theories.

Fairbairn is recognised as one of the originators of the (British) object relations theory of psychoanalysis. Furthermore, synoptic studies of the development of object relations theory (Greenberg and Mitchell 1983; Hughes 1989) agree that his is the most consistent of the object relations theories. His work has been widely influential but not widely acknowledged, as Scharff and Fairbairn Birtles (eds) (1994; 1997) have argued, and because he had no 'school' this influence has rarely been explicit or pursued within a consciously Fairbairnian frame of reference. The reasons for this are complex, not least of which is his dry and dense style of writing. Despite, or maybe because of, Guntrip's efforts to popularise Fairbairn's theory, whilst incorporating aspects of his own theory (Kernberg 1980), there seems to be the feeling that we know Fairbairn, that he was important, but that there is nothing left to know.[2]

'Personal Relations Theory' is the name that Ronald Fairbairn was going to give his developed object relations theory (Sutherland 1989). His mature object relations theory was developed in a series of papers in the 1940s that were a 'progressive development of a line of thought' (Fairbairn 1952a: Introduction). Despite being accepted as the most thoroughgoing object relations theory by those who have studied this strand of psychoanalysis, there is no definitive statement of his mature theory as a whole. Fairbairn's critique of Freud and Klein, which led to his own theory, which has itself been used by contemporary Freudians and by Klein to develop their own theories, was based on principles drawn in part from his Edinburgh-based philosophical training. However, the idea that Fairbairn was an isolate stuck away from the main centre of psychoanalytic training and development, as represented by Ernest Jones in his preface to Fairbairn's book, is only a part of the story. Similarly his 'isolation' in Edinburgh based upon his personal difficulties in travelling long distances (Sutherland 1989) is, similarly, a partial view. At the beginning of his career as a psychoanalyst he travelled to Oxford for the 1929 conference which included Klein, Anna Freud, Ferenczi, Jones, Glover and many others. It is true that he lived and worked in Scotland, and in particular Edinburgh, for all of his life but I would argue that this was conditioned by the deep roots he had in Scotland and the Scottish inflection that much of his theory has, once one looks beneath the surface and at the wider social milieu out of which it grew. I first became aware of this when I was looking for contemporary sources that might share some of Fairbairn's attitudes and feelings, for example when I was looking for those people who had influenced him. There is a strand of Scottish thinking and writing about schizoid phenomena that goes back at least to James Hogg's *Confessions of a Justified Sinner* (1992) and includes such iconic works as *Dr Jekyll and Mr Hyde* (Stevenson 2004) and, after Fairbairn, Ronald Laing's work *The Divided Self* (Laing 1965) and some of his other work on making the schizoid intelligible (Laing 1964, 1967), something that was the subject of Fairbairn's first mature paper (Fairbairn 1940). Trevarthen suggests that aspects of this strand of thinking go back to the Scottish Enlightenment and the work of Hume. More recently, within this strand of Scottish thought that may be deeply conditioned by the

Calvinism of the Kirk and its domination of public life, two contemporaries of Fairbairn stand out: Ian D. Suttie who died as his book *The Origins of Love and Hate* was being published in 1935, and John Macmurray, the philosopher, who acknowledged the influence of Suttie on him in his book *Persons in Relation* (1961). Macmurray met Fairbairn in the 1930s and knew him in the 1940s when he was teaching at Edinburgh University, where Fairbairn had also taught. Harry Guntrip knew both men and discusses Macmurray's relation to Fairbairn (Guntrip 1961, 1968) but there are no references, one to the other, in any of their published works that I have been able to find. The coincidence of their views across a wide range of issues needs some explanation but at present there seems little hope that we can clearly distinguish how these similarities developed. Macmurray's biographer, Jack Costello, only mentions Fairbairn once in his biography of Macmurray, suggesting that it was Guntrip who introduced Fairbairn to Macmurray's work. In a recent book of essays on Macmurray (Ferguson and Dower 2002), Fairbairn is mentioned three times, the most significant of which is a note in Kirkpatrick's paper saying, 'It may be no accident that Macmurray's work and the development of object relations theory both occur at the same time and in the same place: W.D. Fairbairn was a contemporary Scot and Harry Guntrip was Macmurray's student' (Ferguson and Dower: 207). It is this coincidence that interests me.

A close look at both men's work reveals a surprising degree of consonance between their view of things and with Suttie's viewpoint. Whilst Sutherland (1989) acknowledges Fairbairn's debt to Suttie, there is nothing in Fairbairn's work itself to indicate that this was an important or significant influence on him. There has never been any attempt, that I know of, to bring these different strands of thought together through the work of these three men and produce a coherent theory incorporating them all. I know that Ellinor Fairbairn Birtles (personal communication) has looked at some of these connections and that Allan Harrow (1998) of the Scottish Institute of Human Relations has looked at the importance of these thinkers in relation to each other, as has Colin Kirkwood. It was at a conference in Edinburgh in 2003 on the legacy of Fairbairn and Sutherland where I suggested that there ought to be something called 'Personal Relations Theory' to distinguish Fairbairn's form of object relations theory from Klein's, in particular. There I met Colin Kirkwood and it became clear that he and I had been exploring very similar lines of thought over the past few years. This is therefore the second sense in which I would like the term 'Personal Relations Theory' to be read. It is in no sense an established theory as yet but still has the feeling of being a contemporary experience without having a proper term or theory to describe it. It is, I think, what Raymond Williams called a 'structure of feeling' that unites these thinkers – Fairbairn, Suttie and Macmurray – and some of Fairbairn's followers too – Guntrip, Sutherland and Padel in particular. Most importantly perhaps it is still in need of development. It remains a 'structure of feeling' and has yet to be thoroughly worked out as a theory. I hope this book will mark the coming to consciousness of this structure of feeling and the beginning too of that working out.

It is interesting also to note the degree to which the concept of a structure of feeling reflects important aspects of the approach I am describing, aspects that will become clearer as the account of personal relations theory progresses.

Williams discusses the term 'structures of feeling' thus:

> The term is difficult, but 'feeling' is chosen to emphasise a distinction from the more formal concepts of 'world-view' or 'ideology' ... we are concerned with meanings and values as they are actively lived and felt, and the relations between these and formal and systematic beliefs. ... An alternative definition would be structures of experience: in one sense the better and wider word but with the difficulty that one of its senses has the past tense which is the most important obstacle to recognition of the area of social experience which is being defined. We are talking about ... specifically affective elements of consciousness and relationships: not feeling against thought, but thought as felt and feeling as thought; practical consciousness of a present kind, in a living and interrelating continuity. We are then defining these elements as a 'structure': as a set, with specific internal relations, at once interlocking and in tension ... we are also defining a social experience which is still *in process*, often indeed not yet recognised as social but taken to be private, idiosyncratic, and even *isolating*.
>
> (Williams 1977: 132; final emphasis added)

It seems to me that personal relations theory is a set of ideas and practices, a structure of feeling, whose time is yet to come.

Part I

Chapter 1
Why Fairbairn?

Throughout my research the most frequent question I have been asked, either explicitly or implicitly, is 'Why Fairbairn?' The assumption seems to be that Fairbairn is either already completely known and understood or has had his day and is no longer relevant. My intention is to argue that neither of these viewpoints is correct.

In answer to the question 'Why Fairbairn?' there are a number of points that I think need to be made:

1 The overwhelming majority of psychoanalytic theories and practices now are explicitly, or can be seen to be, based fundamentally on object relationships.
2 It follows that the atomic concept of psychoanalysis should be the object relationship – a self, an object and an affective relationship between them. This is the *lingua franca* of all social relationships.
3 Fairbairn's object relations theory is widely regarded, by those who have made the comparisons, to be the most coherent and thoroughgoing object relations theory. It has been influential on major object relations theories of the British and American schools.
4 Fairbairn's complex conceptualisation of the self foreshadows this idea of a non-unitary subject constituted through internalised relationships.
5 Fairbairn traces the development of the (potentially pathological) splitting of the self, his own original contribution to psychoanalytic theory, regarding it as the earliest and most fundamental of defences.
6 Conjoint splitting of the object and the ego, in Fairbairn's model of endopsychic structure, leads to the creation of a complex inner world of object relations between alternative selves. This idea of a dynamic internal world of structures in relationship is another of Fairbairn's original contributions to psychoanalytic theory.
7 Fairbairn's theory contains a potentially liberating social message that, while splitting can kill, these splits in the self can be resolved and an integrated self achieved through creativity, psychic growth, therapy and a benign environment, which can be generalised.

8   Affective object relations, as the basis of psychoanalysis, pre-exist language and therefore supersede psychoanalytic theories founded on language alone.
9   Due to the complex permutations and versatility of its components, and particularly when seen as a dynamic structure, Fairbairn's object relations theory is capable of explaining the findings of some other forms of psychoanalytic theory.
10 Similarly, Fairbairn's object relations theory is capable of contributing to the explanation of some social and cultural products.
11 In sum, Fairbairn's 'psychology of dynamic structure' is capable of providing a common model for psychoanalysis.

When one turns to work referencing, representing or directly studying Fairbairn (and the number of texts is not large, reflecting in part Fairbairn's *oeuvre*) there are distinctly different interpretations of his work. Fairbairn himself stated, quite explicitly, that his principal published work – the book, *Psychoanalytic Studies of the Personality* (1952a) – was the 'development of a line of thought' rather than a finished system of thought. In many ways it is remarkable that he has had the influence that he has, given his limited output, his lack of interest in founding a school and his living and working in Edinburgh – his physical distance from the epicentre of British psychoanalytic practice. This, however, is something that might have been to his advantage, as Ernest Jones suggests in his preface to Fairbairn's book. In 1994 the original source material of *Psychoanalytic Studies* was considerably and significantly expanded by the publication of the invaluable *From Instinct to Self*, edited by David Scharff and Ellinor Fairbairn Birtles (1994), a collection of Fairbairn's previously uncollected and/or unpublished papers. Even so, his total *oeuvre* is small compared to Freud, Klein, Winnicott or Lacan and, to his credit, it is with these important psychoanalytic thinkers that he is most often compared.

There are a number of serious and important Fairbairn scholars including Stephen Mitchell,[1] James Grotstein, David Scharff, Richard Rubens and Otto Kernberg, but in my view the most important of these is the late John Padel since he more than any of the others has offered us an account of the dynamics of Fairbairn's 'psychology of dynamic structures' (1991, 1994).

My first task then, as I conceived it, was to try and develop an account of Fairbairn's mature theory that was faithful to the original texts and captured the *dynamism* of the theory that was implicit but mostly unaddressed by Fairbairn himself. My attempts to do this have convinced me of a number of fundamental aspects of his theory. Perhaps the most important is the deep significance he gave to our most passionate and emotional relations internally and externally; his awareness of the dark destructive side of our nature as well as the vibrancy of our erotic life and imagination. I say this in particular because his writing, the writing of a trained philosophical mind, sometimes gives the impression of lacking passion or emotion and thus flattening the account. Compared to Klein, Fairbairn spends very little time discussing in any detail the sorts of aggression one finds in the imagination and activity of children and adults alike. It would, however, be wrong to think that his understanding of personal relations simply elided this problem. Throughout the 1930s Fairbairn was influenced by Klein and her work: showing the importance of aggression in inner and outer reality. Fairbairn did, however, differ fundamentally from Klein in thinking that this aggression was a reaction to frustration rather than an inborn attribute, but he did not disown or deny aggression. Indeed love and aggression are the principal dynamics of his final model of endopsychic structure (1952a: 82–136). In his 1939 paper on psychoanalysis as 'a Prescribed or a Proscribed Subject' (1952a: 247–55) within British universities he accounts for the, then current, proscription of psychoanalysis by what he calls 'the true nature of the objections to psychoanalysis'. For Fairbairn these are: '(1) that psychoanalysis reveals the presence in human nature of primitive and destructive forces which human nature would fain disclaim; and (2) that it gives an account of the nature and origin of the psychological defences erected by human beings as a protection against such forces in the main' (252).

Fairbairn's account of these defences, developed over the next five years (1940–45) and forming the basis of his mature theory, later published in *Psychoanalytic Studies* (1952a), places splitting of the self at the centre of this process. This, the first introduction of splitting of the self as *the* major defensive mechanism, has had a profound influence on the subsequent development of psychoanalysis, even if that influence is neither adequately acknowledged nor understood. Fairbairn's 1929 MD thesis, comparing Janet and Freud, called 'Dissociation and Repression', arrived at the conclusion that repression is a special form of dissociation of the unpleasant, where the 'defence is directed against tendencies which form part of the mental structure of the individual' (Scharff and Fairbairn Birtles 1994: 77). Considering the emotional turmoil that one faces when presented with difficult choices between highly desirable but morally difficult ends, or, at times when we are resisting deeply felt and motivated intentions that conflict with our moral principles and our view of ourselves, something of the violence of this inner division is apparent. The idea of wrestling with one's conscience, like that of Jacob wrestling with an angel, indicates potentially self-shattering encounters between conflicting aspects of oneself. Where an immovable object meets an irresistible force something has to give and this is not a painless and abstract duplication of selves so much as the painful and diminishing shearing and tearing of the self along the lines of least resistance. In many ways this process of splitting has been represented too tamely – it is closer to the more or less invisible process of tectonic shifts in the earth's crust, with the life-shattering consequences we are all too familiar with, than the over-simplified 'one becomes two' of some representations of splitting. For Fairbairn such far-reaching and subterranean shifts of immense emotional significance occur during the early formation of the personality. These processes take place in the context of a real but contingent family, class, society, history. There are no universals outside the mechanisms themselves and the overall categories of acceptable, libidinal (over-exciting) and anti-libidinal (over-rejecting). It is the relations within and between these selves that will mediate the individual's relations with a contingent outer reality. This schema can therefore be used to analyse the variety of human accommodations to anterior conditions without depending upon any predetermined notion of symbolic structure.

There is philosophical support for the fundamental part played by splitting of the self in the work of Donald Davidson in 'Paradoxes of Irrationality' (1982). There is neurological support for the fundamental importance of object relations in Damasio's work on the development of the self and consciousness from a neurological perspective (2000), though Damasio does not address the question of splitting and the autobiographical self. Fairbairn's work, however, contains both, and seems to me to be a good candidate for providing a unifying account of psychoanalysis.

Like Lacan's theory, Fairbairn's account is of a defensive, potentially pathological, structuring of selves. However, the Lacanian Subject can never be securely established because forever riven by unfulfillable desire, whereas the Fairbairnian counterpart of the subject is the pristine original ego/self, and the potential integration of the split-off sub-selves that can be (re)unified with the achievement of mature dependence. Fairbairn opposes Freud's, Klein's and Lacan's notions of some essential and inevitable shortcoming in human nature that can never be resolved – an unfulfillable desire, or an ever present and active, destructive or insatiable substrate that can never be finally overcome. For Fairbairn the social order is malleable and can be so ordered to avoid or help repair most of the splitting that we are forced to do in order to preserve our relations with others upon whom we depend totally. This is an optimistic message even if the reality, as he knew from his studies of child abuse and the war neuroses, gave him no illusions as to how difficult such a process might be to put in train and sustain. The lucidity of his writing has led some to comment upon an underlying sadness which I think properly reflects the immense difficulties there are to turning the social order upside down and producing a world in which pathological splitting would no longer be an essential or enduring feature of being human.

PADEL

My understanding of Fairbairn's mature theory is heavily influenced by the work of John Padel, psychoanalyst and Fairbairn scholar, in particular Padel's description of the process of psychic change, a crucial aspect of which is his understanding of psychic growth within a Fairbairnian model. Padel's understanding of psychic change was, in part, stimulated by Richard Rubens' insightful essays on Fairbairn (1984, 1994, 1996, 1998) where Rubens' careful attempts to draw out the dynamics of Fairbairn's model have also been invaluable. The notions of structuring and non-structuring internalisations and the ways in which the relative balance between the central self and the subsidiary selves (libidinal and anti-libidinal) are integral to notions of psychic change are central to this understanding and clearly divide a number of Fairbairn's most interesting commentators. (For example, Mitchell (1994) and Rubens (1994) seem happier with the 1943 version of Fairbairn's model, where the 'moral defence', based upon the internalisation of good relationships with significant others, accounts for growth rather than the fully developed model of endopsychic structure which Padel and Grotstein, among others, have accepted and worked within.)

Part I of the book puts forward my interpretation of Fairbairn's mature theory incorporating Padel's work on psychic change and its bearing on a personal relations theory of creativity as a process akin to psychic growth. It represents my original synthesis of Fairbairn and other thinkers and develops a multiple-self model of inner reality. It includes work on the ways in which a Fairbairnian personal relations theory might provide an alternative explanatory framework for Kleinian clinical work and a theory of creativity, and it concludes by considering the importance of the preconscious as a dynamic and descriptively unconscious area of inner reality within Fairbairn's model (see Figure 2.1).

Because Fairbairn's theory is still not widely known or grasped in any detail, I have attempted to give a brief but comprehensive outline of my understanding of it (Chapter 2) before looking in detail at different aspects of its relationship to other models and problems. In Chapter 3 I make use of some philosophical approaches to psychoanalysis to further develop the multiple-self model established in the first chapter, in particular, the work of Donald Davidson on 'partitions of the mind' (splitting) which seems to reinforce the central position that Fairbairn gave to the phenomenon and has become much more widely recognised in recent decades, and the idea of the splitting of the self which Fairbairn was first to introduce in a fundamental way into psychoanalytic theory. I also look at Richard Rorty's development of Davidson's view that it is *self-enlargement* rather than purity or perfection that is the goal of psychic growth and the mark of maturity (1991). This represents the rounding out of the model of mind developed in Chapter 2.

My interest in rehearsing Fairbairn's 'psychology of dynamic structure' meant looking initially at the object relations core of Freudian psychoanalysis and then comparing Fairbairn with Klein, with whom he was more or less contemporary, and between whom there was a mutual influence (Chapter 4).

Fairbairn's theory of art was written just before the period in which he developed his own distinctive personal relations theory though the preparatory work for this development had been done some ten years earlier. In book reviews (on Milner (Fairbairn 1950) and Kris (Fairbairn 1953)) written after the mature theory had been developed, Fairbairn gave some clues and hints as to how he would change his own theory of art but, despite planning to write a book on art,[2] he never made the space to pursue this possibility. In Chapter 5 my attempt to reconcile Fairbairn's mature theory with his theory of art leads to my proposing a personal relations theory of creativity. I also consider in some detail the relationship between the model proposed and the role of the preconscious as described by Kris (1950).

There have been a number of suggestions as to how Fairbairn's theory might be amended, all of which I have resisted on the grounds that the actual theory itself has not been adequately considered in detail. However in Chapter 6, when thinking about the role of the topographical categories (*Cs, Pcs, Ucs*) in relation to Fairbairn's structural theory, I did consider the possibility of a change that involves placing the split-off ego-structures, or aspects of them, in the preconscious, which does seem to make sense. This was then looked at in relation to accounts of preconscious processes in the literature. This proposal is consistent with the view that a dynamic unconscious, like the preconscious, is of central importance to Fairbairn's theory where, as I understand it, the system unconscious disappears as mature dependence is achieved.[3]

FREUD

I have not elaborated on Freud explicitly. One reason is that I believe that the contemporary Freudian position is in reality an object relations position, based upon a modification of the structural model, consistent with Fairbairn's critique but still using classical Freudian language. Another is that all of the approaches described above will involve considerable Freudian content whatever their official designation – it will be impossible to give an account of these options without at some point assuming the Freudian project. Fairbairn was a Freudian. It is also the case that there is a readily identifiable object relations subtext to much of Freud's work after 1914 (Ogden 1994b; Padel 1994), perhaps most clearly visible in 'Group psychology and the analysis of the ego' (Freud 1921). Klein picked up on the object relations aspect of Freud's work and both she and Fairbairn developed it, using the superego as an exemplar, into their different but related mature object relations theories.

UNCONSCIOUS PHANTASY

It was during the 'Controversial Discussions'[4] that the concept of unconscious phantasy was most fully discussed as a major topic of disagreement between the (Anna) Freudians and the Kleinians. The Kleinian view of unconscious phantasy was developed substantially by Sylvia Payne. In Fairbairn's only substantive contribution to the Controversial Discussions he suggested that the phenomenologically based concept of unconscious phantasy should be superseded by a structurally based model of endopsychic structures and the dynamic relations within and between such complex structures. This is a view that was derived in part from Klein's work on internal objects. I think that Fairbairn's objection was as much about the scientific coherence of a structural versus a phenomenologically based theory as it was about the merits of unconscious phantasy. Fairbairn accepted that there was unconscious phantasy but, as he argued in his paper on endopsychic structure, unconscious phantasy is best understood as the dynamics of the underlying endopsychic structures, and one needs to look at these structures and their dynamics in order to make sense of the unconscious phantasies produced.

In the classic Kleinian definition of unconscious phantasy, 'Unconscious phantasies underlie every mental process, and accompany all mental activity. . . . Phantasy is the mental expression of the instinctual impulses and also of defence mechanisms against instinctual impulses' (Hinshelwood 1991: 32). Fairbairn, by contrast, because of his views on Freud's instinct theory, which might best be summarised by Macmurray's statement that we are ' "adapted" . . . to being unadapted' (1995b: 48), did not think that we come into the world with the burden of pre-existing unconscious phantasies of an aggressive and envious hue that we need to contain in some way. On the contrary, Fairbairn believed that we are born with a pristine ego – an essentially unitary, preconscious, bodily ego – and only after our earliest relations with others in the world do we actually begin to establish what might be called a system unconscious through the splitting off and repression of introjected aspects of our relations with others, which we want to disavow, since they threaten essential relationships with significant others.

Because these early relationships form the core of the disavowed and repressed sub-selves and necessarily have less chance to mature along with the rest of the self, they are characteristically primitive. Fairbairn argues that this accounts for the classic distinction between primary and secondary process (1953b: 167).

For Fairbairn, unconscious phantasy is the dynamic aspect of internal object relations, what Henri Laborit (1977: 24–7) in describing an information control system calls the *circulating information* between the *information structures* that are the equivalent of Fairbairn's dynamic structures.

PROJECTIVE IDENTIFICATION

The use by Klein and her followers of projective identification as an analogue of unconscious phantasy apparently suffusing all mental activity is also in stark contrast to Fairbairn's approach to the same subject. Klein proposed the concept of projective identification after reading some of Fairbairn's papers, one of which was 'A revised psychopathology of the psychoses and the psychoneuroses' written in 1941. This paper contains Fairbairn's attempt to make sense of specific patterns of projection and introjection of good and bad objects in relation to the four characteristic techniques of, what he called, the *transitional period* between *infantile* and *mature dependence*. These techniques – hysteria, phobia, paranoia and obsession – were each analysed from an object relations point of view and a table of characteristic patterns of projection and introjection of good and bad objects suggested (Chapter 2). In taking up one aspect of this approach Klein recognised the importance of these processes, but, by not relating this process specifically to characteristics of particular transitional defences, the term has now become a portmanteau concept that has lost much of its potential for useful analysis. Clearly some pattern of projective identification might be taking place, but if it is not stipulated that specific techniques imply characteristic forms of projection and introjection, the scientific value of the concept is diminished. Similarly, if 'good' and 'bad' objects are created willy-nilly, rather than representing aspects of real world relations with others resulting in a determinate (essentially tripartite) intrapsychic structure, then the ability to, and the importance of, identifying specific patterns is also reduced.

LIBIDO AND LOVE

For Fairbairn libido is the dynamic aspect of an action by a reality-oriented object-seeking self and not separable from that self or ego, as in Freud's original concept of the id. The child is initially object-seeking which also means object-loving. Libido is a wider concept than sex and is more like Eros as Marcuse and others have interpreted it. Fairbairn (1952a: 83) cites Freud's argument that 'Love strives after objects' (Freud 1930: 117). For Fairbairn, when the free flow of the infant self's activity towards the world and the (pre-ambivalent) original object is interrupted or frustrated in some way, so that the relationship becomes unsatisfactory to some extent, then the child internalises the original (pre-ambivalent) object. This might be open to scientific investigation but for Fairbairn there is no abstract metric – a quantum of rejection that necessarily crystallises out the basic endopsychic structure or sparks the first internalisation of an object. The world will appear frustrating or rejecting to the child in early infancy but this is likely to be coloured by constitution as well as circumstance. In 'civilised society' where the relationship between primary caregiver and child is not continuous this is more likely to be the case.

As the relationship between the child and his/her original object develops, and the personal relations are experienced as ambivalent, so too does the internal object become ambivalent. Splits emerge between the acceptable set of personal relations between the child and the caregiver, and the over-exciting and over-rejecting relationships between the child and the caregiver, producing what Fairbairn calls the basic endopsychic structure. This splitting is a consequence of the real experiences of the child in relation to its primary caregiver and not, as with Klein for instance, a product of inborn aggression and phantasy. The central self's object, shorn as it is of the over-exciting and over-rejecting aspects of the real relationships with mother, constitutes a preconscious ideal that subsequently forms the basis for Fairbairn's version of the positive superego (ego ideal/ideal ego). After the basic endopsychic structure is formed, one way in which this tripartite structure can be stabilised and strengthened is by internalising experiences with good objects into the ideal-ego; this forms part of what Fairbairn called the *moral defence* (1952a: 65).

PATHOLOGY

One criticism of Fairbairn's theory is that it is a theory of pathology and lacks a theory of normality or psychic health. I think this is a mistaken view based upon the fact that Fairbairn's work has not been properly understood. It is true that he did not develop as well as he might the importance of psychic growth, though he delineated the means whereby it might be achieved. It is also true that his concept of mature dependence is only briefly sketched but it is by looking at both psychic growth and mature dependence in Fairbairn's work that the positive side to his theory will be found. Carveth has pointed out the similarities between Fairbairn and Lacan in regard to their insistence upon the pathological nature of the split self. Fairbairn argues that this splitting is an inevitable aspect of civilised society but also suggests that it can be substantially undone, something with which Lacan would not agree. Indeed, Fairbairn's concept of mature dependence would seem to *require* that the system unconscious is capable of being undone, on pain of falling into incoherence. Mitchell (1994: 81) and Rubens (1984: 428–40) have, I think, accepted that the benign effect of internalising relationships with the good object into the ego ideal as a form of psychic growth towards mature dependence, is all that is required. Only John Padel has fully developed Fairbairn's own view that psychic growth in structural terms means that the increase in scope and power of the central self is *at the expense of* the subsidiary libidinal and anti-libidinal selves, the logical consequence being that the system unconscious, which is constituted by the repressed subsidiary libidinal and anti-libidinal selves in Fairbairn's theory, disappears with the achievement of mature dependence. Not that the *dynamic unconscious* (that is, the preconscious) disappears but the *system unconscious* does. This view seems to be very similar to that developed by Ferenczi in 1928 in his description of the fully analysed person. If mature dependence is realistic as an aim then there has to be some suggestion that the unconscious is a social product. I argue that the degree and severity of splitting in the endopsychic structure is *culturally dependent*. This being the case, it is possible to sustain the potentially revolutionary view that the (pathological) system unconscious is a social artifact that can be undone. This, of course, contrasts strongly with Freudian, Lacanian and Kleinian views that the system unconscious pre-exists us, is both pathological and the source of all creativity, and cannot be undone (a necessary evil one might say) – this is the equivalent of the Christian notion of original sin. Fairbairn is an optimist about the human condition, not a pessimist; his is a tragic rather than a fallen universe.

THE SYSTEM UNCONSCIOUS

This view that the system unconscious can be dissolved, apart from being distinctive to Fairbairn, has interesting consequences for other aspects of his personal relations theory and its consequences for other disciplines. If, as the Kleinians claim, perception always involves some degree of unconscious phantasy or projective identification into the world around you, then the world you perceive is always in some sense a product of your imagination. It would follow that there is *no basis* for anything like an objective view of the world – that the senses are not a bridge to the world honed by millennia of evolution, but some sort of obstacle. This clearly has ramifications beyond psychoanalysis and seems to be making strong claims about the nature of science itself. However empirically precise or careful you are, there would still be no reason to argue that science was anything more than an ideology, a way of looking at the world with no special claims to understanding it. While Fairbairn shares part of this viewpoint, by regarding science as a particular way of looking at the world that is not itself exhaustive (1952b), the concept of mature dependence relies upon the possibility of seeing the world objectively, a view that Fairbairn shares with Macmurray, and which opens the way to arguing for a psychoanalytic basis for scientific objectivity. I believe that this connects Fairbairn's theory with a realist theory of science. In Part II of the book I consider the critical realist approach to science and the work of John Macmurray, both of which seem to me to have strong affinities with Fairbairn's action-based, realistic, object-oriented approach. Fairbairn does recognise the animistic roots of our relations with the world but he believes that these can be overcome in order to give the real objects of our experience their due. The alternative is to remain forever more or less misled about everything, since unable to ever distinguish between direct perception and wish fulfilment.

GUNTRIP

One question that many students of Fairbairn will probably ask concerning this book is why there is not more about Guntrip here. There are a number of reasons for this but the main one is that, unlike many others, I came to Fairbairn via Neville Symington's *The Analytic Experience* (1986) and had read all of Fairbairn's work long before I had read anything by Guntrip. During the course of reading commentators upon Fairbairn, I came across a number of critical comments concerning what Guntrip had done to Fairbairn's theory and in particular the fact that he had introduced changes to Fairbairn's theories without adequately distinguishing between these and Fairbairn's own work. Further, the changes he had made to Fairbairn's theory, if taken seriously, would seem to completely subvert Fairbairn's model. Guntrip's idea of a pre-natal, regressed ego, without an object, as the origin of the self, has a Winnicottian ring about it. He seems to have developed this idea at about the time he moved from being analysed by Fairbairn to being analysed by Winnicott. This idea would totally contradict Fairbairn's views that (a) pre-natal existence did not make sufficient difference to predetermine the development of the basic endopsychic structure, or (b) that the original pristine ego was whole and not burdened by built-in preconceptions, or (c) that you couldn't have an ego-structure without a closely linked internal object structure (that is, selves are based upon internalised relationships), a criticism Fairbairn made of Freud's model and so is unlikely to have agreed with. It is significant that Fairbairn's last published work in 1963 shows no indication that he had changed his view – first developed in the 1940s – of the central place that the basic endopsychic structure has for our relationship to each other and the world.

I recognise, as do many of those who are nonetheless critical of Guntrip, that his work did both help keep alive and introduce others to Fairbairn's work when opposition to him was high following the publication of his book in 1952 and the hostile review by Winnicott and Khan in 1953. Guntrip's *Personality Structure and Human Interaction* (1961) contains a comprehensive explanation and defence of Fairbairn's theory and the context from which it arose. It is only in the last section of the last chapter that Guntrip introduces his modification to Fairbairn's theory. This modification has all the hallmarks of being an attempt to combine Winnicott's idea of regression with Fairbairn's structural theory by splitting the libidinal self pre-natally, which seems to contradict Fairbairn's own account of the origins of the libidinal self. While Guntrip does in general present Fairbairn fairly and comprehensively he does not go any further than Fairbairn had already gone, and neither throws any useful light on, nor stresses the underlying dynamism of, the theory. In *Schizoid Phenomena, Object-Relations and the Self* (1968) Guntrip's Winnicott-influenced theory of the regressed ego is the central focus, and although Fairbairn is widely referenced it is always within Guntrip's modified version of his theory.

To his credit Guntrip did note the connection between Fairbairn and Macmurray but his approach is in part coloured by his own religious convictions so that it is Macmurray's comments on religion that occupy him as much as Macmurray's insistence upon a distinct realm of the 'personal'. Macmurray's *Persons in Relation* (1995b), which I would argue shows the strongest evidence of a deep parallel between Fairbairn and Macmurray (which I look at in some detail in Part II of the present book), was published at the same time as Guntrip's book on personality structure which contains a number of references to Macmurray. However, there is much less evidence that Guntrip was interested in these parallels subsequently, since, in the second book, there are just two references to Macmurray, the second of which I was unable to find. The first reference, however, is a quote regarding H.V. Dicks where Guntrip writes 'his stress on man's humanity as a "person" reinforced my previous philosophical training in the "human relations philosophy" of Professor John Macmurray and prepared me for understanding the theoretical and clinical work of Fairbairn and Winnicott' (1968: 13). This seems to me to be a retrospective view of Guntrip's previous work rather than a living issue for him.

Fairbairn's work is generally regarded as being highly condensed and difficult, with little in the way of clinical examples to sustain the reader. He was trained as a philosopher and wrote at a level of abstraction that is unusual to find in a psychoanalyst. He did, however, think rigorously and clearly about many fundamental problems of psychoanalytic theory. So, thanks are due to Guntrip who, during the 1950s and 1960s, along with Sutherland and Padel, managed to keep Fairbairn's approach alive. However, I do not think that Guntrip went any further than Fairbairn in terms of the development or defence of his theory whereas Padel, prompted by Rubens, did pick up on the difficult problem of psychic growth and produced an enhancement and clarification of Fairbairn's theory which makes the whole understanding of the 'psychology of dynamic structure' easier and leads to a more flexible and accessible theory than hitherto.

CLINICAL ASPECTS

The relative dearth of clinical work in Fairbairn's opus is consistent with his overriding interest in theory, which is where his main contribution lies. However, he did talk in passing about aspects of the clinical setting and was open to varying the length of sessions and modifying the classical setting, which he thought was overprotective of the analyst (1952b). He also made suggestions, explicit and implicit, about how clinical material might be looked at and the importance of the clinical setting. The most notable product of the former might be Grotstein's dual-track hypothesis (1998) where he suggests that Klein and Fairbairn are two sides of the same coin, a hypothesis that I investigate when looking at Meira Likierman's work on the tragic and moral aspects of the depressive position in Klein (Chapter 4). I also suggest that the project implicit in Fairbairn's characterisation of the typical distribution of objects for each of the transitional techniques could open up the possibility for a non-clinician like myself to analyse clinical material from other analytical traditions to see if the sort of patterns described can be supported from these clinical reports.

Because, politically, Fairbairn was not an organiser, because he was always on the margins of the British Psychoanalytic Society, and because he did not seem to be interested in power or influence, other than the publication of his ideas, there is no corpus of specifically Fairbairnian literature from a clinical point of view. This is a matter for regret and one can only hope that there is greater recognition of the implicitly Fairbairnian approaches that are widely used so that a more conscious appreciation of his continuing contribution to clinical work might be made (Scharff and Fairbairn Birtles 1997). Fairbairn argued for the crucial importance of the clinical setting as the laboratory of the science of psychoanalysis and he also argued that it was the whole relationship between the people involved (analyst and analysand) that mattered for therapy, not just transference relationships.

PHENOMENOLOGY AND STRUCTURE

I think that the distinction introduced earlier between Klein's phenomenological approach and Fairbairn's structural approach is what allows Grotstein to maintain his dual-track hypothesis. While it is always possible, within a structural model, to look at the circulating information rather than the information structures, it is not a simple matter to derive structures from phenomenology, which is why there are a plethora of objects, good and bad, within Kleinian theory without any obvious ordering or underlying structure. The argument goes further than this, however, in that scientifically a structural model is a deeper and more explanatory model, and thus preferable.

THE IMPORTANCE OF THE PRECONSCIOUS

Having looked in great detail at Fairbairn's theory, compared it in various ways to other theories, and sought to apply it myself to the analysis of dramatic narrative (Clarke 1994, 2003a, 2003b), I have looked again at the way in which Fairbairn first describes it and his subsequent use of it. In particular, his use of the topographic categories – *Ucs, Pcs, Cs* – in conjunction with the dynamic structures of the model led me to think about a consistent use of the structural and topographic categories and what consequences this might have for Fairbairn's model (Chapter 6). The most important consequence is, I think, the revaluation of the preconscious as a dynamic unconscious aspect of mind. If one considers the concept of mature dependence offered earlier, then the disappearance of the system unconscious might seem like a fatal flaw for a psychoanalytic theory whose major claim to attention is the concept of the unconscious mind. I argue here that it is the *preconscious* (descriptively unconscious) that becomes the theatre of the self with the three ego fragments – ideal, libidinal and anti-libidinal – dynamically interacting as partitions of the mind to determine the ways in which a person will respond to (a) the world outside – conscious ego and the world of direct perception, and (b) the world inside – the system unconscious – the repressed but dynamic libidinal and anti-libidinal objects. It is the preconscious that is the crucible of the self in this model, a view that has resonances with both Grotstein, and Scharff and Fairbairn Birtles, who have suggested that there must be preconscious representations of the libidinal and anti-libidinal selves in Fairbairn's model.

In this attempt to clarify Fairbairn's model we start *without* a system unconscious as *essentially unitary, preconscious, bodily and personal selves*. We develop a structured internal world including a *system unconscious* as a consequence of our earliest experiences of *infantile dependence* – defensively maintaining essential relations to a primary caregiver in the face of ambivalence. As we grow towards maturity through the *transitional phase* the system unconscious is dissolved, if we are lucky, and we achieve *mature dependence* with a *dynamic, preconscious, realistic, integrated and interdependent self*.

Is this a counter-revolutionary position, as commentators, like Marcuse (1969: 190 *passim*), seem to imply? They argue that having a biologically based unconscious that is not subject to social manipulation is a guarantee of some objective basis for revolution or liberation. My argument would be that if we were always in some sense shackled by a biological endowment that could not be undone, whilst it might appear revolutionary in the dark days of oppression, there is nothing to stop it becoming oppressive when material circumstances are better. What seems to me to be more liberating is to argue that there are no intrinsic reasons for supposing that we are incapable of *freedom, creativity* and *decency* in a world of *mature dependence*, and that until we have organised ourselves to administer things to that end we will never know for sure.

Chapter 2
Fairbairn's model of mind

In this chapter I am going to provide a simple and accessible guide to Fairbairn's model of mind based on his mature works (Fairbairn 1952a; Scharff and Fairbairn Birtles 1994). This is similar in intention to Sandler *et al.*'s *Freud's Models of the Mind* (1997). I shall use as overall guidance two lists Fairbairn gave in outline of his object relations theory (1954: 105–25; 1963: 224–5) supplementing this as necessary from his own work and from the work of John Padel (1985) who has added to our understanding of the dynamic aspects of the model. This model will provide an essential background to the overall argument of the book as it is developed.

Fairbairn analysed Freud's libido theory and reached the conclusion that pleasure-seeking is an inadequate and inaccurate theory of human motivation. He proposed that the motivational rationale of human beings is object-seeking and object-relating and that pleasure-seeking for its own sake is a sign of disturbed object relations. Fairbairn also analysed the concept of the superego in great detail and concluded that this concept, as a prototype of an internal object, was very important. He subsequently founded his mature thinking on a consistent use of the concept of internal objects which he initially derived from Melanie Klein. His analysis of the superego led him to propose a model of inner reality as a dynamic structure of three ego–object dyads, in many ways similar to the tripartite division of mind in Freud's structural theory but based upon the concept of internal objects as complex dynamic structures.

'OBSERVATIONS ON THE NATURE OF HYSTERICAL STATES' (1954)

In his 1954 paper 'Observations on the nature of hysterical states' Fairbairn puts forward a 17-point list summarising 'the general views which I have come to adopt regarding the development and differentiation of the personality'. This list, combined with the diagram of endopsychic structure which he uses in his book *Psychoanalytic Studies of the Personality* (1952a), will provide us with the basic model Fairbairn had of inner reality, and shows the central importance of the development of this dynamic structure during the first year of life. I shall quote here directly from his summary:

1. The pristine personality of the child consists of a unitary dynamic ego.
2. The first defence adopted by the original ego to deal with an unsatisfying personal relationship is mental internalisation, or introjection, of the unsatisfying object.
3. The unsatisfying object has two disturbing aspects, viz. an exciting aspect and a rejecting aspect.
4. The second defence adopted by the ego is to reject and split off from the internalised object two elements – one representing its exciting aspect, and one representing its rejecting aspect.
5. The internalised object is thus split into three objects, viz. 'the exciting object', 'the rejecting object', and the nucleus which remains after the exciting and rejecting elements have been split off from it.
6. This residual nucleus represents the relatively satisfying, or at any rate tolerable, aspect of the internalised object, and is therefore not rejected by the ego, but remains actively cathected by it under conditions which render the term 'ideal object' appropriate for its description.
7. The rejection and splitting-off of the exciting and rejecting objects constitutes an act of '*direct and primary repression*' on the part of the ego.
8. Since the exciting and rejecting objects remain cathected while in process of being repressed, their repression involves a splitting-off, from the substance of the ego, of two portions representing the respective cathexes of the two repressed objects.
9. The splitting-off of these two portions of the ego from its remaining central portion represents an act of '*direct and secondary repression*' on the part of the latter.
10. The resulting endopsychic situation is one in which we find a central ego cathecting the ideal object as an *acceptable* internal object, and two split-off and repressed ego-structures each cathecting a *repressed* internal object.
11. The terms 'libidinal ego' and 'anti-libidinal ego' have been adopted to describe respectively the repressed ego-structure cathecting the exciting object and that cathecting the rejecting object.
12. The term 'anti-libidinal ego' has been adopted on the grounds that the repressed ego-structure so designated, being in alliance with the rejecting object, has aims that are inherently hostile to those of the libidinal ego in its alliance with the exciting object.
13. Being a dynamic structure, the anti-libidinal ego implements its hostility to the aims of the libidinal ego by subjecting the latter to a sustained aggressive and persecutory attack which supports the repression already exercised against it by the central ego, and which it thus seems appropriate to describe as a process of '*indirect repression*'.

14 Although direct and indirect repression of the libidinal ego are two processes of a very different nature, they are both included under the single term 'repression' as understood by Freud; but it is to be noted that Freud took no account of the direct repression of the *anti-libidinal* ego by the central ego, except in such incidental references as are contained in the passages in *The Ego and the Id* in which he raised the questions why the superego is unconscious, and whether, in the case of the hysterical personality at any rate, this instigator of repression is not itself subject to repression – questions to which the exigencies of his own theory did not permit of a satisfactory answer.

15 Although the anti-libidinal ego, the rejecting object and the ideal object are all independent structures playing different roles in the economy of the psyche, they are all included by Freud in the comprehensive concept of 'the superego'; and this source of confusion may be obviated by recognition of their independent character.

16 The endopsychic situation resulting from the twin processes of repression and splitting, which have just been described, is one which, in its general outlines, inevitably becomes established in the child at an early age, and in this sense may be regarded as 'normal'; but, especially in its dynamic aspect, it contains within it the potentialities of all psychopathological developments in later life.

17 The conception of this basic endopsychic situation provides an alternative, couched in terms of personal relationships and dynamic ego-structure, to Freud's description of the psyche in terms of id, ego and superego, based as this is upon a Helmholtzian divorce of energy from structure no longer accepted in physics, and combined as it is, albeit at the expense of no little inconsistency, with a non-personal psychology conceived in terms of biological instincts and erotogenic zones.

This 17-point list provides us with a summary of the development of the basic endopsychic structure at the point at which Fairbairn had more or less completed the development of his mature object relations theory.

Figure 2.1 is based on Fairbairn's own graphic representation of the internal world.

'SYNOPSIS OF AN OBJECT RELATIONS THEORY OF THE PERSONALITY' (1963)

Towards the end of his life Fairbairn produced a related list of axioms and expanded observations for the *International Journal of Psychoanalysis* that were a synopsis of his object relations theory. This outline of the concept of a dynamic system of endopsychic structures is more comprehensive than the list from the previous section, sketching as it does the whole of Fairbairn's

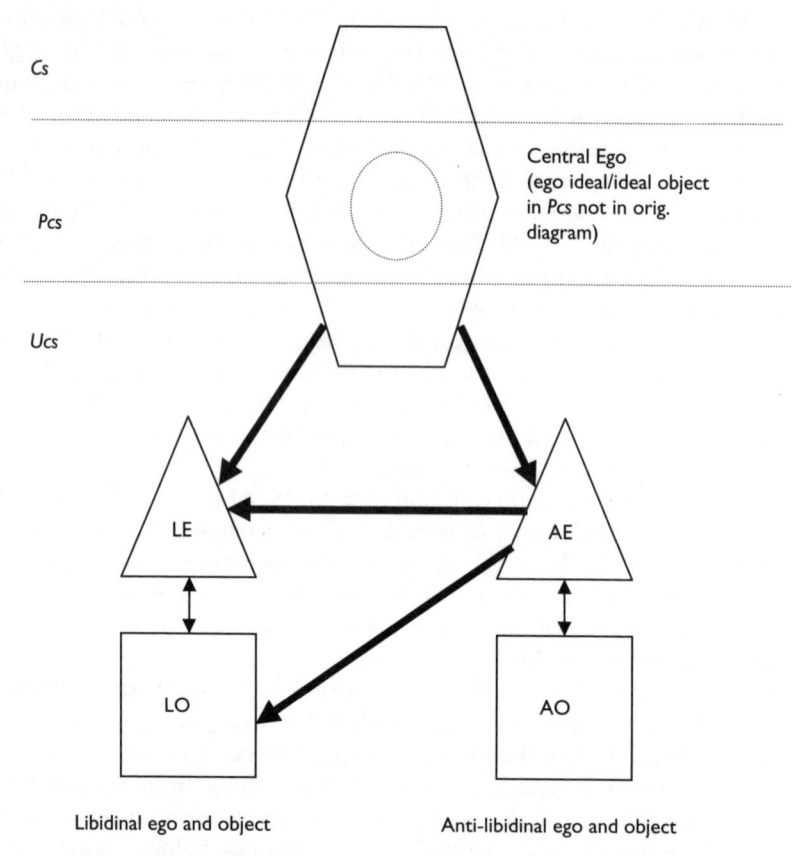

Figure 2.1 Diagram of endopsychic structure based on Fairbairn's diagram.

mature theory of object relations. I will quote this list and add some explanatory text and diagrams where necessary:

1 An ego is present from birth.
2 Libido is a function of the ego.
3 There is no death instinct; and aggression is a reaction to frustration or deprivation.
4 Since libido is a function of the ego and aggression is a reaction to frustration or deprivation, there is no such thing as an 'id'.
5 The ego, and therefore libido, is fundamentally object seeking.

I suggest that the following extract from Fairbairn's 1956 paper 'A critical evaluation of certain basic psycho-analytical conceptions' may help to clarify these first five points:

Psychological hedonism has for long appeared to the writer to provide an unsatisfactory basis for psychoanalytic theory because it relegates object relationships to a secondary place. Indeed it involves the implicit assumption that man is not by nature a social animal . . . as Aristotle described him . . . and that, accordingly, social behaviour is an acquired characteristic. This assumption would appear to be in complete contradiction of the facts of animal psychology. For throughout the animal world social (viz. object-seeking) behaviour is in general exhibited from birth . . . Further, it would appear that the instinctive behaviour of animals . . . is determined by the reality principle rather than the pleasure principle . . . it seems a reasonable assumption that an analogy may legitimately be drawn between the behaviour of animals and the basic behaviour of human beings; and, on this assumption alone, it seems justifiable to infer both that man is by nature object-seeking rather than pleasure-seeking, and that his basic behaviour is determined . . . by the reality principle rather than the pleasure principle.

(1956a: 52)

Figure 2.2 illustrates this propensity.

Further on in the same paper Fairbairn presents a critique of the instinct theory:

As regards Freud's theory of instincts itself . . . whilst it is meaningful to describe basic behaviour as 'instinctive', the conception of separate 'instincts' represents no more than a hypostatisation of trends manifesting themselves in instinctive behaviour. . . . More obvious perhaps is the tendency to treat the 'part instincts' as if they were separate entities; and here we have an example of the atomism which from the first constituted one current in Freud's thought. Such atomism is implicit in Freud's view that the adult sexual attitude is the product of a process of development whereby the various part instincts become organised under the supremacy of the genital impulse. . . . It is to be noted, however, that physical development is characterised, not by gradual integration of a number of separately functioning organs, but the gradual differentiation of a unified

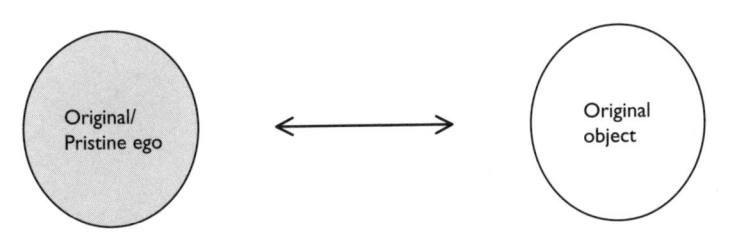

Figure 2.2 The original object relationship.

functioning structure; and it would seem reasonable to assume that mental development is characterised by a similar process.

(1956a: 53)

6 The earliest and original form of anxiety, as experienced by the child, is separation anxiety.

Fairbairn comments on the stages the person has to go through from infantile dependence to mature dependence, where infantile dependence is 'primary identification with the object' and 'the more mature a relationship is, the less it is characterised by primary identification' so that *'the abandonment of infantile dependence involves an abandonment of relationships based upon primary identification in favour of relationships with differentiated objects'*. (1952a: 42 emphasis in original) (see Figure 2.3).

He goes on to say:

> The process of differentiation of the object derives particular significance from the fact that infantile dependence is characterised not only by identification, but also by an oral attitude of incorporation. In virtue of this fact the object with which the individual is identified becomes equivalent to an incorporated object, or, to put the matter in a more arresting fashion, the object in which the individual is incorporated is incorporated in the individual.... Such then being the situation, the task of differentiating the object tends to resolve itself into a problem of expelling an incorporated object, i.e. to become a problem of expelling contents.
>
> (1952a: 42)

7 Internalisation of the object is a defensive measure originally adopted by the child to deal with his original object (the mother and her breast) in so far as it is unsatisfying.

It is important to note particularly that this internalisation is a defensive measure to help preserve the vital relationship with the caregiver. In 'Observations on the nature of hysterical states' (1954) Fairbairn includes a long

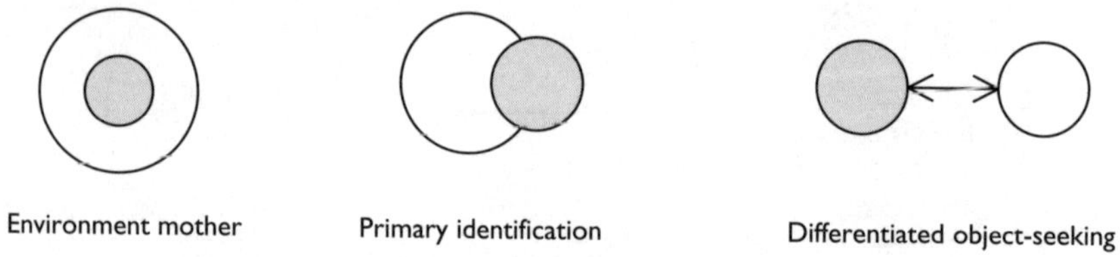

Environment mother   Primary identification   Differentiated object-seeking

Figure 2.3 The movement from fusion to separation.

footnote explaining this point of view and distinguishing it from the view of Melanie Klein and her followers:

> I can think of no motive for the introjection of an object which is *perfectly satisfying*. Thus, in my opinion, it would be a pointless procedure on the part of the infant to introject the maternal object if his relationship with his actual mother was completely satisfying ... it is only in so far as the infant's relationship with his mother falls short of being completely satisfying that he can have any conceivable motive for internalising the maternal object. This is a view which appears to present considerable difficulty for Melanie Klein and her collaborators, especially since the introjection of 'good' objects plays such an important part in their theoretical system.
>
> (107n)

Fairbairn then makes the final revision to this part of his theory:

> in previous formulations of my views ... I expressed the opinion that it was always 'bad' objects that were introjected in the first instance ... I have now revised my previous opinion to the effect (1) that the differentiation of objects into categories to which the respective terms 'good' and 'bad' can be applied only arises after the original (pre-ambivalent) object has been introjected, and (2) that this differentiation is effected through splitting of an internalised object which is, in the first instance, neither 'good' nor 'bad', but 'in some measure unsatisfying', and which only becomes truly 'ambivalent' after its introjection.
>
> (42)

8 Internalisation of the object is not just a product of a phantasy of incorporating the object orally, but is a distinct psychological process.

This process may be depicted as in Figures 2.4, 2.5 and 2.6.

9 Two aspects of the internalised object, viz. its *exciting* and *frustrating* aspects, are split off from the main core of the object and repressed by the ego. (Emphasis added)
10 Thus there come to be constituted two repressed internal objects, viz. the exciting (or libidinal) object and the rejecting (or anti-libidinal) object.
11 The main core of the internalised object, which is not repressed, is described as the ideal object or ego ideal.
12 Owing to the fact that the exciting (libidinal) and rejecting (anti-libidinal) objects are both cathected by the original ego, these objects carry into repression with them parts of the ego by which they are cathected,

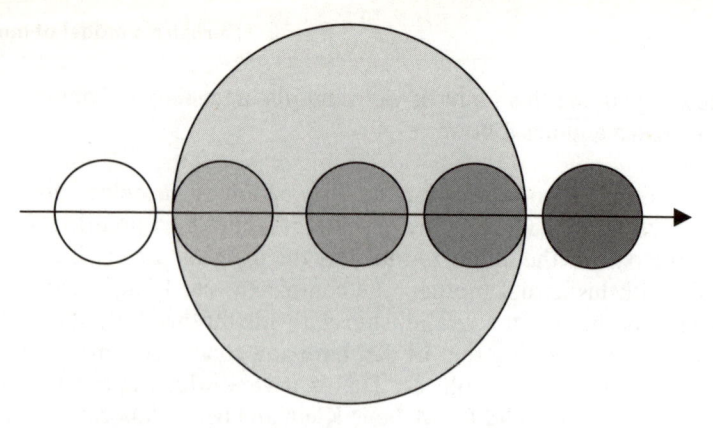

Figure 2.4 Physical processing of a real incorporated object.

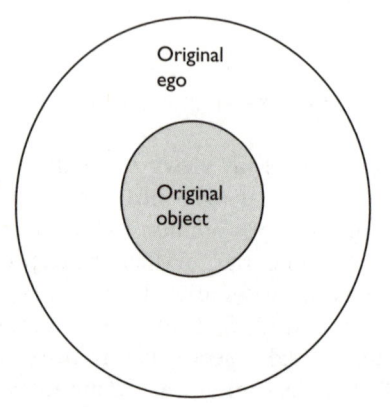

Figure 2.5 Psychological incorporation: the original object is incorporated into the original ego.

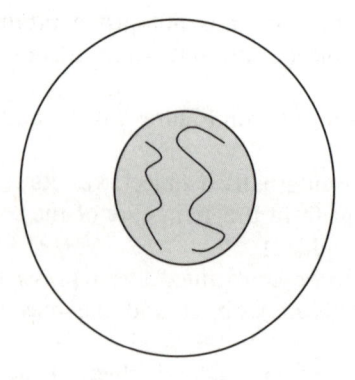

Relationships with the object are clustered according to the nature of the experience. This grouping of related experiences can lead to splits within the object.

Figure 2.6 Splitting of the original object based upon the infant's experience.

leaving the central core of the ego (central ego) unrepressed, but acting as the agent of repression (see Figure 2.7).

13 The resulting internal situation is one in which the original ego is split into three egos – a central (conscious) ego attached to an ideal object (ego ideal), a repressed libidinal ego attached to the exciting (or libidinal) object, and a repressed anti-libidinal ego attached to the rejecting (or anti-libidinal) object (see Figure 2.8).

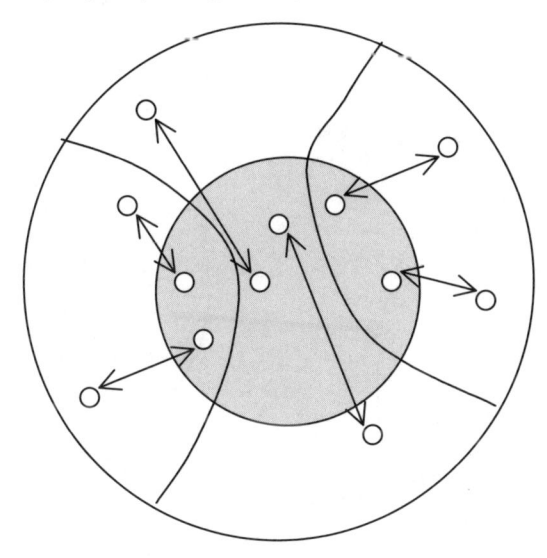

Figure 2.7 The object relations origins of the basic endopsychic structure.

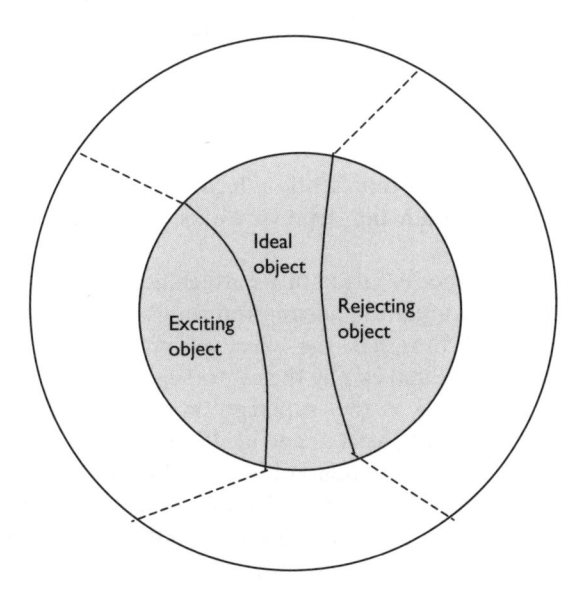

Figure 2.8 Splitting of the ego.

32 Fairbairn's model of mind

We can now represent the whole endopsychic structure as the dynamic relationships between three ego–object pairs where the ego–object pairs are linked together by libidinal relationships and the relations between the three are mediated by aggressive relationships (see Figure 2.9).

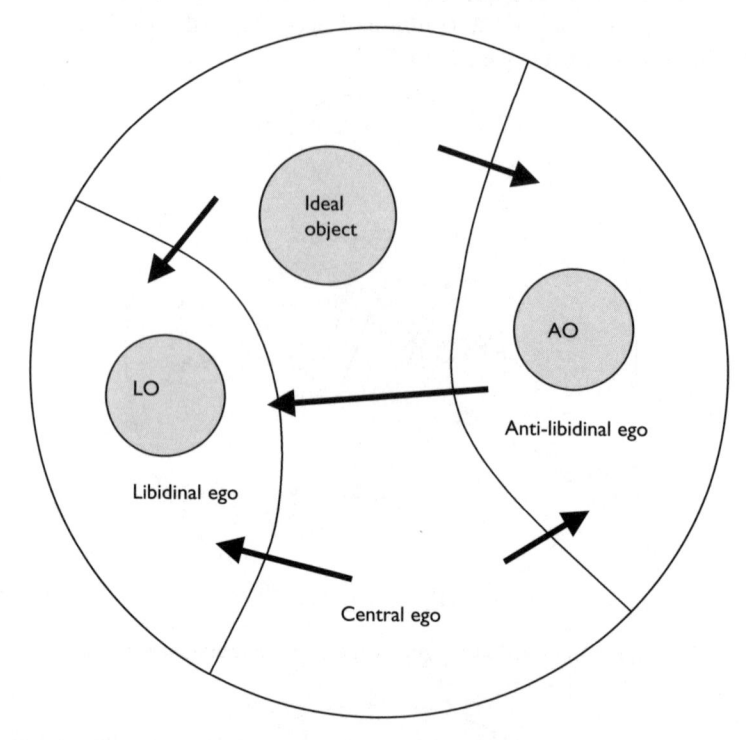

Figure 2.9 An alternative diagram of Fairbairn's basic endopsychic structure based on diagram in Scharff (1982).

14 This internal situation represents a basic schizoid position which is more fundamental than the depressive position described by Melanie Klein.
15 The anti-libidinal ego, in virtue of its attachment to the rejecting (anti-libidinal) object, adopts an uncompromisingly hostile attitude to the libidinal ego, and thus has the effect of powerfully reinforcing the repression of the libidinal ego by the central ego.
16 What Freud described as the 'superego' is really a complex structure comprising (a) the ideal object or ego ideal, (b) the anti-libidinal ego, and (c) the rejecting (or anti-libidinal) object (see Figure 2.10).
17 These considerations form the basis of a theory of the personality conceived in terms of object relations, in contrast to one conceived in terms of instincts and their vicissitudes.

The ego-ideal/ideal object, the anti-libidinal ego and the anti-libidinal object are all parts of Freud's notion of the superego.
The ego ideal is the positive preconscious aspect of the superego while the anti-libidinal self (ego + object) is the unconscious punitive aspect of the superego.

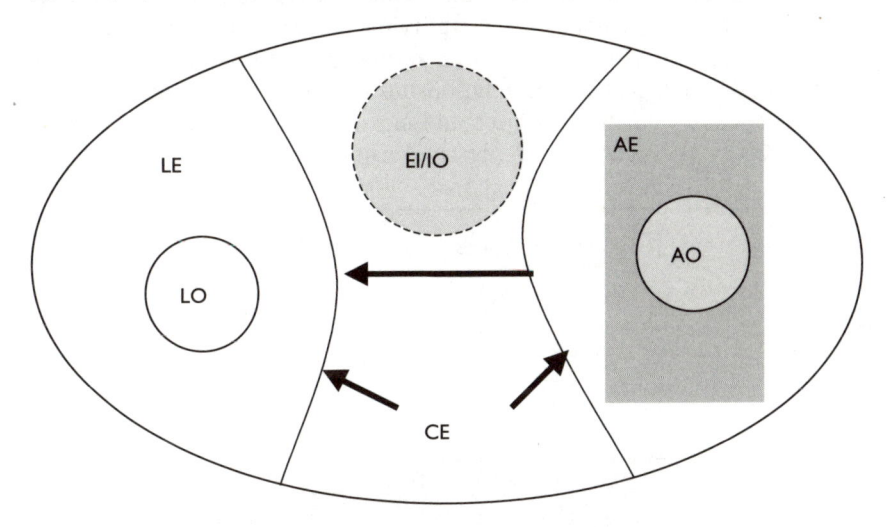

Figure 2.10 The Freudian superego and Fairbairn's ego-ideal.

Figure 2.11, which takes elements from Fairbairn's original diagram and Scharff's more recent version of the same diagram, has libidinal relationships represented as internalisations and aggressive relationships represented as directed vectors between putative selves.

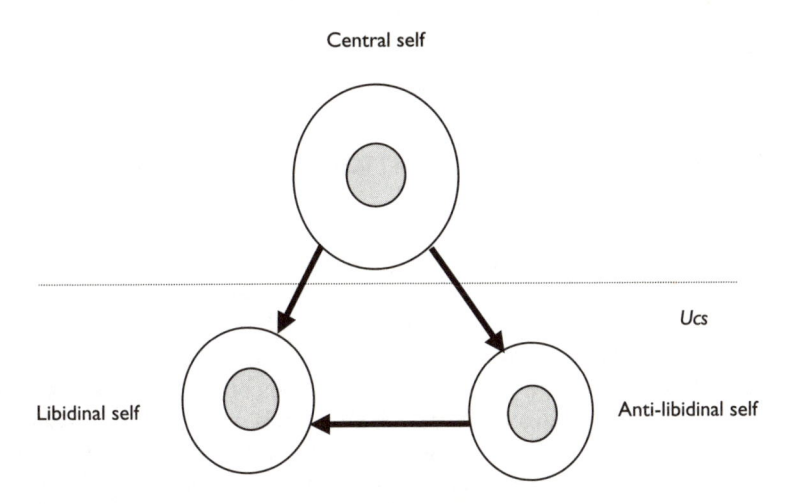

Figure 2.11 The basic endopsychic structure.

RELATIONSHIP TO A KLEINIAN MODEL

I want to suggest that there is a deep connection between the model that Fairbairn developed and the working model of inner reality used by some Kleinians. We can schematise and simplify the diagrams introduced so far to produce a diagram (Figure 2.12) that corresponds to a model that some Kleinians use to represent the relationship between the paranoid-schizoid and the depressive positions (objects in the paranoid-schizoid position being part-objects and objects in the depressive position being whole objects).

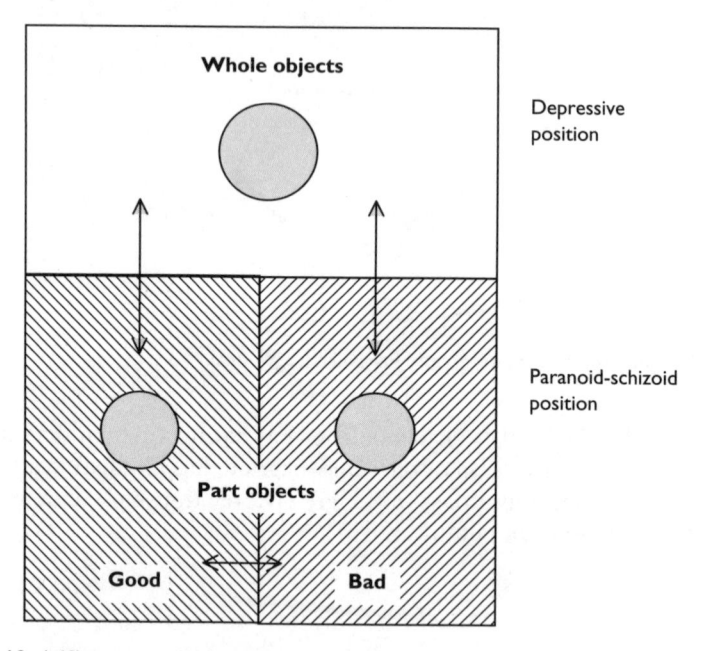

Figure 2.12 A Kleinian model based upon 'positions'.

DIAGRAMMATIC REPRESENTATION OF MODELS OF THE MIND

I have not discussed the problems of representing an essentially dynamic process of great complexity through the use of diagrams. I have presented other people's diagrams – Fairbairn's, Scharff's – and then used one of my own without discussing in any detail how it has been constructed. Freud did attempt to give his model a representation in terms of the actual anatomy of the brain, both in his 'Project' (1895), where there is some attempt to depict a neuronal description of the processes involved, and in the structural model where ego, id and superego are mapped onto a brain. The model I am discussing here is of a different logical type (Bateson 1973) to a neuronal or brain function model. It may be that in the future advances in neurophysiology and cognitive science will be able to identify areas of the brain that might be said to carry out mind-like processing but until that day arrives these models are separate from any issues of implementation.

I could have used a far more 'fuzzy' representation (see Figure 2.13) of the differences between the three selves so far defined, so as to represent more directly the reality, where there are no hard and fast divisions between these different selves so much as negotiable boundaries. The dynamism of the whole would become completely impossible if there was such a rigid demarcation as Figure 2.12 represents, but what it loses in exactness of representation it gains in its ability to help us think about each of its facets.

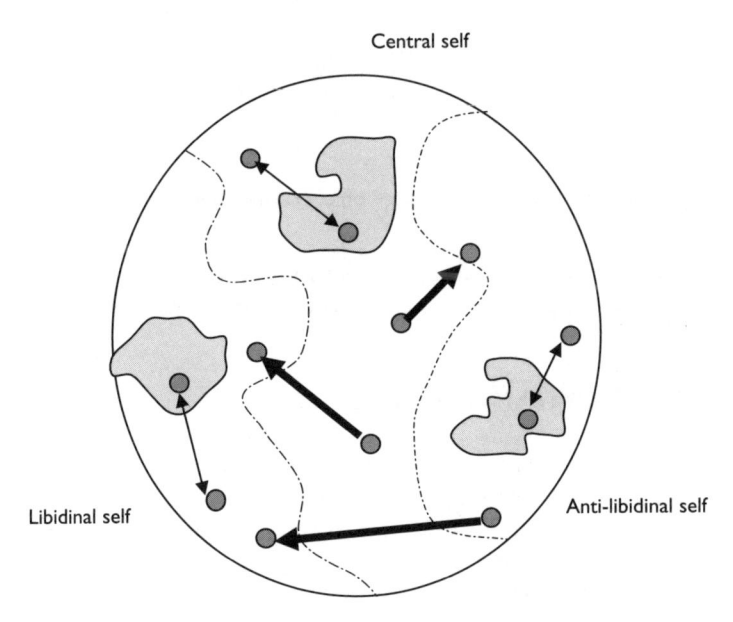

Figure 2.13 A 'fuzzy' diagram of the internal world.

It is important to note that each of the aggressive relations between ego-like entities in Figure 2.13 is also a higher-level relationship between two object relationships as is shown in Figure 2.14. This relationship between object relationships is akin to the triangular relationships that characterise the Oedipal situation.

Quite clearly chains of complex relations between object relations can form and have ramifications throughout the dynamic structure. For the sake of simplicity in Figures 2.15–2.27 I will be using the model of the central, libidinal and anti-libidinal selves which I introduced earlier. In this model libidinal object relationships are represented implicitly by including the

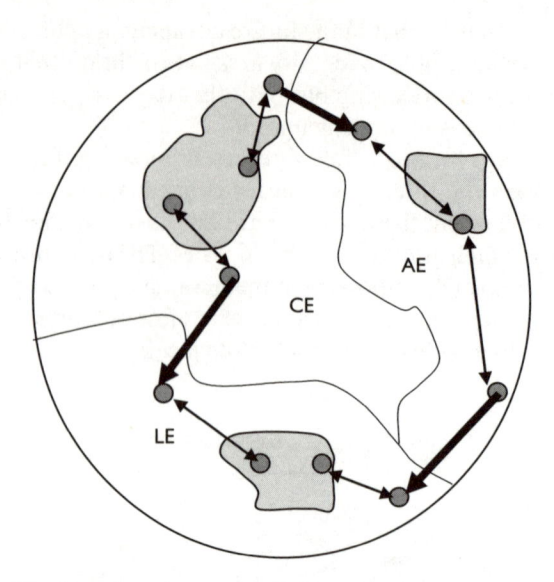

Figure 2.14 Possible dynamics of internalised object relationships.

object within the ego and directed vectors between the selves represent aggressive – repressing, dissociating – object relationships.

A MODEL OF DYNAMIC STRUCTURE

I will attempt to represent some aspects of the dynamics of the system as a whole by using Figure 2.11 based on Fairbairn's own diagram which I introduced previously in Figure 2.1. So, for example, Figure 2.15 is intended to represent the way in which a previously repressed or dissociated object relationship might overcome the repression barrier and come under conscious consideration. The circumstances surrounding such an occasion do not concern us here but could be part of a dream, or a daydream, or a therapeutic session, or an hallucination, or under stress, or whilst creating something, etc.

STRUCTURATION AND PSYCHIC CHANGE

Rubens (1984) is very clear about the process of development of the structures of inner reality in Fairbairn's theory and the fact that they are evidence of pathology, which in this case means the internalisation and splitting-off of particular object relationships as we have already seen with the development of libidinal and anti-libidinal selves. He then relies upon what he calls non-

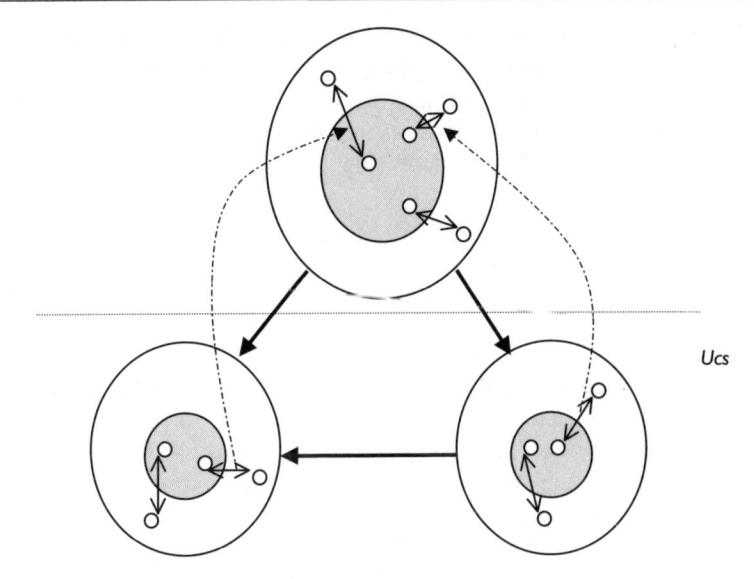

Figure 2.15 Object relations crossing the repression barrier and becoming conscious.

structuring internalisations to account for psychic growth, a view that is discussed in the next section.

First there is the incorporation of an unsatisfactory pre-ambivalent object, then there is splitting of this original object and the original ego leaving three ego–object dynamic structures in an unstable and potentially dangerous state. This is the schizoid forerunner to the stable basic endopsychic structure where the central self is in overall control of the disavowed and unruly sub-selves. I believe that the process of moving from the originally split self to a stable basic endopsychic structure is a precursor of what is called the manic defence. The process is likely to be manic as the search for a stable way of organising the three ego–object fragments proceeds. This preconscious manic precursor to the first stable sense of self is going to reappear in creativity as the manic womb of Milner and Ehrenzweig in Chapter 5 and is clearly also a precursor to the structured preconscious seat of the self that I hypothesise in Chapter 6. Ricardo Rey (2005), at a recent conference on Fairbairn and Sutherland, suggested this should be called the 'intuitive position'.

PADEL'S ACCOUNT OF PSYCHIC GROWTH WITHIN FAIRBAIRN'S THEORY

In response to a paper by Rubens (1984) Padel comments:

> Without doubt Rubens has pointed to an important incompleteness in Fairbairn's theory of psychic structure: although Fairbairn insisted on

'dynamic structure', he has no image for psychic growth and gives no account of the ongoing interchange there must be between the central ego and the split-off libidinal and anti-libidinal selves. Also, his formulas for cure do not go beyond diminishing the splitting, reconciling the split off elements of the self, and accepting a more open relationship with the world.

(1994: 296–7)

Padel then goes on to try and make good this lacuna by suggesting how psychic growth may occur within Fairbairn's dynamic structure:

During each night the day's ego–object relations will be worked over, and, ... will be established in the central ego by means of associative bonds. The new ego–object relations so accepted are likely to have the tripartite structure of libidinal, neutral and anti-libidinal aspects acquired during the provisional sorting; so that the whole of the central ego will have been, and will continue to be, built up of a mosaic of more or less closely integrated ego–object relations. Any mosaic is likely to have lines of potential cleavage under stress; in which identifications that have been formed in relationships are still unstable or have remained in potential conflict with other earlier-made identifications. A 'false self', for instance, will be an individual who early in life over-emphasised certain anti-libidinal identifications at the expense of the libidinal, and may even have taken a spurious libidinal pleasure in doing so; a psychopath will have emphasised the libidinal at the expense of the anti-libidinal.

(1994: 297)

In another paper Padel poses himself the questions 'what is the structure of the Central Ego, and how has it grown?' (1991: 607). I think the answers he gives supplement the account quoted above and give an indication of the content of the dynamic structure of inner reality:

I conceptualise the Central Ego as an emotionally rich and complex store of available relationships – and also relational possibilities, given an imaginative use of splitting and recombining ... The subsidiary ego–object relationships cannot be lacking in complexity (witness the way in which we come to know them in so many different guises in dreams); nor can they be absolutely split off from the Central Ego ... If analytical therapy works, it does so by making more exchanges available between the Central Ego and its subsidiaries, which allows the whole personality more possibilities of exchange with other people in the outside world ... The Central Ego may to some extent grow by internalising fresh relationships from the outside world, but these are likely to be shorn of their unacceptable and new aspects, which get sorted and filed in the categories 'libidinal' and 'anti-libidinal' ... we do this sorting and filing largely unconsciously in sleep. The growth of the Central Ego must rather take place by working over and accepting elements from the repressed structures.

(1991: 608)

It is important to recognise here that Padel implicitly proposes that aspects of the repressed sub-selves can become both *preconscious and conscious* and it is through this process that they can, under the right circumstances, be thought about and transformed so that they can become incorporated into the central self.

PROJECTIVE IDENTIFICATION

In Padel's discussion of the criticism of Fairbairn's theory he shows how the transitional techniques necessarily involve processes akin to what Klein calls projective identification (Hinshelwood 1991: 179–208):

If, as Fairbairn held, the very dynamic of the self (he spoke of the 'ego') is its object-seeking and object-attachment, it is impossible to internalise an object without internalising an aspect of the self affectively and purposively attached to that object; also, it is impossible to split off versions of the already internalised object without splitting off the appropriate versions of the self along with them. Therefore every internalised object would have been, for Fairbairn, a Kohutian 'selfobject' (though he might not have approved of the term). The purpose of internalising objects is twofold; first, to control and refashion them as required; secondly, to use them in projective-introjective exchange as a basis for external relationships. Clearly the repressed elements are less available for this purpose than those in the central self, but clinical experience shows that it is inevitable, once therapy gets under way, for the repressed elements, both libidinal and anti-libidinal, sooner or later to devolve upon the relationship of therapist and patient.

(Padel 1994: 295–6)

Similarly the distinction between the depressive and the paranoid-schizoid positions can be seen as equivalent to the distinction between the central ego and its ideal object and the subsidiary egos and their objects, where the emergence of the central ego, or third, is a necessary forerunner to mature dependence. This suggests that the move to the depressive position has structural consequences.

Padel provides an alternative account of psychic growth and transference from the point of view of the psychology of dynamic structure:

> The growth of the Central Ego must . . . take place by working over and accepting elements from the repressed structures. This requires interpretive links between the two-person and the three-person system. The only way in which the two-person system can be activated in such a manner that new experience does not become internalised, sorted, and filed in the old closed system of relationships is by the other person making some interpretative links in a two-person relationship. That is the crucial importance of transference interpretation.
>
> (1991: 608)

Padel goes on to describe how he thinks these links are made:

> First, the therapist shows understanding of the three-person situation presented by the patient, with some recognition of the problems it presents for him; to that extent the therapist is accepting what is brought but also differentiating the libidinal and anti-libidinal elements in it which have made the patient reject the whole libidinal–anti-libidinal relationship. . . . Next the therapist's strategy depends upon his assessment of the 'static' relationship. The repressed relationships in it, libidinal and anti-libidinal, cannot be equally bad – *or equally repressed* – at the same time: the libidinal is 'bad' when it threatens basic stability, which the anti-libidinal ensures; the anti-libidinal is 'bad' when it prevents or inhibits the basic enjoyment which gives meaning to living. So each of these rejected relationships will need to be looked at from the point of view of the other one, the therapist showing that the patient is putting him in the role now of seducer or disturber, now of the disapprover or inhibitor. Finally the previously rejected libidinal–anti-libidinal relationship may be reviewed for its reality-based badness or desirability.
>
> (1991: 608–9; emphasis added)

Padel notes that this is not intended to be prescriptive but 'when we feel we have been effective in a therapeutic episode, these are likely to be the passages in it that we can distinguish' (1991: 609). Again it is quite clear that, for Padel, aspects of the repressed sub-selves can become both *preconscious and conscious* under certain circumstances.

The transference is a common thread of the papers considered above but not the only occasion for psychic growth. I will end this section with the generalised account of psychic growth that Padel gives:

> The conditions for acceptance of a newly internalised relationship into the central ego and for its integration there will be positive and negative. The positive condition is that we have been able to reflect upon it and to regard each of its elements from the point of view of the other. . . . The negative condition . . . is the judgement that there are no

Fairbairn's model of mind   41

obstacles to reflection on it, no elements in it that conflict with the ego's established nature, and nothing to prevent regard of each element from the point of view of the other or to prevent free identification with each element.... Reflection, regard and judgement are according to this account the central activities which maintain growth of self. We turn these powers upon other selves which have the same capacities but different identities. When asleep we turn our reflection upon the ego–object's relationships we have internalised in the course of the day and also upon those previously repressed; this can lead to our acceptance of the new but also to the modification and acceptance of items previously rejected and repressed.... To employ our power of reflection, regard and judgement in waking life, we need as well the capacity to perceive, recall and anticipate and to act in ways suited to a situation, but especially to apprehend, survey and respond to others similarly capable of reflection and of apprehending and responding to us.

(1994: 299–300)[1] (see Figure 2.16)

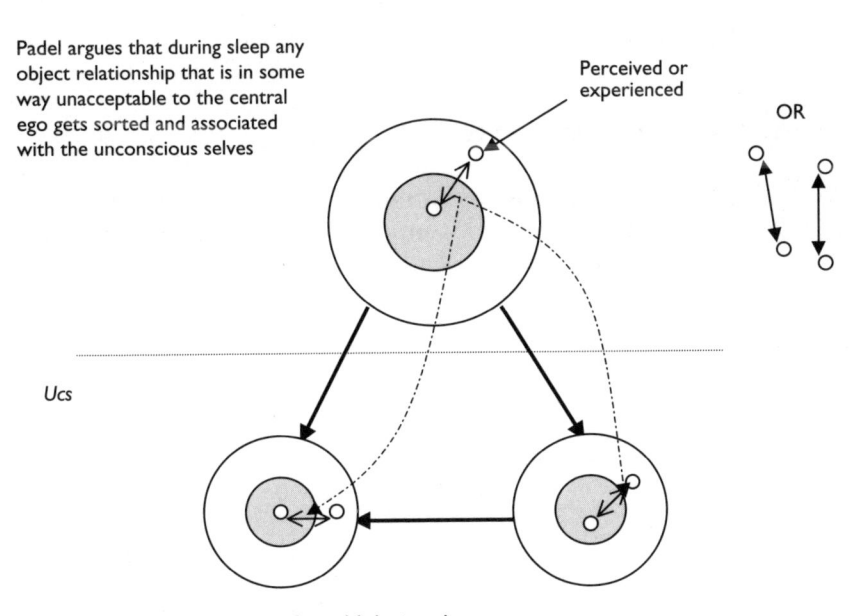

Padel argues that during sleep any object relationship that is in some way unacceptable to the central ego gets sorted and associated with the unconscious selves

Perceived or experienced

OR

Ucs

Figure 2.16 Sorting the internal world during sleep.

PSYCHIC GROWTH

Psychic growth within this model is represented by an ability to accept certain aspects of object relationships that were previously repressed. This means that aspects of object relationships from the repressed (dissociated) selves are (re)incorporated into the central self (see Figure 2.17).

42 Fairbairn's model of mind

Object relations from the split-off (unconscious) selves are (re-)integrated into the central self

Object relationship acceptable

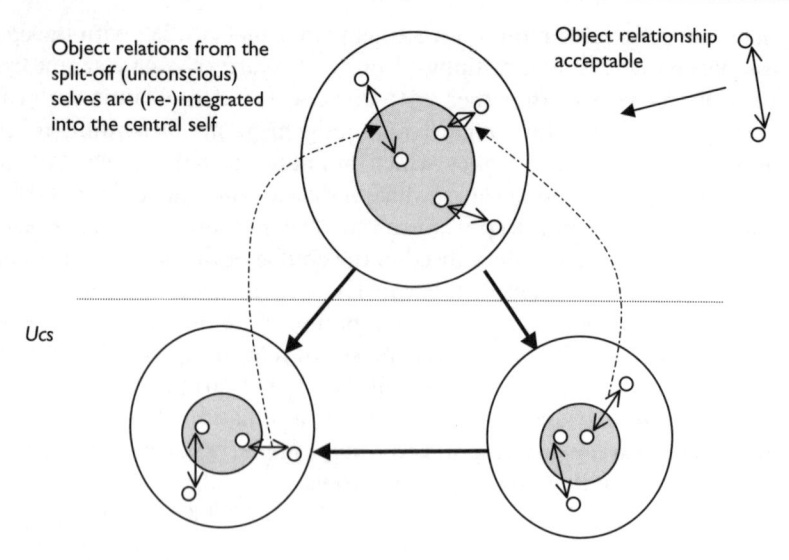

Ucs

Figure 2.17 Psychic growth.

DREAMS AND DAYDREAMS

In dreams, object relationships appear that reflect the relationships between the different parts of the endopsychic structure. Dreams are for the most part non-volitional (see Figure 2.18).

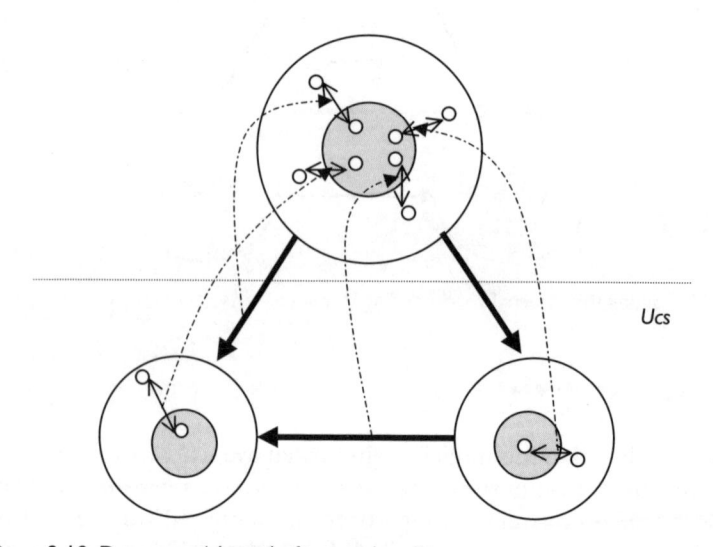

Ucs

Figure 2.18 Dreams as 'shorts' of internal reality.

Fairbairn's model of mind

In his paper on endopsychic structure Fairbairn explains how he views dreams from an object relations point of view:

> Dreams are essentially not a wish-fulfilment, but dramatisations or 'shorts' (in the cinematographic sense) of situations existing in inner reality ... so far as figures appearing in dreams are concerned ... such figures represent either part of the 'ego' or internalised objects ... the situations depicted in dreams represent relationships existing between endopsychic structures; and the same applies to situations depicted in waking phantasies.
>
> (1952a: 99)

PHYSICAL SYMPTOMS (OF MENTAL ORIGIN)

If we follow the logic of Fairbairn's theory through, at the centre of each psychosomatic symptom is some object relationship that has been repressed. Symptoms are non-volitional (see Figure 2.19).

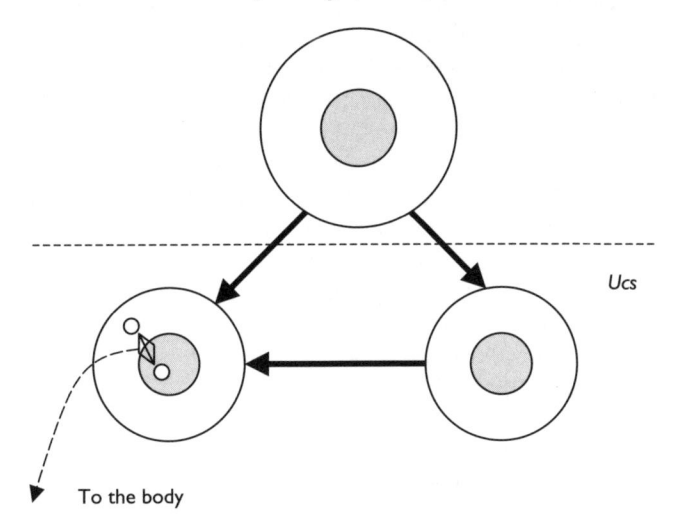

Figure 2.19 Hysterical conversion symptoms.

In his paper 'Observations on the nature of hysterical states' (1954) Fairbairn discusses the way physical symptoms can be used as a defence:

> Hysterical conversion is, of course, a defensive technique – one designed to prevent the conscious emergence of emotional conflicts involving object relationships. Its essential and distinctive feature is *the substitution of a bodily state for a personal problem,* and this substitution enables the

personal problem as such to be ignored. All personal problems are basically problems involving personal relationships with significant objects; and the objects involved in the conflicts of the hysteric are essentially internal objects.

(117)

CREATIVITY

Thomas Kuhn (1964) suggests that there are two paradigms for scientific development. One, which he called normal science, involves working within an established paradigm, or set of theories, and developing all the ramifications that such theories give rise to, exploring what might be called the 'phase space' of the currently acceptable set of scientific theories. An alternative scientific practice, which he calls revolutionary science, characterises a period in which a new set of theories is being introduced and the currently dominant scientific paradigm is being overthrown and replaced, with all the attendant difficulties and resistances. For example, the introduction of Darwin's theory of evolution, or Einstein's theory of relativity might represent historically recent examples of such a process.

I suggest that one can apply a similar sort of thinking to the notion of creativity. One could argue that there are two modes of creativity based upon a similar distinction to that used by Kuhn. The first one would involve central self operation only, that is, be the equivalent to normal science in that it operated totally within the established (conscious and preconscious) view of the person concerned. The other option, equivalent to Kuhn's revolutionary science, would involve aspects of object relationships from the unconscious becoming available (in the preconscious) and being incorporated into the (conscious) central self. That is, during the process of making the finished work, changes would occur in inner reality akin to those described earlier for psychic growth (see Figure 2.20).

PSYCHIC GROWTH REVISITED

When object relations from the unconscious (repressed/dissociated) selves are (re)incorporated into the central self these relegated object relationships can now be thought about and acted upon rather than being put into the system unconscious sub-selves. This leads to a decrease in the *complexity, size and power* of these unconscious sub-selves and an increase in the *complexity, size and power* of the central self, and, as such, an increase in the person's freedom to feel, think and act in accordance with the real complexity of their experience (see Figure 2.21).

Fairbairn's model of mind 45

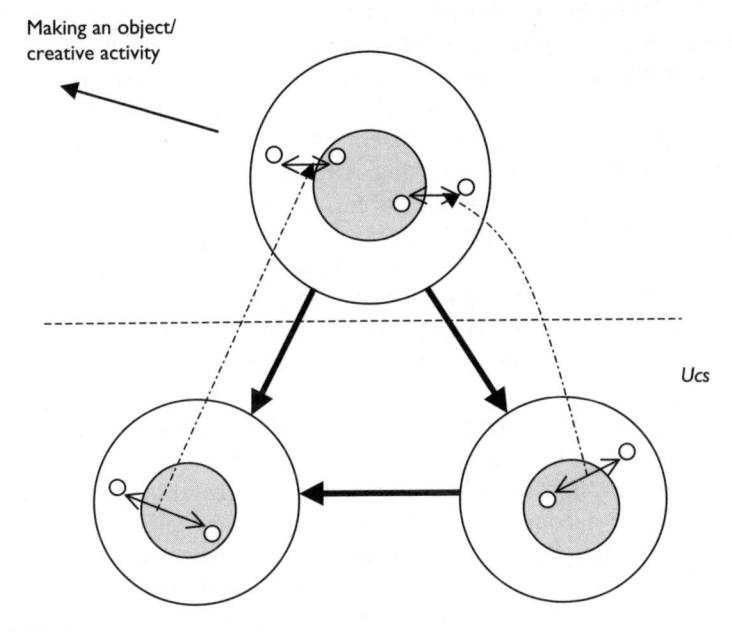

Making an object/
creative activity

Figure 2.20 Creativity.

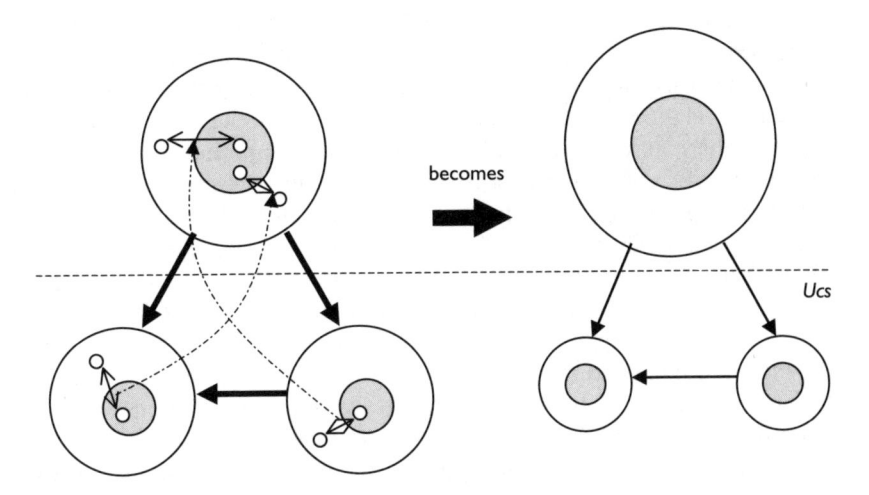

becomes

Figure 2.21 The process of psychic growth.

THE OEDIPUS SITUATION

In a section of his classic 1944 paper 'Endopsychic structure considered in terms of object-relationships' called 'The significance of the Oedipus situation', Fairbairn explains his own concept of 'indirect repression': 'the technique whereby aggression is employed to subdue libido is a process which finds a commonplace in Freud's conception of "repression" and my own conception of "indirect repression" ' (1952a: 119) and that his understanding of the origin of this technique is different from Freud's. For Freud 'the technique originates as a means of arresting or reducing the expression of libidinal (incestuous) impulses towards the parent of the opposite sex and aggressive (patricidal) impulses towards the parent of similar sex in the setting of the Oedipal situation' (119). However, for Fairbairn 'the technique originates in *infancy* as a means of reducing the expression of *both* libido and aggression on the part of the infant towards his *mother*, who at this stage constitutes his only significant object, and upon whom he is wholly dependent' (119–20; emphasis added).

Fairbairn explains that he has dispensed with the Oedipus situation as an explanatory concept in his account of the origins of repression, the genesis of the basic endopsychic structure, and of the differentiation of endopsychic structure: 'These accounts have all been formulated exclusively in terms of the measures adopted by the child in an attempt to cope with the difficulties inherent in the ambivalent situation which develops during his infancy in his relationship with his mother as original object' (120).

So, for Fairbairn: 'The Oedipus situation is ... a phenomenon to be explained in terms of an endopsychic situation which has already developed' (121). He considers how the child deals with the Oedipus situation as it materialises in outer reality as he develops a relationship with his father. Fairbairn suggests that the same processes used to deal with the mother are deployed in relation to the father. He suggests that the paternal exciting object and the paternal rejecting object are 'partly superimposed upon and partly fused with' the maternal exciting and rejecting objects. He argues that the relationship with the father has to be almost exclusively emotional in that the child is necessarily precluded from the experience of feeding at the breast of the father. He asserts that it is precisely because the child has the experience of a physical relationship with his mother's breast that his need for mother persists beneath his need for his father and subsequent genital needs.

As the child comes to recognise, in some measure, the genital differences between the parents as his own genital needs develop, so his need for his mother includes a need for her vagina and his need for his father includes a need for his penis. The more satisfactory his emotional relations with his parents the less urgent are his physical needs for their genitals. Since these needs are never satisfied directly, although substitute satisfactions may be sought through sexual curiosity, nevertheless a measure of ambivalence towards the mother's vagina and the father's penis is necessarily developed. This ambivalence is reflected in sadistic conceptions of the primal scene.

By the time the primal scene is envisaged, the relationships of his parents to one another has become important to the child and jealousy of each of his parents in relation to the other asserts itself. This jealousy is partly determined by the biological sex of the child and partly determined by the emotional relationships with each of his parents: 'The result is that he internalises both a bad maternal genital figure and a bad paternal genital figure and splits each of them into two figures which are embodied retrospectively in the structure of the exciting object and the rejecting object' (122). These internal objects have then already become complex composite structures built up partly by:

> superimposition of one object upon another and partly on a basis of the fusion of objects. The extent to which the internal objects are built up respectively on a basis of *layering* and on a basis of *fusion* differs ... from individual to individual and the extent to which either layering or fusion predominates ... would appear to play an important part in determining the psychosexual attitude of the individual in so far as this is not determined by biological sexual factors ... it would [also] appear to be the chief determining factor in the aetiology of the sexual perversions.
> (122–3)

It is important to try to make clear what these concepts of layering and fusion might mean within the object relations model we are developing. My view is that fused object relations are those with an object that is both mother and father, while layered object relations are of an object relationship with an object that is closely linked with another object with which this object relationship was first formed (see Table 2.1).

Table 2.1 Fusion and layering

Fusion	Layering
Self => mother/father	Self => mother Becomes Self => father (<=> mother) The link to mother being hidden

Fairbairn notes that although his explanation throughout refers to a boy child the explanation applies equally to a girl child too.

He draws attention to the fact that the classic Oedipus situation has not yet emerged in his description and suggests that it is determined by the constitution of the exciting and the rejecting object. That is, '*The Oedipus situation is not really an external situation at all, but an internal situation*' (123) since 'the nuclei of both the internal objects are derivatives of the original ambivalent mother and her ambivalent breasts ... *a sufficiently deep analysis of the Oedipus situation invariably reveals that this situation is built up around figures of an internal exciting mother and an internal rejecting mother*' (124). He argues that a deep analysis of the positive Oedipus situation should take place at three levels – the Oedipus situation itself, the ambivalence towards the heterosexual parent, and ambivalence towards the mother. All of these stages, he argues, can be found in 'Hamlet', and the Queen, as both the exciting and rejecting object, is the real villain of the piece.

The child finds it difficult enough to deal with one ambivalent object, so when he is called upon to deal with two ambivalent objects he seeks to simplify this complex situation by:

> converting it into one in which he will only be confronted with a single exciting object and a single rejecting object; and he achieves this aim ... by concentrating upon the exciting aspect of one parent and the rejecting aspect of the other ... for all practical purposes [he] comes to equate one parental object with the exciting object and the other with the rejecting object ... *the child constitutes the Oedipus situation for himself*.
>
> (124)

In the Oedipus situation, as described by Fairbairn, the initial structuring of inner reality takes place in relation to the original object, so the first exciting, rejecting and accepted/ideal objects are all based upon object relationships with the mother (M) or primary caregiver (119 *et passim*) (see Figure 2.22).

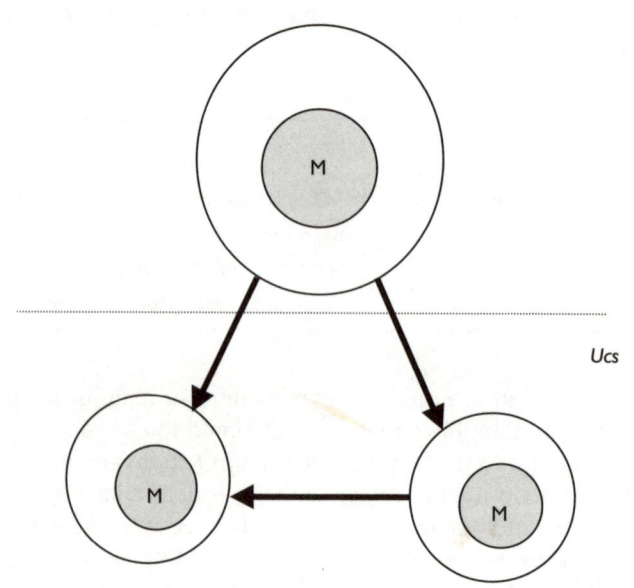

Figure 2.22 Basic endopsychic structure (prior to the Oedipus situation).

Fairbairn's model of mind

As the child grows up and comes to know the father (F), so object relationships with the father (or secondary caregiver) are added to those already established with the mother. Object relationships with the father lead to his being internalised in his exciting, rejecting and acceptable aspects too. Identifications with both mother and father (or primary and secondary caregivers) are combined (fused) (M/F) (119 *et passim*) (see Figure 2.23).

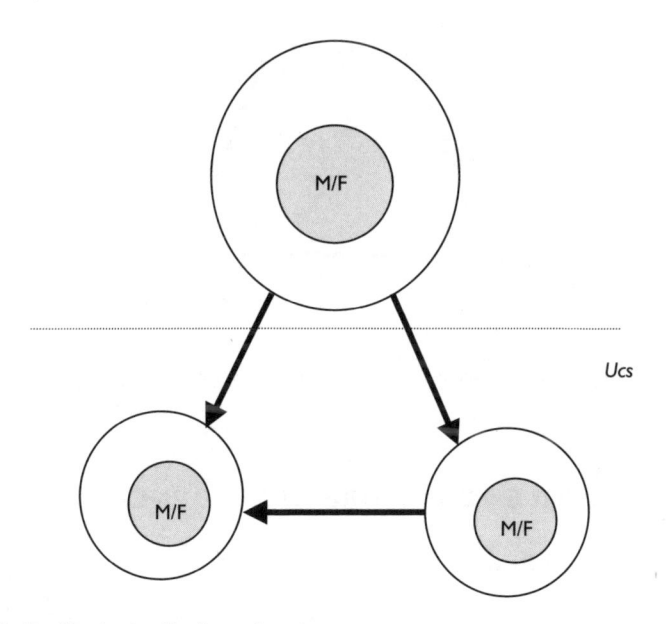

Figure 2.23 Conflict in the Oedipus situation.

At the time of the Oedipus situation, according to Fairbairn's account, there are no new structuring internalisations, but existing internalisations are weighted differentially according to whether they originate with mother or father. This can lead to a layering of the object relations.

If you take the top half of each object depicted in Figure 2.24 as being the dominant identification then you have something close to the resolution of the Oedipus situation for boys according to Freud. Similarly if you take the bottom half of each object as the dominant identification you get something like the resolution of the Oedipus situation for girls according to Freud.

Given that the mix of identifications is dependent upon the particular experience of the child, there is clearly room in this model for a wide variety of gender identifications to result (119 *et passim*).

50 Fairbairn's model of mind

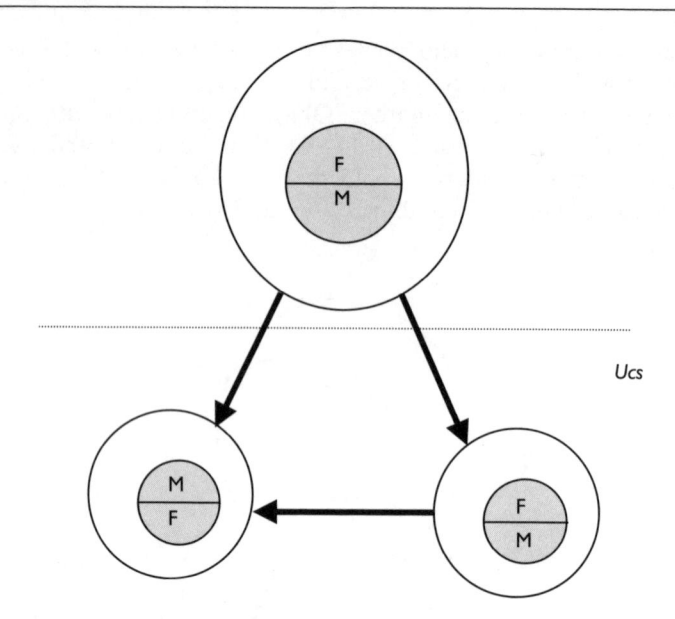

Figure 2.24 Oedipus situation resolved in a specific way (one of many).

FROM INFANTILE TO MATURE DEPENDENCE

Infantile dependence

This is characterised by primary identification, that is the unconscious selves are much more active and stronger than later, and also simpler (1952a: 38 *et passim*) (see Figure 2.25).

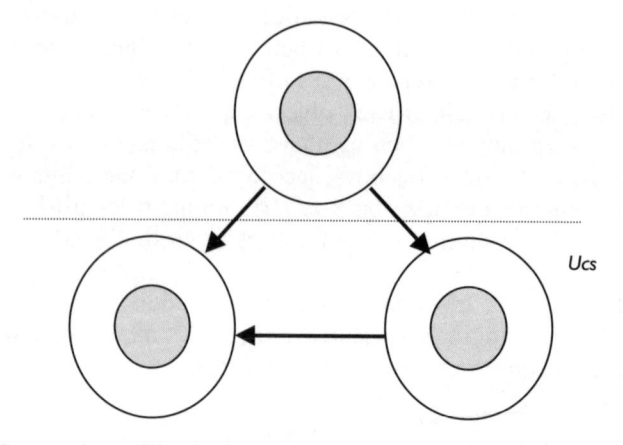

Figure 2.25 Basic endopsychic structure with similar strength sub-selves.

The transitional period

During the transitional period the central self is consolidated but the unconscious dissociated selves are still active. This is a period where the major defences are forms of neurosis appearing as transitional techniques – phobia, hysteria, paranoia and obsession. Each of these techniques is characterised by a specific way of projecting and/or introjecting objects (see below) (1952a: 38 *et passim*) (see Figure 2.26).

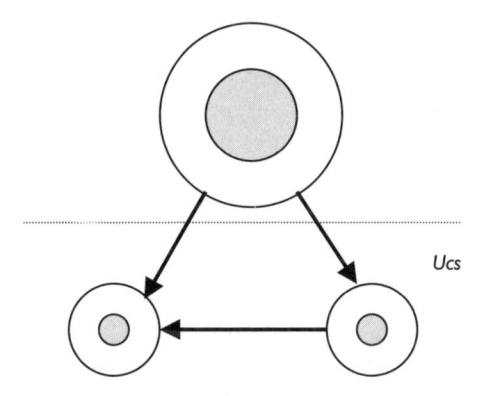

Figure 2.26 Basic endopsychic structure with central ego firmly in control.

Mature dependence

This is Fairbairn's equivalent of the Freudian 'genital character'. It is characterised by the fact that all external objects are treated as differentiated others. There is an absence of the projection and introjection of internal objects. This is an ideal and perhaps unattainable limit where the unconscious selves have disappeared, where everything can be thought about consciously and rationally. Here the internal object would be potentially conscious and represent a realistic reflection of outer reality; the ideal object would have become a realistic object. Relations would be with real external objects (see Figure 2.27).

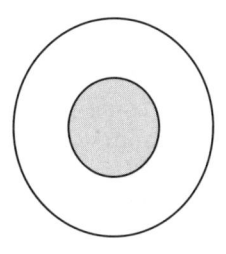

Figure 2.27 Mature dependence.

THE TRANSITIONAL TECHNIQUES AND THE DISTRIBUTION OF INTERNAL OBJECTS

In his 1941 paper 'A revised psychopathology of the psychoses and psychoneuroses', in a section called 'The stage of transition between infantile and adult dependence, its techniques and psychopathology', Fairbairn sets out to explore in some detail the transitional techniques associated with the transitional period. He argues that infantile dependence is characterised by primary identification with the object and that abandonment of infantile dependence involves abandonment of relationships based upon primary identification in favour of relationships with differentiated others. In mature dependence it is assumed that all relationships are with differentiated others. Since primary identification coincides with a period of oral incorporation, the task of differentiation from the object 'tends to resolve itself into a problem of expelling an incorporated object, i.e. to become a problem of expelling contents' (1952a: 43). He suggests that much of the rationale of Abraham's 'anal phases' is based upon this process. Fairbairn is opposed to Abraham's scheme of specific stages of libidinal development and makes use of only the early (sucking) and late (biting) oral stages in his work. He warns that 'it is not the case of the individual being preoccupied with the disposal of contents at this stage because he is anal, but of his being anal because he is preoccupied at this stage with the disposal of contents' (43).

Fairbairn defines the underlying character of the transitional stage as:

> a conflict between a progressive urge to surrender the infantile attitude of identification with the object and a regressive urge to maintain that attitude. During this period ... the behaviour of the individual is characterised both by desperate endeavours ... to separate himself from the object and degenerate endeavours to achieve reunion with the object.
>
> (43)[2]

Fairbairn looks at the anxieties associated with this conflict to see how they manifest themselves in each of the four techniques of the transitional period – the phobic, the obsessional, the hysterical and the paranoid.

The phobic state

'The anxiety attending separation manifests itself as fear of isolation; and the anxiety attending identification manifests itself as a fear of being shut-in, imprisoned and engulfed' (43). Fairbairn identifies these as essentially phobic anxieties and suggests that it is conflict over the progressive urge to separation from the object and the regressive lure of identification with the object that makes the phobic state intelligible.

The obsessional state

Given that primary identification and oral incorporation are so closely linked during infantile dependence, there will also be a close link between separation and excretory expulsion. So, the conflict of the transitional period can also present itself as a conflict between an urge to expel and an urge to retain contents: 'Just as between separation and reunion, so here there tends to be a constant oscillation between expulsion and retention ... the attitude of expulsion being attended by a fear of being emptied or drained, and the attitude of retention by a fear of bursting' (44). This latter can be accompanied or replaced by a fear of some internal disease like cancer. Fairbairn identifies these as obsessional anxieties, and defines conflict between an urge to expel the object as contents and an urge to retain the object as contents as the obsessional state.

Fairbairn comments that the phobic and obsessional techniques can thus be seen as two different methods for dealing with the same basic conflict corresponding to two different attitudes towards the object. The phobic conflict concerns *flight from* and *return to* the object and the obsessional conflict concerns *expulsion* and *retention* of the object. Fairbairn suggests that in the main these represent respectively a passive and an active attitude and suggests that the obsessional technique is predominantly sadistic in nature while the phobic technique is predominantly masochistic.

The hysterical state

Fairbairn suggests that the conflict here is one between *acceptance* and *rejection* of the object. Looking at the characteristics of the hysteric – the propensity for intense love-relationships and dissociative phenomena centred on the hysteric's body – he argues that the hysterical state is one where there is acceptance of the externalised object and rejection of the internalised object. He regards this as equivalent to the externalisation of the accepted object and the internalisation of the rejected object(s).

The paranoid state

By contrasting the hysterical and the paranoid states and their valuation of the externalised and the internalised object, Fairbairn comes to define the paranoid state as representing the *rejection* of the externalised object – seen as persecutors – and the *acceptance* of the internalised object – typified by extravagant grandiosity. He regards this as equivalent to the externalisation of the rejected object(s) and the internalisation of the accepted object.

Having interpreted both the hysterical and the paranoid techniques in terms of the acceptance and the rejection of objects, or the projection and introjection of the accepted and rejected objects, Fairbairn applies a similar interpretation to the phobic and obsessional techniques. His conclusion regarding the disposition of the accepted and the rejected objects in each of the techniques is summarised in Table 2.2. In terms of the development from infantile dependence to mature dependence, the order of the techniques in the Table can be seen to be moving from a situation that is close to infantile dependence to one that is close to mature dependence.

Table 2.2 Distribution of internal objects within the transitional techniques.

	Internal	External
Obsessional	Ideal, Libidinal, Anti-libidinal	
Paranoid	Ideal	Libidinal, Anti-libidinal
Hysterical	Libidinal, Anti-libidinal	Ideal
Phobic		Ideal, Libidinal, Anti-libidinal

○ Ideal object   ● Libidinal object   ● Anti-libidinal object

Fairbairn summarises the nature and importance of the transitional period as follows:

> The transitional period is characterised by a process of development whereby object relationships based upon identification gradually give place to relationships with a differentiated object. Satisfactory development ... depends upon the success which attends the differentiation of the object ... this in turn depends upon the issue of a conflict over

separation from the object – a situation which is both desired and feared. The conflict in question may call into operation any or all of four characteristic techniques – the obsessional, the paranoid, the hysterical and the phobic; and, if the object relationships are unsatisfactory, these techniques are liable to form the basis of characteristic psychopathological developments in later life. The various techniques cannot be classified in any order corresponding to presumptive levels of libidinal development . . . they must be regarded as alternative techniques, all belonging to the same stage of development of object relationships. . . . Which of the techniques is employed . . . would seem to depend upon the degree to which objects have been incorporated, and upon the form assumed by relationships which have been established between the developing ego and its internalised objects.

(1952a: 46)

Chapter 3

Fairbairn's theory and some philosophical interpretations of Freud[1]

Fairbairn, in his only contribution to the 'Controversial Discussions' (King and Steiner 1991), criticises the Kleinian concept of unconscious phantasy and offers an alternative description of inner reality:

> In my opinion the time is now ripe for us to replace the concept of 'phantasy' by a concept of 'inner reality' peopled by the Ego and its internal objects. These internal objects should be regarded as having an organised structure, an identity of their own, an endopsychic existence and an activity as real within the inner world as those of any objects in the outer world.
>
> (King and Steiner 1991: 359)

Susan Isaacs later rejected this view, on behalf of the Kleinian group during the Controversial Discussions. However, support for Fairbairn's view of inner reality can be argued to come, not only from its clinical use by many analysts within the Group of Independents, nor from the fact that contemporary Freudians have reconstructed Freud's structural theory in its image, but from the unlikely source of a philosophical interpretation of Freud developed by Donald Davidson in 1978 as a solution to the problem of irrationality (Wollheim and Hopkins 1982).

I have argued for the importance of psychic change to Fairbairn's model and his hypothesis of mature dependence, a developmental goal state of adulthood equivalent to the genital position in Freud's theory, conceived in object relations terms. I have used John Padel's work (Padel 1991, 1994) to develop an understanding of the processes of psychic growth and mature dependence. Mature dependence is not much talked about by Fairbairn, possibly because he thought it was a goal that we could only approach asymptotically. Richard Rorty's philosophical essay 'Freud and moral reflection' (1991), which builds upon Davidson's work on irrationality, does, however, offer a way to further our understanding of both psychic growth and mature dependence in Fairbairn's theory. I will not attempt to place these two philosophical essays in their proper philosophical context or otherwise relate them to the wider discourse of philosophy and psychoanalysis. I will, however, be using the models that Davidson and Rorty develop to show direct links with Fairbairn's theory and to suggest ways in which these models might help clarify our understanding of the nature of these three concepts of inner reality, psychic growth and mature dependence.

DAVIDSON AND THE STRUCTURE OF INNER REALITY

Davidson's paper, called 'Paradoxes of irrationality', is published in *Philosophical Essays on Freud* edited by Wollheim and Hopkins (1982). It looks at the problem of giving an account of irrational behaviour and related topics like self-deception, wishful thinking and weakness of will. A precursor to this paper was given before the British Psychoanalytical Society and responded to by Dr Edna O'Shaughnessy, from whose comments Davidson says he benefited. Davidson argues that, 'psychoanalytic theory as developed by Freud claims to provide a conceptual framework within which to describe and understand irrationality' (290), and that, 'after analysing the underlying problem of explaining irrationality, I conclude that any satisfactory view must embrace some of Freud's most important theses, and when these theses are stated in a sufficiently broad way, they are free from conceptual confusion' (290). I will be arguing that this developed theory looks more like Fairbairn's model of inner reality than Freud's structural theory.

Davidson argues that the problem of irrationality can be given a satisfactory answer if some central tenets of Freud's mature theory are accepted. He characterises these as follows. The first is that a mind contains, 'a number of semi-independent structures, these structures being characterised by mental attributes like thoughts, desires and memories' (290). The second point is that parts of this mind, 'are in important respects like people, not only in having (or consisting of) beliefs, wants and other psychological traits, but in that these factors can combine, as in intentional action, to cause further events in the mind or outside it' (290). The third point is that, 'some of these dispositions, attitudes, and events that characterise the various substructures in the mind must be viewed on the model of physical dispositions and forces when they affect, or are affected by, other substructures of the mind' (290–1). He hopes that the reader will agree that these doctrines are all to be found in Freud, and that they are central to his theories. As I have already mentioned, there is plenty of evidence that one can draw from Freud's works that supports this view, but Freud's structural theory was criticised by Fairbairn precisely because, in important respects, both the ego and the id did not fit easily into this sort of model, the ego being seen as structured but lacking energy and the id being seen as an unstructured reservoir of desires or wishes or instincts. Fairbairn argued that only the superego had the appropriate combination of structure and energy (beliefs and desires) to act as a model for internal objects. Fairbairn's modification of this starting point, as we have seen, does argue strongly for a number of person-like semi-independent structures.

I will not attempt to rehearse the arguments Davidson uses to produce his explanation of the irrational with a model of inner reality derived from Freudian theory as his premise. I will report some of his findings, however, since he does discuss the unconscious in passing. We also need to consider Davidson's conclusions since the paper by Rorty starts from these and builds upon them. A central part of Davidson's argument implies that the mind is more like a society of minds. This concerns the way in which mental events influence other mental events.

> There is ... a way one mental event can cause another mental event without being a reason for it, and where there is no puzzle and not necessarily any irrationality. This can happen when cause and effect occur in different minds.... But I suggest that the idea can be applied to a single idea and person. Indeed, if we are going to explain irrationality at all, it seems we must assume that the mind can be partitioned into quasi-independent structures.... To constitute a structure of the required sort, a part of the mind must show a larger degree of consistency or rationality than is attributed to the whole.
>
> (300)

He then applies this model to the problem of irrationality:

> the way would be clear for explanation if we were to suppose two semi-autonomous departments of the mind, one that finds a certain course of action to be, all things considered, best, and another that prompts another course of action. On each side, the side of sober judgement and the side of incontinent intent and action, there is a supporting structure of reasons, of interlocking beliefs, expectations, assumptions, attitudes and desires.
>
> (300)

It is interesting to note that one of the conditions that Fairbairn put upon inner reality in the section quoted from the 'Controversial Discussions' is the same as the argument developed above: 'These internal objects should be regarded as having an organised structure, an identity of their own, *an endopsychic existence and an activity as real within the inner world as those of any objects in the outer world*' (King and Steiner 1991: 359; emphasis added). Fairbairn, in 1943, foreshadows the argument that Davidson makes in 1978, and has explicitly included it in his description of inner reality.

To proceed to his overall conclusions then, Davidson argues the following:

> What I have tried to show . . . is that the very general features of psychoanalytic theory that I listed as having puzzled philosophers and others are, if I am right, features that will be found in any theory that sets itself to explain irrationality.
>
> The first feature was that the mind is to be regarded as having two or more semi-autonomous structures . . .
>
> The second feature assigned a particular kind of structure to one or more subdivisions of the mind: a structure similar to that needed to explain ordinary actions . . .
>
> The third feature . . . was that certain mental events take on the character of mere cause relative to other mental events in the same mind. This feature also we found to be required by any account of irrationality. It is a feature that can be accommodated . . . but in order to accommodate it we must allow a degree of autonomy to parts of the mind.
>
> (Wollheim and Hopkins 1982: 303–4)

The components of Davidson's theory are quasi-autonomous and person-like entities, also described as partitions of the mind. These elements, in an object relations theory, would be called internal objects and splitting, and are, incidentally, consistent with Fairbairn's view that what is split off and repressed is not an impulse but a dynamic structure. Davidson also argues that if some of the internal objects were unconscious this would not weaken his theory. So we can include repression and the unconscious in the model too. Splitting, internal objects, repression and the unconscious are the characteristic features of a thoroughgoing object relations theory of the sort developed by Fairbairn from his critique and interpretation of Freud's structural model. I am arguing that Davidson's interpretation and defence of Freud's theory, as it applies to the problems of irrationality, wishful thinking, etc., ends up positing an object relations theory like Fairbairn's.

Davidson ends his paper by suggesting that, 'A theory that could not explain irrationality would be one that also could not explain our salutary efforts, and occasional successes, at self-criticism and self-improvement' (305). This suggests that the theory might be suitable to explain conscience and psychic change as well, a line of thought that is developed by Rorty in his paper on Freud.

RORTY, PSYCHIC CHANGE AND MATURE DEPENDENCE

Before looking at Rorty's paper I want to comment on Fairbairn's concept of mature dependence. This is an important concept in terms of its being an implicit goal state for us all as we attempt to overcome the splitting of our infancy and achieve some sort of wholeness by exteriorisation of the bad objects we have interiorised. However, Fairbairn does not spend much time discussing this. His main comments are that, 'mature dependence involves a relationship between two independent individuals, who are completely *differentiated* from one another as mutual objects' (1952a: 42), and, in the same vein, 'mature dependence is characterised by a capacity on the part of a differentiated individual for co-operative relationships with differentiated objects' (1952a: 145). Rorty's essay allows us to talk about mature dependence in more concrete terms.

Examining Rorty's essay in some detail reveals that the underlying model he is using, based in Davidson's interpretation of Freud, is equivalent to an object relations model similar to Fairbairn's. I also want to demonstrate that for Rorty conscience is best understood as being embodied within an internal object like Fairbairn's concept of the ego ideal. Similarly, I want to show that Rorty's view of change is similar to that developed by John Padel, and that change comes about by opening up the relationships between the ego and its internal objects into some sort of conversation with each other and with the external world, turning the closed system of the inner world into an open system, as Fairbairn argued in his paper on hysteria (1954). A further common feature, between Rorty's interpretation and Fairbairn's model, is that psychic growth and mature dependence are about finding the most comprehensive unified set of beliefs and desires one can, and that an essential aspect of maturity is to turn away from concerns about internal consistency, towards the external world and one's place within it. In Fairbairn's view of mature dependence all the previously bad *internal* objects have become *exteriorised* and the problem then is one of relating to *external* objects, good and bad.

Although Rorty's essay does suggest all these parallels to me, it is also true that he does not deal with the *mechanisms* involved in making these changes. In particular, there is a somewhat simplified and too easy resolution of the problem of externalising bad objects in the process of integrating the self. However, I think that the argument that Davidson and Rorty, taken together, have produced is indicative of and depends upon a thoroughgoing object relations theory consistent with Fairbairn's theory. There is some benefit in comparing the two models if only because Rorty's essay raises the question of mature dependence again in a more detailed form and, like Padel's development of Fairbairn's theory regarding psychic growth, this may lead to an extension of Fairbairn's theory. These parallels between Fairbairn's model (developed in the 1940s) and these philosophical interpretations of Freud (developed in the late 1970s and 1980s) are remarkable because of the degree to which the interpretations have brought to the fore the object relations aspect of Freud, *without* at the same time noting their distance from Freud's structural theory. Nor do they appear aware of any connection with Fairbairn's object relations theory. I believe that these essays can be used to both strengthen a thoroughgoing object relations approach and develop the internal arguments about what exactly that approach is and entails.

If Davidson's problem is the explanation of irrationality then Rorty's is to see what the consequences of the mechanisation of mind might have on morality. Rorty, in his essay 'Freud and moral reflection', in *Essays on Heidegger and Others*, says, 'if humanity is a natural kind, then perhaps we can find our own centre and so learn how to live well. But if we are machines, then it is up to us to invent a use for ourselves' (1999: 144). Contextualising Freud he says, 'in trying to see how Freud fits into this story of decentring-as-mechanisation one should begin by noting that Freud was not the first to suggest that, having mechanised everything else, we mechanise the mind as well' (144). Rorty notes that Hume had also been involved in just such an enterprise. However, 'unlike Hume, Freud did change our self image. Finding out about our unconscious motives is not just an interesting exercise, but more like a moral obligation' (145). In 1955 Roger Money-Kyrle comes to a similar conclusion in his essay 'Psychoanalysis and ethics' when he argues that, 'wisdom – which for our immediate purpose we have now equated with psychological insight – although increasing, is always incomplete. . . . If therefore the ethical question is not to be purely academic, we must stop asking about the ethics of the wise, and ask instead about the changing ethics of those whose wisdom is increasing' (1955: 424). Later he says 'we believe that what we call health is something that can be achieved by insight . . . a normal – that is, healthy – mind is one that knows itself' (438). In a footnote to this comment he adds ' "a mind that knows itself" and "an integrated mind" are I think equivalent' (438).

Having briefly considered Freud's comments that the ego is not even master in its own home Rorty suggests that the Freudian unconscious, 'looks like somebody who is stepping into our shoes, somebody who has different purposes than we do. It looks like a person using us rather than a thing we can use' (1991: 146). At this point Rorty introduces what he calls Davidson's 'remarkable essay'. He describes Davidson's defence of Freud's insistence on 'partitioning the self' which always upsets philosophers who hope to remain faithful to 'the common-sense assumptions that a single body typically contains a single self'. Rorty's description of Davidson's conclusions are as follows:

> He identifies . . . being a person with being a coherent and plausible set of beliefs and desires. Then he points out that the force of saying that a human being sometimes behaves irrationally is that he or she sometimes exhibits behaviour that cannot be explained by reference to a single such set. Finally he concludes that the point of 'partitioning' the self between a conscious and an unconscious is that the latter can be viewed as an alternative set, inconsistent with the familiar set that

we identify with consciousness, yet sufficiently coherent to count as a person.

(147)

This leads on to the following characterisation of Freud's theory: 'Freud populated inner space ... with analogues of persons – internally coherent clusters of beliefs and desires. Each of these quasi-persons is, in the Freudian picture, part of a single unified *causal* network but not of a single person' (147). Rorty comments further that knowledge of this causal network is necessary to predict and control a person's behaviour but that only one of the persons in this network is available to introspection at any given time.

Rorty suggests that if we take this interpretation of Freud seriously we will:

> wish to become acquainted with these unfamiliar persons, if only as a first step towards killing them off. This wish will take the place ... of the religious and metaphysical desire to find one's 'true centre'. It initiates a task that can plausibly be described as a moral obligation – the task whose goal is summed up in the phrase 'where id was, there shall ego be'.
>
> (148)

Rorty then makes an important distinction between two different senses of the term unconscious in the view of Freud he is proposing. The one that he accepts is one which 'stands for one or more well articulated systems of belief and desires, systems that are just as complex, sophisticated and internally consistent as the normal adult's conscious beliefs and desires' (149). He rejects the view of the unconscious as a 'seething mass of inarticulate, instinctual energies, a "reservoir of libido" to which consistency is irrelevant' (149). This description again is directly comparable to an object relations view of internal objects, that can be illustrated here with Fairbairn's depiction of the difference between what Freud called the primary and secondary processes:

> According to the principle of dynamic structure, it is not a case of a structural ego being differentiated under the pressure of the impact of external reality out of an original id which is relatively formless, so much as of an id being a structure with primitive characteristics which is differentiated from an original (and relatively primitive) ego-structure under the influence of repression; and it can be seen that once such a differentiation has occurred, the repressed id-structure will retain primitive features (and acquire exaggerations of such features under the influence of repression), while that part of the ego which remains conscious and in touch with external reality will be free to develop under the influence of relationships with external objects ... The primary process will present itself as a characteristic feature of the activity of the repressed

id-structure, and the secondary process as a characteristic feature of the activity of the conscious ego-structure; and the nature of artistic activity will then come to be described, not as an ego-controlled regression to the level of the primary process but rather as an attempt to reconcile the primitive expression of a repressed id-structure with the requirements of a conscious ego-structure oriented towards external objects in a social mileu.

(1953b: 167)

Similarly Rorty suggests that the application of psychoanalytic notions to normal life might lead to a revision of our self-image and that the unconscious, as he describes it above, substitutes 'transactions between two or more "intellects" for the traditional picture of one "intellect" struggling with a mob of "irrational" brutes' (1991: 149). This leads Rorty to suggest that our self-knowledge will be a matter of enlargement or enrichment:

To say 'Where id was, there shall ego be' will not mean 'Whereas I was once driven by instinct, I shall become autonomous, motivated solely by reason'. Rather, it will mean something like: 'Once I could not figure out why I was acting so oddly, and hence wondered if I were, somehow, under the control of a devil or a beast. But now I shall be able to see my actions as rational, as making sense, though perhaps based upon mistaken premises. I may even discover that these premises were not mistaken, that my unconscious knew better than I did.'

(150)

Rorty suggests that this way of thinking about the passions is equally applicable to conscience: 'It makes conscience like passion one more set of human beliefs and desires – another story about how the world is. . . . More important, it makes it just another story – not one that (in the case of the passions) is automatically suspect nor one that (in the case of conscience) is automatically privileged' (151). This view seems to me to be totally consistent with Fairbairn's view of the ego ideal as an internal object and more generally his psychology of dynamic structure.

Rorty goes on to suggest what the importance of this way of looking at things might be:

Freud gave us a new technique for achieving a genuinely stable character: the technique of lending a sympathetic ear to our own tendencies to instability, by treating them as alternative ways of making sense of the past, ways that have as good a claim to our attention as do the familiar beliefs and desires that are available to introspection.

(152)

Concerning growth he says, 'maturity will, according to this view, consist rather in an ability to seek out new redescriptions of one's own past' (152). Combining these views and looking (ironically) at the practice of psychoanalysis he says:

> The point of psychoanalysis is the same as that of reflection on the sort of character one would like to have, once one ceases to take a single vocabulary for granted and begins to revise and enlarge the very vocabulary in which one is at present reflecting. The point of both exercises is to find new self-descriptions whose adoption will enable one to alter one's behaviour. Finding out the views of one's unconscious about one's past is a way of getting some additional suggestions about how to describe (and change) oneself in the future. As a way of getting such suggestions, psychoanalysis differs from reading history, novels or treatises on moral philosophy in being more painful, in being more likely to produce radical change, and in requiring a partner.
>
> (153)

Rorty distinguishes between public and private morality and suggests that private morality, or the development of character, is his only concern, as it was Freud's. Rorty does not believe that Freud has any contribution to make to social theory: 'His domain is the portion of morality that cannot be identified with "culture"; it is the private life, the search for character, the attempt of individuals to be reconciled with themselves (and, in the case of some exceptional individuals, to make their lives works of art)' (153). Such explorations can take two different forms in Rorty's view: 'a search for purity or a search for self-enlargement' (154). Rorty's view is that 'Freud is an apostle of this aesthetic life, the life of unending curiosity, the life that seeks to extend its own bounds rather than find its centre' (154). I believe that this description, with its parallels to Nietzsche's idea of self-enlargement, as Rorty comments, would also fit Fairbairn and his view of psychic growth and mature dependency. The search for purity is for Rorty a 'nay-saying' approach to life.

Rorty now turns to the consequences of this view of Freud in terms of psychic growth and mature dependence. He says:

> Freud, by helping us to see ourselves as centreless, as random assemblages of contingent and idiosyncratic needs rather than as more or less adequate exemplification of a common human essence, opened up new possibilities for the aesthetic life. . . . It has helped us think of moral reflection and sophistication as a matter of self-creation rather than self-knowledge. Freud made the paradigm of self-knowledge the discovery of the fortuitous materials out of which we must construct ourselves rather than the discovery of the principles to which we must conform. He thus made

the desire for purification seem more self-deceptive, and the quest for self-enlargement more promising.

(155)

He goes on to describe the consequences of our accepting the model he attributes to Freud: 'not until Freud did we get a usable way of thinking ourselves as machines to be tinkered with, a self-image that enabled us to weave terms describing psychic mechanisms into our strategies of character formation' (158). In the same vein he says:

> his work enables us to construct richer and more plausible narratives of this ad hoc sort – more plausible because they will cover *all* the actions one performs in the course of one's life, even the silly, cruel and self-destructive actions. More generally, Freud helped us see that the attempt to put together such a narrative – one that minimises neither the contingency nor the decisive importance of the input into the machine that each of us is – must take the place of an attempt to find the function common to all such machines.
>
> (161)

Rorty argues that this view is neither bleak nor does it imply our separation from others: 'Freud does nothing to diminish a sense of human solidarity that, rather than encompassing the entire species, restricts itself to such particular communal movements as modern science, bourgeois liberalism or the European novel' (163), and 'letting us see the narratives of our own lives as episodes within such larger historical narratives is, I think, as much as the intellectuals are able to do in aid of morality' (163).

These comments, and those that follow, represent a valuable contribution to our attempts to understand what mature dependence might be. I think that it is also imperative that we ask the question as to just how possible mature dependence is. It strikes me that the negative assessment of the possibility of mature dependence that characterises a lot of psychoanalytic thinking is based on a residual perfectionist bent. The maturely dependent person is not perfectly integrated, but they are not pathologically split either; they are living and working productively in their historically contingent situation. I think that this view of mature dependence might be profitably compared to Adam Phillips' view of sanity as developed in his recent book *Going Sane* (2005).

Some work on attachment theory (see Chapter 9 for more detailed consideration of attachment theory) suggests that about two-thirds of the population are securely attached (Ainsworth *et al.* 1978). I interpret this as meaning there is a minimal amount of pathological splitting in these people. This might lead one to hope that mature dependence is a much more common, albeit a much more mundane phenomenon, than we sometimes imagine.

To quote Rorty again:

> We pick up Freud by the wrong handle if we try to find an account of 'moral motivation' that is more than a reference to the historical contingencies that shaped the process of acculturation in our region and epoch.
> Historical narratives about the social and intellectual movements are the best tools to use in tinkering with ourselves, for such narratives suggest vocabularies of moral deliberation in which to spin coherent narratives about our individual lives.
>
> (1991: 163)

Rorty concludes in the same vein:

> narratives that help one identify oneself with communal movements engender a sense of being a machine geared into a larger machine. This is a sense worth having. For it helps reconcile an existentialist sense of contingency and mortality with a Romantic sense of grandeur. It helps us to realise that the best way of tinkering with ourselves is to tinker with something else – a mechanist's way of saying that only he who loses his soul will save it.
>
> (163)

Chapter 4
Internal objects and inner reality: Fairbairn and Klein

There have been many attempts to compare and evaluate the theoretical standpoints of Fairbairn and Klein as two of the most seminal object relations thinkers. One of the underlying stumbling blocks to a full understanding of Fairbairn's theoretical framework has been the tendency to conceptualise his diagram, and thus his model of inner reality, as either a static structure or as a structure that is duplicated in relation to every new object relationship, neither of which are true. The centrally important feature of the model is its implicit dynamics. Fairbairn stresses this throughout his mature work but somehow the message never got through. This attempt to compare the two thinkers is therefore built upon a dynamic model of inner reality based upon animating Fairbairn's diagram and benefiting from Padel's crucial work on the dynamics of endopsychic structure and its role in psychic change.

I hypothesise that for every configuration of Fairbairn's basic endopsychic structure there is a particular dynamic that can account for each of the identifiable Kleinian phenomena. This clearly has limits in that those Kleinians who believe that unconscious phantasy is ultimately of a biological origin and the *fons et origio* of all human thought and feeling will not be able to accept the essentially social, interpersonal view of the unconscious that Fairbairn's theory represents.

Several years ago, at a seminar run by Essex Institute for Psychoanalytic Studies (a group that later formed the nucleus of the Centre for Psychoanalytic Studies at Essex University), Anne Alvarez, a Kleinian child psychotherapist from the Tavistock Clinic, used the diagram of Kleinian positions in Figure 4.1 as an aide to reviewing the relationship between Klein's depressive and paranoid-schizoid positions.

As I was already familiar with Fairbairn's theory and his model of the basic endopsychic structure, and interested in seeing how far this theory might be able to model Klein's theory, I was struck by the fact that this diagram and Fairbairn's diagram were structurally equivalent. So, the depressive position expressed in terms of Fairbairn's model was equivalent to the central ego and its ideal object (ego ideal) functioning independently, that is, with the

68 Internal objects and inner reality

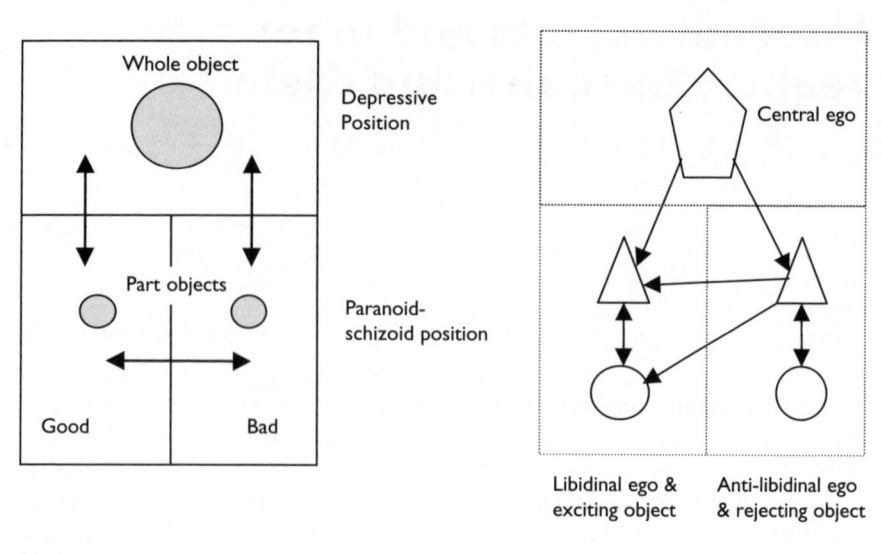

(a) Diagram of the relationship between the Kleinian positions

(b) Fairbairn's diagram of the basic endopsychic structure

Figure 4.1 Kleinian and Fairbairnian models compared.

successful repression of the libidinal and anti-libidinal sub-selves. Similarly the paranoid-schizoid position is functionally equivalent to the basic endopsychic structure when repression is failing and the sub-selves are actively contributing to, that is disrupting, the functioning of the central self. In short the development of the basic endopsychic structure and the achievement of Klein's depressive position seemed to me to be very closely related.

Later, while explaining this interpretation of the relationship between the two models, someone commented that as far as she was concerned Klein's depressive position was much more like the original ego and its object, a view that is similar to Carveth's interpretation (1996) of Fairbairn's model in Lacanian terms, where the original ego and its object are likened to the Lacanian 'subject'. When I came to look at Fairbairn's model in greater detail and tried to understand what it was that he meant by the basic endopsychic structure, which in Fairbairn's view is equivalent to the schizoid position and more fundamental than Klein's depressive position, I was faced with a difficulty. Since I was still viewing the emergence of the central ego as equivalent to the development of the depressive position, I was having trouble locating a distinctive schizoid position separate from the depressive position. This led me to think that there might be an earlier position that Fairbairn meant to indicate by the term schizoid, that I had somehow missed. A recent paper by Rubens (1998), addressing Fairbairn's thought on depression, and showing how his theory might be applied to depression in a way that would account for both Freudian and Kleinian insistence on depression as of fundamental importance, made me realise that what I was failing to do was treat Fairbairn's model sufficiently as a dynamic system. As noted previously, this is a common failing that bedevils many attempts to understand what it is that Fairbairn is getting at. One of the most difficult aspects of interpreting his model in dynamic terms is finding appropriate representations for both the dynamism and the various ways the particular dynamism can manifest itself. So, my intuition that there was a strong similarity between Klein's theory of the depressive and the paranoid-schizoid positions, and two different aspects (dynamics) of Fairbairn's basic endopsychic structure, was based upon the central ego's success, or failure, at sustaining the repression of the subsidiary selves. I was imagining the model with different dynamics, but using the same diagrammatic representation as Fairbairn, which is essentially static, although, as I have argued, his theory is not. I realised that the constant shifting between the depressive and the paranoid-schizoid positions as introduced by Bion (1963) and represented by his 'equation' P/S <-> D could be used to represent the dynamic shifts in Fairbairn's theory on Fairbairn's diagram by replacing the arrows representing the repression of the subsidiary selves with 'two-way' arrows representing both repression and the (possible) failure of repression. This would at least open up the possibility of finding an analogue to Kleinian positions within Fairbairn's model. Fairbairn's thoughts about the disposition of internal objects within the transitional techniques (1941) – the distinctive patterns of the projections and introjection of internal objects (good and bad) – characteristic of hysteria, paranoia, phobia and obsessionality – further opens up the possibility of finding ways of representing clinically significant patterns of relating; as does his description of the growth and development of the sub-selves as the Oedipus situation is negotiated. All this is further enhanced by the variety of possible personifications available to an internal world with both dyadic and triadic structures at its heart, and permutations leading to at least six possible 'characters' in search of a narrative (Grotstein 1994b). The simple elegance of the diagram is also its shortcoming. One problem is that the same representation of the basic endopsychic structure can be used to model a wide variety of different configurations of inner reality. For instance, in a recent paper Celani (1998) has analysed the ways in which the libidinal and anti-libidinal sub-selves can create substantial resistance to therapy in the case of battered women where the central ego is weak and underdeveloped. Similarly Skolnick (1998) has reopened the debate about the internalisation of the good object in Fairbairn's model and has carefully analysed a number of options within the theory to account for some clinical data. His failure to find an adequate explanation within Fairbairn's theory is vitiated in my view by his failure to consider the *layering* and *fusion* of aspects of both mother and father in the development of the internal objects during the Oedipus situation.

There are a number of critiques of the relationship between Fairbairn's and

Klein's theories. The major attempts to look at the similarities and differences between the two are probably Greenberg and Mitchell's *Object Relations in Psychoanalytic Theory* (1983) and Hughes's *Reshaping the Psychoanalytic Domain* (1989). Both of these studies conclude that Fairbairn was the more consistent object relations thinker in that he rejected Freud's libido theory and developed a structural theory based on object relations alone, 'not without a certain rigour', as Lacan has commented (1988: 248). Fairbairn's is a structural theory in the same sense that Freud's later theory of id, ego and superego is a structural theory. Fairbairn's structural theory is, however, built upon the twentieth-century scientific understanding that structure and energy cannot be separated, and this leads to his critique of Freud's structural model and his attempt to build a similar model on consistently *relational* lines. Klein, whilst never formally repudiating Freud's libido theory or rejecting the structural theory, nevertheless went on to develop her own theories, including the idea of the depressive and the paranoid-schizoid positions and projective identification, which largely replaced the classical concepts. Klein was not interested in questions of system and structure as such, being far more concerned with the phenomenology of the analytic encounter. Agreeing with Charles Brenner's view (1996) that Freud's structural theory needs revising, though not by getting rid of separable agencies that compete and cooperate as he argues, Hanna Segal, one of Klein's foremost interpreters, suggests revision in the following ways:

(1) The concept of the id is redundant; the I – the ego has instincts and desires.
(2) On the other hand, the role of the super-ego in mental structure I think is not redundant, but should be revised and enlarged. Our mental structure does not contain one object, internalised at one moment of development, the heir of the Oedipus Complex. There is a whole internal phantasy world of object relationships which get structuralised within the ego. But this structure is not static: it develops and changes as part-and-parcel of the development of the ego.

(1996)

This view is very similar to the one developed by Fairbairn over 50 years earlier on the dynamic nature of the original ego and the development of an inner reality composed of *internal objects as dynamic structures* and the relations between them. Grotstein has suggested (1994a) a 'dual-track' approach to metapsychology, where the same phenomena may be looked at from different perspectives – inner, outer; conscious, unconscious; nature, nurture. In terms of the relations between Fairbairn and Klein I want to suggest that the rich world of Kleinian clinical work, concentrating as it does on the phenomenology of the analyst's and the analysand's experience, might be considered from a Fairbairnian structural perspective. In short, and consistent with

Fairbairn's view on the relation between phantasy and structure, the *generative mechanisms of Fairbairn's dynamic structures account for unconscious phantasy*.

There has been some excellent work by Mitchell, Grotstein and others describing the fundamental *differences* between Klein and Fairbairn in terms of concepts like internal objects, the nature and source of aggression, and the nature and origin of phantasy. In my attempt to argue that Fairbairn's model is capable of providing an underlying mechanism for Kleinian clinical data, I will have to show that some of these fundamental incompatibilities can be overcome and reconciled. Or, if not reconciled, then some decision, one way or the other, can be reached as to which is the better description. Part of this process will involve finding ways to represent different aspects of the *dynamics* of Fairbairn's model. In order to make a start on this process, I will look at Rubens' development of a Fairbairnian theory of depression and then consider how this might be used to model the detailed phenomenology of early infant experience as represented in a paper by Meira Likierman (1995) (also cited by Grotstein 1998). This whole approach is already implicit in Grotstein's 'dual-track' hypothesis (1998) and he, more than any other commentator on Fairbairn that I know of, has made a concerted attempt to find ways of relating particular configurations of Fairbairn's model with clinically identifiable phenomena (1994a, 1994b, 1994c, 1998). Indeed Grotstein's suggestion (1998: 93–4) as to the way in which Fairbairn's model of endopsychic structure might be able to represent the clinical and theoretical distinction that Likierman makes between a 'tragic' and a 'moral' phase of the depressive position, as it emerges, will form a central focus for what follows. Even Grotstein, however, seems to think that Fairbairn saw his model of endopsychic structure as a closed system (1994b: 189). However, it is my conviction that we need to take seriously the numerous references throughout his work on the dynamic nature of *all* the elements of the endopsychic structure (Fairbairn 1956a; 1956b). Fairbairn also explicitly points towards the differences between an open and a closed system way of relating to the world and others in it, and the central importance for mental health of an open relationship to others and the world (1958).

FAIRBAIRN AND KLEIN

Fairbairn was strongly influenced by both Freud and Klein and one can interpret his mature theory as an attempt to rewrite Freud's structural theory to be consistent with Klein's notion of internal objects, of which the superego is the prototype.

In a letter to Marjorie Brierley in 1942 (Scharff and Fairbairn Birtles 1994, vol. II: 443) Fairbairn admits his 'Kleinian lineage' but argues that the logical implications of the Kleinian viewpoint are that instinct theory and classical libido theory should be rejected. He calls the Kleinian refusal to reject the libido and instinct theories in favour of an object relations theory 'muddleheaded'.

In his only substantive contribution to the 'Controversial Discussions' (even then read in his absence by Glover), Fairbairn argues that:

> the explanatory concept of 'phantasy' has now been rendered obsolete by the concepts of 'psychical reality' and 'internal objects' which the work of Mrs Klein and her followers has done so much to develop; and in my opinion the time is now ripe for us to replace the concept of 'phantasy' by a concept of 'inner reality' peopled by the ego and its internal objects. These internal objects should be regarded as having an organised structure, an identity of their own, an endopsychic existence, and an activity as real within the inner world as those of any objects in the outer world.
> (King and Steiner 1991: 359)

He reminds us that the superego was one such internal object. These comments on 'phantasy' need to be noted since his later argument with Klein seems to centre on this:

> The concept of 'phantasy' is purely functional and can only be applied to activity on the part of the Ego. It is quite inadequate to describe inner situations involving the relationships of the Ego to internal objects possessing an endopsychic structure and dynamic qualities. It would still seem legitimate, however, to speak of 'phantasies' in the plural (or of 'a phantasy') to describe specific inner situations.
> (Scharff and Fairbairn Birtles 1994, vol. II: 294)

This suggestion was rejected by the Kleinians but forms the core of Fairbairn's theory of dynamic structure. Taken together with his description of dreams as 'shorts' of internal reality this suggests that *phantasy is an epiphenomenon of relations between dynamic structures* (ego-structures and internal objects).

In his 1949 paper 'Steps in the development of an object relations theory of the personality' (1952a: ch. 6) Fairbairn acknowledges his debt to both Freud and Klein, calling Klein's work, 'an important advance in the development of psychoanalytic theory' (1952a: 154). Commenting, however, on her notion of an internal object he says:

> but she also envisages the presence of a multiplicity of other introjected objects – good objects and bad objects, benign objects and persecuting objects, whole objects and part objects. The introjection of these various objects is regarded by her as the result of phantasies of oral

incorporation occurring primarily and characteristically during the oral phase of infancy . . . it seems to me, Melanie Klein has never satisfactorily explained how phantasies of incorporating objects orally can give rise to the establishment of internal objects as endopsychic structure – and, unless they are such structures, they cannot be properly spoken of as internal objects at all, since otherwise they will remain mere figments of phantasy.

(1952a: 154)

This is the crux of his objection to Klein.

Part of the reason for Fairbairn's antipathy to Klein's concept of 'phantasy' seems to come from his view of it being inadequate to represent the *dynamic and relational* nature of internal objects, that is it does not represent a dynamic internalised object on the model of the superego:

the internalised objects which I envisage are the *only* [emphasis added] parts of the psyche which I have *not* treated as dynamic structures. I have treated the internalised objects simply as *objects* of the dynamic ego-structures, i.e. as endopsychic structures which are not themselves dynamic. I have done this deliberately, not only to avoid complications of exposition, but also to bring into focus the *activity* [emphasis added] of the ego-structures which I find it necessary to postulate, and to avoid all risk of under-rating the primary importance of this activity; for, after all, it is only through this activity that objects ever come to be internalised . . . I must now draw the logical conclusion of my theory of dynamic structure and acknowledge that, since internal objects are structures, they must necessarily be, in some measure at least, dynamic . . . this . . . step will enhance the explanatory value of my theory of mental structure by introducing additional possibilities into the endopsychic situation by way of permutation and combination . . . however . . . in practice it is very difficult to differentiate between the activity of the internalised objects and the activity of the ego-structures with which they are associated.

(1952a: 132)

Clearly finding ways of describing and charting these differences, and how they manifest themselves, would be an important area for the extension of Fairbairn's theory. This would require a concerted effort to apply Fairbairn's theory clinically or to the analysis of clinical findings.

In his reply to some responses to his 1956 paper on the re-evaluation of certain basic psychoanalytic concepts, the structure and dynamics of internal objects are again addressed:

I find no difficulty in accepting the proposition that the internal objects are composite structures; and indeed it would be my contention that this is so. Thus the internal objects which I envisage may be composed of maternal and paternal components in all proportions and in all degrees of integration; and for that matter, they may undergo both disintegrative changes under pathological conditions and integrative changes under therapeutic conditions.

(Scharff and Fairbairn Birtles 1994, vol. I: 154)

Again, showing clearly how these differently structured and integrated objects manifest themselves would constitute an important contribution to Fairbairn's theory and would depend upon the analysis of clinical work for its development.

MITCHELL'S VIEW OF THE DIFFERENCES BETWEEN FAIRBAIRN AND KLEIN

Mitchell, in his 'The origin and nature of the object in the theories of Klein and Fairbairn' (1994), can be taken to represent a wider spectrum of opinion (see also Grotstein) when he summarises the differences between Klein and Fairbairn as follows:

1. Regarding the function of internal objects.
For Klein, the internal world is a natural, inevitable and continual accompaniment of all experience. Internal objects are established at the beginning of psychological life and they become the major content of phantasy. (82)
    For Fairbairn, internal objects are neither primary nor inevitable (theoretically). They are compensatory substitutes for unsatisfactory relations with real, external objects, the 'natural' primary objects of libido . . . In Fairbairn's vision of emotional health and analytic cure, internal objects are abolished altogether. (82)
2. Regarding the contents of internal objects.
[Klein] . . . stresses the a priori origins of object images as: part of a phylogenetic inheritance built into the experience of desire itself, construed from early sensations or derived from the drives through projection . . . Klein also stresses the importance of real people in the child's life; however, here it is the universal features of these real objects that are most important – their anatomical characterisation as representatives of the human species, their durability in the face of phantasied attacks against them, their inevitable mixture of gratifying and depriving features. (83)
    For Fairbairn, the content of internal objects derives completely from real external objects, fragmented and recombined to be sure, but always derived from the child's experience of his actual parents. (83)

3. Regarding the source of pathology.
For Klein, the root of evil lies in the heart of man himself, in the instincts, particularly in the death instinct and its derivative, aggression. (84)

For Fairbairn ... the root of psychopathology and human suffering is maternal deprivation. Ideally perfect mothering results in a whole non-fragmented ego, with its full libidinal potential available for relations with actual external objects. Inadequate parenting poses grave threats to the integrity of the ego. The central anxiety for Fairbairn involves protecting the tie to the object in the face of deprivation, and all psychopathology is understood as deriving from the ego's self-fragmentation in the service of protecting that tie and controlling its ungratifying aspects.

(84)

Mitchell comments further that these differences are reflected in the different meanings the term 'bad objects' has for each. For Klein the badness of an object, internal or external, derives ultimately from the child's own inherent destructiveness projected onto others. For Fairbairn badness means unsatisfying or depriving:

> For Klein, 'bad objects' are reflections, creations derived from the child's own inherent and spontaneous destructiveness. For Fairbairn, 'bad objects' are aspects of the parents which make them unavailable to him, and frustrate his inherent longing for contact and relation.

(84)

OGDEN'S CONCEPT OF INTERNAL OBJECT RELATIONS

In his 'The concept of internal object relations' (1994b) Thomas Ogden reviews the concept of the internal object as it relates to the work of 'Freud, Abraham, Melanie Klein, Fairbairn, Winnicott and Bion'. He derives a view of the internal object that seems to me to come directly from Fairbairn's own account of the internal object. He quotes Fairbairn's comments regarding the dynamic nature of the internal object but argues that this is a 'reluctant admission' and offers an explanation of this dynamism based in Bion's theory of the formation of bizarre objects. This leads him to the following conclusions:

> I would like to suggest that the internalisation of an object relationship be thought of as necessarily involving a dual subdivision of the ego. *Such a dual split would result in the formation of two new suborganisations of the ego, one identified with the self in the external object relationship and the*

other thoroughly identified with the object. This formulation accounts for the dynamic nature of the internal object and also defines the relationship between the concept of the ego and the concept of the internal objects. In brief, internal objects are subdivisions of the ego that are heavily identified with an object representation while maintaining the capacities of the whole ego for thought, perception, feeling etc.

(99; emphasis in original)

a view that he notes goes no further than Freud and the superego, and no further than Fairbairn or Klein either, in my opinion.

Ogden goes on to suggest a logical extension of Fairbairn's notion of dynamic structure that seems to me to be already present in Fairbairn:

> The logical extension of Fairbairn's notion of dynamic structure is the idea that the ego is the only source of dynamism and that further dynamic structures are formed only by means of a subdivision of the ego. The dynamism of an internal object must in every case reflect the fact that an aspect of the ego has been split off and is at the core of the new structure. The fact that this structure (the internal object) is experienced as non-self is accounted for by means of a profound identification with the object. Internalisation requiring a splitting of the ego only occurs in early development and as a result, the identification with the object is of a poorly differentiated nature, i.e. the experiential quality of the identification is one of 'becoming the object' as opposed to 'feeling like' the object. Adult 'internalisations' are built upon existing splits in the ego and do not involve the creation of new ones.
>
> (100)

HINSHELWOOD'S VIEW OF FAIRBAIRN

There are many superficial similarities between what I understand of Fairbairn's mature theory of object relations and Hinshelwood's description of Klein's concept of internal objects in his *Dictionary of Kleinian Thought* (1991). This is not surprising because Fairbairn took the concept from her and then tried to take it further. Klein was also deeply influenced by Fairbairn, as Padel explains:

> Fairbairn's 1940 paper, which urged the fundamental importance of the 'schizoid position', points to the splitting of the ego in the phenomena of dreaming and of the superego; but in his 1944 paper he made a tripartite split in the ego the central feature of his thought on 'Endopsychic structure', and, as we know from Phyllis Grosskurth's examination of the letters between Klein and her colleagues in 1944–5, it was that paper of

Fairbairn's which spurred Klein to write 'Notes on some schizoid mechanisms' (1946). Although she acknowledged her adoption of Fairbairn's term, which she combined with hers in formulating the 'paranoid-schizoid position', it was more than his term that she took over; it was the very concept of ego-splitting, subsumed in her new notion of 'projective identification'.

(1991: 593)

We have seen, however, that there are some obvious differences between Klein and Fairbairn (as described by Mitchell). And since Klein never gave up either the instinct theory or the libido theory, however much she may have altered them, this remains one fundamental disagreement between herself and Fairbairn.

However, when it comes to Fairbairn there are at least two ways in which Hinshelwood's understanding of his theory are at variance with the mature theory described in Chapter 2. One concerns the reiteration of an early formulation of Fairbairn's theory in which he said that the only reason he could see for internalising objects was if they were bad. Fairbairn modified this view at least twice on the way to his mature theory, as I have explained. The initial structure-generating internalisation of the early object (breast with mother) in the pre-ambivalent phase is of the entire original object (prior to its being split into good and bad objects).

The second misconception about Fairbairn's theory concerns the nature of the basic endopsychic structure and its vicissitudes. Hinshelwood interprets this structure as a *fixed* structure, which is quite contrary to Fairbairn's psychology of dynamic structure described above. I hope I have already indicated that Fairbairn's model of mind is centrally and necessarily dynamic. In my view, if one was to try to show how the Kleinian model of internal relations and their transformations could be mapped into Fairbairn's dynamic structures, one would be faced with the task of mapping Kleinian 'good' objects into the ideal object of the central ego, and distributing Kleinian 'bad' objects between the exciting (libidinal) and the rejecting (anti-libidinal) objects and egos. That is, Fairbairn's model represents an *ordering* of Klein's internal objects at a more complex, by which I also mean a deeper, level that is more unconscious, to include ego splits.

The fact that there are fundamental differences across the whole range of concepts that are required to construct a model of mind means that rapprochement between a Kleinian and a Fairbairnian approach, at the level of a systematisation of internal objects, is unlikely to be attempted. However, it would be an important achievement for any research programme seeking to establish that there was some substance to Fairbairn's model to show that this higher (deeper) level ordering of Kleinian bad objects was both possible and cogent. As far as I know Kleinian theorists do not distinguish between aspects of bad objects in the way that Fairbairn's theory suggests they might.

RUBENS' MODEL OF THE DEPRESSIVE POSITION

Rubens (1998) looks closely at Fairbairn's theory of repression with a view to developing a theory of the depressive position in terms of endopsychic structure. He prefaces his remarks by noting that Fairbairn's theory of endopsychic structure 'turned all of psychoanalytic theory on its head' (215). This is because it involves the basic assumptions that: (a) relationships are not the result of drive discharge but that self-expression in relationship is the foundation of psychic functioning; (b) psychic growth is not progressive structuralisation but that the structuring of self is pathological; and (c) the biological theory of vicissitudes of instinct is inappropriate and that health and pathology should be understood in terms of our ability to make and sustain attachments (215).

Rubens notes that Fairbairn did not articulate a distinct theory of depression but adopted a theory from Melanie Klein, and that in general, and increasingly, he ignored depression. Reviewing Fairbairn's theory of depression starting with his comments in papers from the 1930s (1936, 1939), Rubens notes that Fairbairn adopted the (Kleinian) position that aggression and oral sadism were the main issues. When in 1940 Fairbairn proposed the schizoid position, he took over the depressive position from Klein 'whole cloth'. Rubens argues that the metapsychological importance of the schizoid position is as a 'fundamental pattern of interaction that characterises a person's relations to another' (1998: 216). The schizoid position is of crucial importance to Fairbairn, and its origins in the early oral phase, before the development of (late oral) ambivalence, means that the basic endopsychic position is more fundamental than the depressive position which is post-ambivalence. Since Fairbairn's 1941 paper outlined a developmental trajectory that meant we were unlikely to escape early splitting, or be able to ever finally undo or overcome splitting (1941), Fairbairn regarded the schizoid position as truly fundamental. Rubens concludes that, 'depression was viewed by him as a reaction in which hate and aggression are turned inwards against the self when circumstances disturb the object relations of the depressive type ... someone whose basic endopsychic structure is founded on the ambivalence of the later oral phase of development as opposed to ... schizoid endopsychic structure' (1998: 218). In Rubens' view Fairbairn saw the schizoid position as being 'more basic and universal' (219) and concludes that 'the schizoid position, representing as it did the fundamental state of the existence of split-off subsystems within the self, was the position that underlay *all* of human psychopathology' (219). Rubens argues that Fairbairn lost interest 'in the dynamics of depression as they relate to psychic structure' (220), since he had taken:

> Klein's notion of the paranoid position, separated it from its original foundation in instinct theory, and transformed it into his own notion of a

schizoid position. This schizoid position, representing as it did the fundamental pathological outcome of the unavoidable ego splitting that was engendered by intolerably bad experience of the infant with its absolutely important attachments, became the cornerstone of his entire theory of development and of endopsychic structure, as well as of his theory of psychopathology.

(220–1)

Rubens believes that Fairbairn did not look at depression as closely as he might have done (221) and suggests that 'it is not necessary or useful to understand depression as a position in the developmental organisation of the psyche . . . Fairbairn's theory of endopsychic structure is entirely adequate without any such addition' (221). He goes on to make the important point that *'depression should be viewed as a very general mechanism of conservation of the endopsychic situation and stasis in the closed system of experiencing the world'* (221). Rubens adds 'in this view, depression is a technique for avoiding, or at least denying, the existence of change' (222) since 'it represents the ultimate closed-system attempt to maintain the existing endopsychic situation' (222). Rubens comments that the sense of futility that Fairbairn so closely associates with the schizoid position is also a characteristic feature of depression. Rubens suggests that depression, like the transitional techniques (paranoia, hysteria, phobia and obsession), can apply over wide areas of developmental time. He makes the interesting and important observation that, 'sadness represents the healthy affective recognition and acceptance of loss, whereas depression represents the neurotic attempt to deny loss' (224), an insight that he has previously discussed in a paper on tragedy (a view shared by many including Freud in 'Mourning and melancholia' (1917) and Julia Kristeva in *Black Sun*).

Consistent with Fairbairn's position, Rubens suggests that living is all about living in an open-system way, where there is change and movement and growth and there is also inevitable loss as we move from one position of integration to another superior one – if we are lucky. He reminds us of Fairbairn's definition of psychopathology as 'an attempt to live in a closed system' (Rubens 1998: 224). He reminds us too of the internal dynamics associated with such a closed system. 'The maintenance of such a closed system involves the perpetuation of the relationships prevailing between the various ego-structures and their respective internal objects, as well as between one another' (Fairbairn 1958: 380). It is worth reminding ourselves that the basic endopsychic structure in Fairbairn's 1944 description has the maximum of libido tied up in the libidinal ego and the exciting object, and the maximum of aggression tied up in the anti-libidinal ego and the rejecting object. The overall dynamics are that all other aggression is used by the central ego to repress the libidinal and anti-libidinal sub-selves, and by the anti-libidinal ego to repress the libidinal self.

Rubens develops this view of the closed-system nature of depression: 'depression becomes something that one experiences in response to a loss – or a change – that threatens to affect the shape of one's inner world. Any change that does not fit with the expectations of one's closed system can precipitate depression' (1998: 225). He suggests that, 'depression is a defence that actively attempts to maintain the stasis of this closed system' (226), even though loss is inevitable. However, the depressed person is avoiding loss, and thus psychic change.

In relation to the therapeutic importance of the appearance of depression, Rubens suggests that sadness and depression are inversely related. Depression is a positive sign in therapy since it suggests that change is imminent, but, he argues, the emergence of sadness is a much better sign, since it represents a recognition, and acceptance, of loss. This means that the endopsychic structure is not static, rigid and closed, but open to change. 'Sadness' here is consistent with the concept of 'mourning' used by many psychoanalysts, starting with Freud, to indicate acknowledgement and working through of loss, as distinct from the defensive depression of 'melancholia'.

SKOLNICK AND THE INTERNALISATION OF THE GOOD OBJECT

In a recent paper Neil J. Skolnick (1998) raises a question that has been raised ever since Fairbairn first formulated his object relations theory of the mind, that is the question of the internalisation of the good object. This is something that is fundamental to Klein's view and was part of Winnicott and Khan's objection to Fairbairn's theory, in the review they wrote of his book. Lacan, in his comments on Fairbairn (1988: 248), agrees with Fairbairn that there is no need to internalise the good object. Skolnick addresses what he calls 'Fairbairn's difficulty' by locating the good object in the repressed endopsychic structures in an attempt to reconcile Fairbairn's views with those of Melanie Klein. 'I find both Klein's and Fairbairn's ideas equally useful in informing my thought about and actions towards patients. I ignore . . . the gross and at times grotesque inconsistencies and incompatibilities between these two theoretical systems' (Skolnick 1998: 138). He argues for a 'possible integration of one aspect of Fairbairn's and Klein's differing conceptions of the internal world . . . the somewhat glaring discrepancy between the two in their place for good objects in this world . . . Klein puts them there and Fairbairn does not' (139). Skolnick elaborates: 'The difference that I focus a spotlight on in this paper is Fairbairn's idea that the internal unconscious world of objects is devoid of good objects. I propose that a clarification and alteration in Fairbairn's theory of development can allow for the place of good objects in the unconscious while maintaining the basic integrity of his fundamental concepts' (139–40). Skolnick suggests that, as a corrective to

Fairbairn's model, there is an 'argument to be made for including a process by which good objects are internalised, identified with and structured into the endopsychic self and where these remain out of conscious awareness but where they exert an active influence on interactions with the external world in much the same way bad internalised objects do' (141). He characterises Fairbairn's model in the following terms: 'For Fairbairn our unconscious exists as a kind of intrapsychic hell, populated only by split-off pieces of bad objects (either exciting or rejecting) along with the fragments of ego structure they abscond with and relegate to the unconscious, in particular, the libidinal and the anti-libidinal egos' (141), and: 'Identifications with good objects are ... structured into the central ego ... [they] remain conscious and readily available for open flexible interaction with worldly matters and people. Thus according to Fairbairn (1944), good objects are nowhere to be found in the internal, unconscious. Good objects ... remain integrally connected to our central ego' (141–2). Skolnick agrees that, as far as development is concerned, Fairbairn's view is consistent with current mother-infant research and describes how original splitting and formation of sub-selves occurs by reference to Ogden's (and Padel's) already quoted notion that what is internalised is a relationship, a view that originates with Freud and is central to Fairbairn's thinking.

Skolnick looks at the different accounts that Fairbairn gives of the place of the good object in his model. He notes that Fairbairn in his 1943 paper does have the good object internalised, which he called the ego ideal, as an early form of the superego and part of the moral defence. In Fairbairn's 1944 paper there is the argument that internalisation is a defensive move in order to *control* bad objects in some way, which would clearly mean there was no need to internalise the good object. There is no mention of the good object in his diagram of endopsychic structure in this paper. However, in the 1951 addendum to the paper (1952a) Fairbairn puts forward his later view on the good object which allows for its early internalisation as part of the preambivalent object that is in some way unsatisfactory. This forms the preconscious core of the ego ideal or ideal object associated with the central ego. Skolnick confirms Fairbairn's final view that, 'while good objects may be internalised ... they are never repressed ... never forced by the central ego to dwell in the unconscious endopsychic structures ... but take the form of an ego-ideal informing the core of the superego' (1998: 144) (we should remember here that, for Fairbairn, Freud's notion of the superego is a composite structure made up of ego ideal, anti-libidinal ego and anti-libidinal object).

Using Rubens' distinction between structuring and non-structuring internalisations of good and bad objects, Skolnick says that in Fairbairn 'good objects are never subjected to structure-generating repression' (144). Skolnick looks at Rubens' account of non-structuring internalisation, which Rubens describes as resulting in 'an alteration of the integration of the self, or in the production of a thought, memory or phantasy within the self' (1984: 437), and argues that this fails 'to account for a repressed good object' (Skolnick 1998: 145).

Skolnick looks at a clinical example of what he believes is the 'Return to consciousness of a heretofore unconscious, yet decidedly good, object relationship' (145). The assumption here seems to be that *what is not available to consciousness is necessarily part of the system unconscious*. I would point out that while the preconscious is in principle accessible to consciousness it is clearly not the case that everything in the preconscious is easily brought to consciousness.

The case Skolnick describes concerns a patient who recovered fond memories of his father after he died, despite regarding him as tyrannical whilst alive. Skolnick suggests that 'attempts to understand these (loving) memories within the framework of Fairbairn's split self and object systems lead to unsatisfactory dead ends' (147). However, I would argue that Skolnick does not consider the process whereby different aspects of mother and father are incorporated into each of the objects (exciting, rejecting and ideal) during the Oedipal situation, nor the reordering of these fused and layered relationships when the Oedipus situation is resolved. In my reading of Fairbairn's description of this process it would be perfectly possible for a memory of a good relationship with father to become fused with what became the dominant good relationship with mother, and to disappear from conscious recall because of the dominant memory of a good relationship with mother at the time the Oedipus situation was resolved. The death of father and the need to rework all the relationships with the now dead object (Freud 1917) could return the relationship to consciousness without it ever having been repressed as such.

Skolnick's solution, since he believes that there are repressed good objects, is to review Fairbairn's account of the development of the basic endopsychic structure and suggest an alternative. His conclusion is that Fairbairn's account of the development of the endopsychic structure is wrong and that he failed to take sufficient account of the difference between what he calls split object experience and ambivalent object experience:

> the feelings of both love and hate towards the same person present the child with an enormous problem. It is just this struggle to maintain a good connection with a whole but failing object that ushers in the experience of ambivalence, with its concomitant feelings of unbearable conflict. It is this conflict, then, that propels the child at Fairbairn's later oral stage to split off and repress good part objects.
>
> (1998: 156)

Skolnick's suggestions, if taken seriously, would turn Fairbairn's model of endopsychic structure into a variant of Klein's model of the depressive position, where both good and bad objects are internalised and play their part in the dialectic of projection and introjection that constitutes a major part of the life of the mind. Since the existence of repressed good objects is central to Skolnick's argument, but not conclusive given the case example referred to earlier, this might be a question that could be referred to a wider clinical 'court'.

GROTSTEIN'S USE OF FAIRBAIRN'S MODEL OF ENDOPSYCHIC STRUCTURE

Grotstein, in discussing Fairbairn's 1943 paper on the return of bad objects, looks in detail at 'demoniacal possession' and suggests that we should consider the whole of the unconscious endopsychic structure as one:

> Fairbairn's portrayal of endopsychic structures belies their demoniacal nature insofar as he dissociates the Rejecting Object from the Exciting Object and the Anti-libidinal Ego from the Libidinal Ego. When we see his endopsychic configuration as a totality ... we too readily compare it with Freud's (1923) tripartite psychic apparatus. If, on the other hand, we picture the Rejecting Object and Exciting Object as 'Siamese twins', connected and yet paradoxically disconnected (rather than absolutely and clearly split-off from each other) – the same for the Libidinal Ego and Anti-libidinal Ego – then the full appearance of the Devil would be evident. The Libidinal Ego is haunted, not merely because of its fatal desire for the Exciting Object, but because the Exciting Object is also the Rejecting Object. The same applies for the 'Siamese twinship' between the Libidinal Ego and the Anti-libidinal Ego. The former's awareness that its 'alter ego' has totally succumbed to the Devil's influence results in its abject demoralisation and fatal hopelessness – as damned.
>
> (1994c: 128; abbreviations expanded)

So a particular configuration of the endopsychic structure as a whole is used to account for and explain the strength of a sense of possession by demons or the devil, and in particular the underlying idea that both split-off sub-selves are originally based upon different bad aspects of the mother.

In his 1994 paper called 'Endopsychic structure and the cartography of the internal world' Grotstein gives several examples of the way in which specific configurations of the endopsychic structure might be used to describe and identify clinical phenomena. Earlier in the paper he includes a more elaborated discussion of demoniacal possession than that referred to above (1994b: 185–7) and in the preceding section called 'The dialectics of endopsychic relationship' he describes briefly a number of configurations of the endopsychic structure and the ways they might be interpreted:

The Libidinal Ego, for instance, may ignore its relationship with the Exciting Object and relate instead to the Rejecting Object or to the Ideal Object. A direct cross-relationship between the Libidinal Ego and the Rejecting Object would involve the experience of sadomasochism. A triangular competition of the Libidinal Ego with the Anti-libidinal Ego for the affection of the Rejecting Object (or a competition of the Anti-libidinal Ego with the Libidinal Ego for the affection of the Exciting Object) would constitute the phenomenology of Klein's manic defence or of Kohut's and Kernberg's narcissistic grandiose self in relationship to slave selfobjects.

(183–4; abbreviations expanded)

A little later he says, 'in manic psychosis, as well as in schizophrenia, the Libidinal Ego is totally identified with the Exciting Object (having incorporated it intact) and has taken over the agency of subjective "I"-ness. Thus, the Libidinal Ego behaves as if it were the same ego repressing or splitting off the other egos and objects, which are all experienced as being entrapped in the manic's unconscious' (184; abbreviations expanded), and, again, 'in depressive psychosis . . . one might postulate that the Anti-libidinal Ego and the Rejecting Object now occupy the position of the Central Ego and the Ideal Object. The Libidinal Ego and the Exciting Object may be experienced as either regressed or split off and projected into others' (184; abbreviations expanded). He refers to a recent study of adult survivors of child abuse:

> these patients show an invariant dissociation between an 'adult self' and a 'child self', the latter of which can be further subdivided into a 'good – perfect child' and a 'naughty – omnipotent child' and the 'terrified – abused child'. The 'good – perfect child' may derive from a false central self (Central Ego) repressing a victimised self (Libidinal Ego), which is simultaneously being abused by an abused self (Anti-libidinal Ego) while in a corrupt, collusive relationship with an 'idealised omnipotent rescuer' (Exciting Object).
>
> (184; abbreviations expanded)

Grotstein summarises what he calls the '*Weltanschauungen* of the endopsychic structures' in the following terms:

> the pathological 'libidinal self' (the Libidinal Ego and Exciting Object) represent a licentious self that pursues wanton pleasure, tantalisation and frustration, whereas the 'rejecting self' (Anti-libidinal Ego and Rejecting Object) pursues a perversely destructive mode and becomes a tormenting self. I believe, and understand Fairbairn to have believed, that these four repressed endopsychic entities (Libidinal Ego, Anti-libidinal

Ego, Exciting Object and Rejecting Object) are created by default and represent the breakdown in a basic trust with the primal caretakers. The licentious self is what Freud meant by the id and the rejecting self is what Klein meant by the operation of the death instinct.

(185; abbreviations expanded)

In my view the systematic investigation and application of this sort of analysis is both long overdue and absolutely essential to the development of Fairbairn's theory.

LIKIERMAN'S NEW PERSPECTIVE ON KLEIN'S CONCEPT OF THE DEPRESSIVE POSITION

In a recent paper Meira Likierman (1995) makes a close reading of Melanie Klein's concept of the depressive position as represented in primary texts. She argues that Klein showed how, 'the event of ego integration triggers the depressive position' (150), and reviews post-Kleinian developments, where the relationship between the paranoid-schizoid and the depressive position, as represented by Bion's 'equation' P/S<->D, becomes part of an everyday process of dis- and re-integration. But, she argues, in Klein's view it was crucial to overcome the depressive position.

Likierman discusses what she calls 'two contradictory motifs in Klein's vision of the depressive position' (150). These are the 'tragic' and the 'moral'. According to Likierman 'the "tragic" motif centres on an experience of *irrevocable* loss or damage. This is felt to have been brought about through the subject's own aggression' (150). At the same time, 'the "moral" motif centres on the infantile capacity to acknowledge guilt and responsibility for aggression with the resulting capacity to engage in reparation' (150). (This is on the Kleinian assumption that aggression originates in the person.)

As she goes on to describe the circumstances in which the initial loss of the loved object takes place, Likierman couches her explanation in terms of the internalisation of the good object:

> The good internal object is structured on the basis of the introjected maternal goodness and represents the phantasy objectification of such goodness, hence an endowment of a central aspect of the psyche, its 'core', with an identity that can be experienced in primitive phantasy. Losing such an object amounts to the profound loss of the life-orientated, self-nourishing aspect of the psyche, the 'core' of the self. Thus the 'loss of the loved object' is an external event related to the internal object, as well as being bound up with the perceived loss of the external object or its qualities due to separation and weaning.

(150–1)

She quotes Segal, Riviere and Klein herself on the catastrophic implications of the loss of the good object and notes the parallels with Greek tragedy. However, she also notes that ' "morality" in the Kleinian texts reverses the results of "tragedy" ' (151), and goes on to consider how this move from irrevocable loss to a restored and safeguarded object might be possible. She acknowledges that Klein's concept of the depressive position 'requires us to accept the fractured nature of experience, the lack of a subjective sense of continuity in the present experiencing of evolutionary phases that only become "a development" retrospectively' (151). The early experience of tragedy – the loss of the loved object – is a 'total situation' for the infant, with its limited perspective and sense of reality, and cannot be ameliorated by the future possibility of developing into the later 'moral' phase of the process which is unknown to the infant.

Likierman describes the relationship between the 'tragic' and the 'moral' in the following terms:

> Underlying the narrative of morality with its power of hope and continuity, and with its measure of control over events, is a hidden stratum of a completely different order – the tragedy that ends in destruction and loss and leads to despair and madness . . . Klein's vision of the psyche suggests that a continual underlying level of tragedy ensures that the secondary, 'higher' level of morality retains its sense, for morality must assume the possibility of irrevocable loss all the time.
>
> (152)

The notion of ambivalence is introduced as an indicator of the achievement of the moral phase of the depressive position: 'ambivalence thus evolves gradually from early splitting and is in organic continuity with it' (153), and again, 'such states of volatile fluctuation between uncontrollable aggression and the resulting "nightmare of desolation" (Riviere 1936) are gradually outgrown, but this depends on the infant's secure instating of the good object within his inner world (Klein 1935)' (1995: 153). So we have splitting preceding ambivalence and the instating of the good object in the inner world taking place *after* the development of ambivalence and as a defence against internal bad objects in Likierman's interpretation of Klein's depressive position; a picture that is consistent with Fairbairn's view of the process.

Likierman cites the literature on the commonly held view of the depressive position as a progressive phenomenon and links this to an ambiguity in Klein's work: 'Klein herself made no explicit differentiation between two levels that nevertheless emerge in her textual descriptions. Whilst at times she equated the depressive position more with "morality" describing a *fear* of losing the loved object and the simultaneous urge to regain it, at other times she conveyed the sense of "tragedy" proper' (156).

Likierman looks closely at the process of 'overcoming', a process that Klein thought of as extending over the entire period of early childhood. In Likierman's reading, 'the term "overcoming" does not imply an annihilation of early psychical states, but addresses the facet of experience that involves the outgrowing of primitive modes of psychical functioning, the latter manifest in both paranoid-schizoid and tragic/depressive perceptions of the world' (157). Perhaps drawing on Winnicott, Likierman argues that it is the ability of the external world (and especially the mother) to survive the infant's attacks upon it (and fears for her) that is crucial in Klein's view to overcoming: 'There is as we know, no better means of allaying a child's fears than the presence and love of his mother ... the accumulation of such beneficial experiences is one of the main factors in overcoming his infantile neurosis' (157).[1] Thus Likierman argues that external reality is of 'marked importance' in Klein's view and 'what matters about external reality is not merely its actuality, but the fact that through it the infant discovers a version of events that is governed by alternative principles' (158).

Likierman closes the paper with a quotation from Klein in which Klein argues that persecutory and depressive anxieties originating in earliest infancy are the fixation points for severe mental illness, a viewpoint we find expressed in similar terms in Fairbairn's work. In Fairbairn it is the schizoid position, which is closer to Klein's paranoid-schizoid position, or the tragic aspect of the depressive position as described by Likierman, that is the fixation point for schizophrenia, while the depressive position, or moral aspect of the depressive position in Likierman's terms, is the fixation point for depressive illness.

GROTSTEIN'S INTERPRETATION OF LIKIERMAN

In a number of papers Grotstein (1994a, 1994b, 1994c, 1998) gives a sympathetic reading of Fairbairn's theory and locates it internationally in such a way as to sustain and develop the claims that are made for its importance to psychoanalytic theory as a whole. He has also suggested that it might be seen as complementary to Kleinian theory, his dual-track hypothesis. He constructs a Kleinian analysis of the dream[2] that prompted Fairbairn to develop his model of endopsychic structure, and reaches the following conclusions: 'I believe that Fairbairn's model of endopsychic structure is incomplete insofar as it fails to represent the normal situation; but ... I also believe that his model is able to accommodate Klein's internalised objects as well as his own endopsychic structure' (1998: 81). Earlier Grotstein suggests that:

> Fairbairn may well have come around eventually to postulating a normal endopsychic structure but one situated topographically in the preconscious rather than the unconscious – because of his injunction, with

which I am in agreement, that good objects do not need to be internalised (except for defensive purposes), only unsatisfactory ones. The system preconscious would be the reservoir for the legacy or memory of satisfying experiences with reliable objects as opposed to the unconscious, which is the reservoir for the concrete internalisation of unreliable but needed objects that putatively need to be controlled and processed dissociatively.
(1998: 79–80)

My own feeling about Grotstein's description of the 'normal' is that it sounds like Fairbairn's concept of mature dependence. The questions of *structure as pathology* and Fairbairn's pessimism about the *unavoidability* of some splitting and the difficulty of finally overcoming such splitting are ignored. In fact, Grotstein's paper itself is centrally concerned with both the similarities and differences between Fairbairn and Klein, seeking to find a way of engaging the one with the other dialectically. Grotstein ends by suggesting that a practical attempt at combining the two views might be attempted in relation to Likierman's recent rethinking of the depressive position through a close reading of the Kleinian primary sources (1998).

Grotstein continues to investigate the use of Fairbairn's model of endopsychic structure to represent clinically identifiable situations. He suggests that:

> Central Ego and Ideal Object collude to scapegoat the four denizens of endopsychic structure; Anti-libidinal Ego and Rejecting Object likewise collude against Libidinal Ego and Exciting Object; and finally Libidinal Ego and Anti-libidinal Ego collude against Exciting Object, the latter of which, after all is not only the other side of Rejecting Object but, more importantly, is the other side of Ideal Object. Further Central Ego/Ideal Object may collude with Anti-libidinal Ego/Rejecting Object against Libidinal Ego/Ideal Object in melancholia, whereas Libidinal Ego/Ideal Object may collude with Central Ego/Ideal Object against Anti-libidinal Ego/Rejecting Object in mania.
> (1998: 80; abbreviations expanded)

At the end of this paper Grotstein suggests that this approach may prove fruitful in modelling Klein's concept of the depressive position based on Likierman's careful investigation of the concept. Grotstein suggests that the early 'tragic' position identified by Likiermann could be represented in terms of Fairbairn's endopsychic structures, 'where Libidinal Ego is the ultimate underdog under a double repressive attack – by Central Ego/Ideal Object and Anti-libidinal Ego/Rejecting Object' (94; abbreviations expanded), or in other words by Fairbairn's *basic* endopsychic structure. He later suggests that the later 'moral' stage of the depressive position could be seen as 'the beginning of a benign coalition between Libidinal Object and Central Ego/Ideal

Object in which the latter would come to the former's aid in conducting reparations and restorations of the damaged object, which amounts to allowing an integration between Rejecting Object, Exciting Object and Ideal Object – and thus with Libidinal Ego, Anti-libidinal Ego and Central Ego' (94; abbreviations expanded). This is the process of psychic growth described by Padel and is a move to *an open-systems view of the self* (endopsychic structure) where psychic growth can occur by the internalisation of good experiences with others along the lines I have described earlier. I think that Grotstein's suggestion that Fairbairn's theory might be able to explain Klein's theory is potentially very important since the idea that a structural explanation is deeper than a phenomenological one is an important aspect of a scientific approach (Will 1986).

I want to bring some of the strands of the previous sections together by considering in some detail the extent to which Grotstein's suggestions can be borne out concerning a Fairbairnian interpretation (that is a paradigmatic explanation in terms of Fairbairn's model of endopsychic structure) of Likierman's identification of the 'tragic' and 'moral' aspects of Klein's depressive position. In addition this involves reference to Rubens' Fairbairnian interpretation of the depressive position and Skolnick's argument about the need to modify Fairbairn's theory to include an internalised good object on the model of the internalised bad object. This will also give concrete expression to Grotstein's dual-track hypothesis, which seems to me to imply that there is a Fairbairnian model state for all the psychic phenomena Klein identifies, a view I would like to see developed further.

Likierman suggests that, for Klein, ambivalence evolves out of overcoming early splitting, which is consistent with Fairbairn's view and at the root of Skolnick's attempt to make Fairbairn's theory more like Klein's by having the good object internalised and repressed. It is true that Likierman recognises the importance of internalising the good object for the development of the moral phase of the depressive position, and subsequently, to allow the infant to overcome the depressive position. But, in her interpretation of Klein, there is nothing to say that this good object is necessarily unconscious, as opposed to preconscious, which would be quite consistent with Fairbairn's view.

Grotstein uses two different configurations of the basic endopsychic structure as analogues of the tragic and the moral aspects of the depressive position described by Likierman. Interestingly these two different model states are precisely those identified by Rubens when he gives his interpretation of Fairbairn's model as it applies to the depressive position. Rubens' distinction between the endopsychic structure under depression and that structure under sadness maps very neatly into both Grotstein's and Likierman's views of the tragic and moral aspects of the depressive position. The initial configuration of the endopsychic structure, where the maximum of libido is bound in the libidinal self, and the maximum aggression is bound in the anti-libidinal self, and any surplus aggression is used to hold these two sub-selves as separated repressed entities, where the anti-libidinal self also directs aggression towards the libidinal self, is what Fairbairn defines as the basic endopsychic structure and the schizoid position. As Rubens describes it, it is equivalent to the *closed* internal world that resists change in therapy (defence against recognition of loss) and is here associated with the tragic phase of the depressive position. Grotstein associates the moral phase of the depressive position with an endopsychic structure with different dynamics, and a stronger, and more obvious, representation of the good object as part of the ideal object. However, both Grotstein and Rubens have chosen to represent the 'moral' phase of the depressive position by a model of the endopsychic structure that clearly has an *ideal object* playing an important role. This is the internalised good object that both Skolnick and Likierman stress the importance of, but the difference between the two configurations of the model is that in the former the ideal object has little if anything to do, whereas in the latter it is active in the dynamics of the self. In my view the absence of the ideal object from an active part in the basic endopsychic structure as initially developed by Fairbairn could be interpreted as the equivalent of the 'dead' internal object Klein refers to in the 'tragic' phase of the depressive position. The binding of a maximum of libido and aggression in other structures would effectively reduce the ideal object to an empty cipher or a dead object. Only later in the moral phase when the dynamic is less punitive, and the ideal object can contain aspects of the libidinal and aggressive potential of the self, can the ideal object figure as an aspect of reparative strivings; indeed without such a possibility there could be no reparation.

Chapter 5

Fairbairn's theory of art in the light of his mature model of mind

In 1938 Fairbairn published two linked papers on art (Fairbairn 1938a, 1938b) written within a broadly Freudian metapsychology with a significant contribution from Melanie Klein's theory of early aggressive phantasies. Two years later, during the Second World War, Fairbairn produced the first of the papers in which he formulated his own object relations theory or 'psychology of dynamic structure' as he called it. When these and other papers were collected in *Psychoanalytic Studies of the Personality* (1952a) Fairbairn chose *not* to include the art papers amongst them. Fairbairn did publish two critical notices on art (Fairbairn 1950, 1953b), one on Marion Milner's *On Not Being Able to Paint* (1950) and one on Ernst Kris's (1993) *Psychoanalytic Explorations in Art*, and in each of these short notices he refers back to his papers on art in a manner that suggested he thought they were worth developing. In the paper on Kris in particular, he gave some suggestions of how his pre-war theory of art might be amended in the light of his psychology of dynamic structure. I have suggested elsewhere (Clarke 1994, 1995, 2003a, 2003b) that Fairbairn's psychology of dynamic structure might be used to analyse film and drama with particular reference to the description of psychic growth in Fairbairn's mature theory developed by Padel (1991, 1994). It was in response to Ken Wright's (1995) Winnicottian view of creativity, based in a multiple-self model and critical of Segal's Kleinian account, that I came to see how Fairbairn's mature multiple-self model and Padel's description of psychic growth within that model (see Chapter 2) could provide an account of creativity that would, in effect, be a rewriting of Fairbairn's theory of art in the light of his mature theory.

ARTISTIC ACTIVITY

In the 'Prolegomena to a Psychology of Art' Fairbairn (1938a) begins by looking at art as a social phenomenon with four components – the artist, the percipient, the work of art and technique. He dismisses both the work of art and technique as suitable places to begin his investigations, and notes that in the past the choice of the psychologist has usually fallen upon the percipient with the consequence that the psychology of art has been largely a psychology of art appreciation. Fairbairn feels this approach has been barren even though it is more suitable to psychological investigation than artistic creation. He notes that, strictly speaking, art does not need an audience so that it is his first task to determine the nature of *artistic activity*, and, since the work of art is its outcome, this approach must also determine the nature of the work of art.

Fairbairn suggests that all activity can be classified into one of two types – activities undertaken for the satisfaction provided by the activities themselves and activities undertaken as a means of providing satisfaction independent of those inherent in the activities in question. He associates the former with the pleasure principle and fun, and the latter with the reality principle and work. He says, 'pure artistic activity, which is free from all ulterior motives, is seen to fall automatically into the class of play activities' (291).

He goes on to point out that artistic activity is also characterised by making something, not just doing something: 'a work of art is something that is made for fun; and, conversely anything that is made for fun must be regarded as a work of art. Art appreciation consists in perceiving something that has been made for fun. And furthermore, aesthetic pleasure may be defined as the fun of perceiving something that has been made for fun' (291). Fairbairn is aware that this expands the field of art to a much wider set of activities than is common and comments upon the culturally specific way in which 'the senses of sight and hearing are exalted at the expense of senses like taste and smell, which are more closely related to the libidinal gratifications of childhood, and, further, that this cultural process is intimately related to the process of repression in the individual mind' (292).[1]

Fairbairn sets out next 'to reach some understanding of the psychological significance of the work of art in terms of the psychology of the artist' (293). He compares the work of art with the dream, and puts forward the notion of a 'process of "art-work", which performs a function in relation to the work of art similar to that performed by dream-work, art-work must be regarded as essentially unconscious' (294). Like dream-work 'art-work ... provides the means of reducing the psychical tension in the artist's mind by enabling the repressed urges to obtain some outlet and satisfaction without unduly disturbing his equanimity' (294). He also notes that, like dream-work, art-work can fail and when it does both the equanimity of the artist and the quality of the work of art will suffer. He argues that the complexity of the art-work is determined by the relative strength of the repressed urges and the factors responsible for repression and concludes that 'there can be no doubt that art-work, like dream-work, is dependent upon repression, and that without repression no *high achievement* in art is possible' (295; emphasis added).

Fairbairn goes on to review some psychoanalytic findings from an essentially Freudian point of view, and then introduces Melanie Klein's work on destructive phantasies. He starts by citing the findings of Freud on the life and death drives, which he refers to as the life principle and the denial of life principle. He points out that the co-existence of these two incompatible groups of impulses leads to mental conflict particularly in early childhood, when libidinal and destructive impulses are directed towards the same person in the shape of the mother or primary caregiver: 'It is to deal with the anxiety and guilt engendered by destructive phantasies regarding love-objects that repression is originally instituted in childhood; and it is owing to the persistence of such phantasies in the unconscious that it is maintained in adult life' (296). He notes that this involves considerable repression of libido, and, since artistic activity is essentially creative, you would expect art to be determined by libidinal urges. Fairbairn discusses Klein's work on destructive phantasies and points out that she found that these were characteristically accompanied by compensatory phantasies of restitution, which arise as a means of alleviating the guilt and anxiety engendered by the destructive phantasies. The function of these phantasies of restitution is to provide reassurance regarding the integrity of the threatened love-object, 'since the preservation and enhancement of its objects of attachment is the great concern of the libido' (297). Fairbairn argues that we should regard phantasies of restitution as libidinal manifestations despite their owing their origin to the presence of destructive urges. He comments upon the cultural importance of phantasies of restitution which are at the root of notions of perfection and the ideal, and he goes on to argue that the principle of restitution is the governing principle in art. This is where his original argument is most like Segal's view that reparation is the governing principle of art.

Finally Fairbairn reviews aspects of Freud's structural theory where the notion of the agent of repression was developed. He returns again to the concept of dream-work and says 'dream-work is . . . a function of the ego, which . . . modifies phantasies engendered by the instinctive id-impulses in deference to the demands of the superego' (301). In this account dream-work is both negative and positive; not just a way of allowing hidden and unacceptable wishes some expression but also a positive gesture towards the superego:

> Art-work modifies repressed phantasies in such a way as to enable them to elude the vigilance of the superego and so to become available for embodiment in works of art . . . relieving the tension between the repressed impulses and the ego . . . art-work enables the ego to convert phantasies unacceptable to the superego into positive tributes to its authority and so relieves the tension existing between the ego and the superego.
>
> (301)

Thus, 'art is . . . not only a sublimated expression of repressed urges, but also a means whereby positive values are created in the service of an ideal' (302).

He rounds off the paper by returning to some of his opening remarks, saying again that, in so far as the act of restitution is determined by a need for the relief of inner tension, then the creation of a work of art can be regarded as 'making something for fun'. As to the artist's audience, in the light of the notion of restitution, it consists in the objects to whom restitution is made, in some cases real or phantasised external objects and in other cases internal objects represented in the artist's own superego.

AESTHETIC EXPERIENCE

In his second paper on art, 'The ultimate basis of aesthetic experience', Fairbairn (1938b) explains that the paper is a sequel to the 'Prolegomena...' and says it addresses the psychology of the beholder where the beholder is the subject of aesthetic experience:

> It is only when we seek our clue to the psychological significance of art in artistic activity (i.e. the motives of the artist) that it becomes possible to establish a definite criterion by which to differentiate between what is a work of art and what is not. Such a criterion is to be found, however, in the conclusion reached in my previous paper that anything that is 'made for fun' is a work of art. This conclusion, together with the conclusion that the work of art represents a tribute of restitution paid by the artist's ego to his superego, provides a means of surmounting the difficulties inherent in prevalent conceptions in aesthetics.
>
> (168–9)

Fairbairn turns to Dali's notion of the surrealist object, that is, of objects functioning symbolically: 'the "found objects" of the surrealist consist in external, and for the most part natural, objects, in the appearance of which he discovers a hidden symbolic significance, and which he therefore preserves and, so to speak, "frames" ' (170). What is interesting to Fairbairn about the found object is that it represents an intermediate point between the attitude of the artist and that of the beholder and that it also represents what he calls a *minimal work of art*.

Fairbairn uses this idea of the found object to speculate about the origins of art, quoting Herbert Read who had noted that many of the earliest cave drawings are based around a natural (rock) feature. Fairbairn believes that these natural features are comparable to found objects and suggests that the found object represents 'a union between the outer world of reality and the inner world of wish fulfilment' (170–1). The natural feature, as found object, becomes the nucleus of the picture, the next step being to make a picture without a natural feature at its core.

Fairbairn considers the origins of a specific work of art. He describes the way in which Dali came to make *Visage Paranoiaque* on the basis of a postcard of an African village that he had mistakenly interpreted as a picture of a head by Picasso. Fairbairn considers the process of creating a work of art, and describes the following stages in this process. The artist is confronted with an object in which he discovers symbolic significance, a significance that is *not* inherent in the real nature of the object. Due to this object possessing features enabling it to represent, for the artist, a fulfilment of his emotional needs – a 'wish fulfilment' – this is tantamount to the discovery of a new object. The artist seeks to perpetuate what he has found in a work of art. But because it represents a wish fulfilment it cannot exist apart from the act of discovery, it has been created by the discovery, and the discovery represents a creative act on the part of the artist. And so the artist embodies the discovery in a formal work of art. Fairbairn says that the process he has described 'may be taken to represent what happens in all artistic creation' (172).

Since the emotional needs, which determine the significance of the 'found object' for the artist, are predominantly unconscious, there has to be a certain amount of disguise of the object, even for the Surrealists who want to bring the world of the unconscious into the world of reality. The comparative poverty of the art-work in surrealist works of art, Fairbairn argues, is evidence of the relative failure of repression. In most schools of art it is usual for the ultimate significance of the 'found object' to be unconscious.

Fairbairn makes a general statement about artistic creation, which he describes as *the discovery and perpetuation of an object which symbolises, for the artist, the fulfilment of unconscious emotional needs*. He goes on to describe aesthetic experience as follows: aesthetic experience represents a specific emotional reaction, which occurs when a symbolically significant object is discovered in the external world. Individuals vary both in terms of their emotional needs and in the amount of disguise necessary to enable an object to function symbolically for them – that is to function as a 'found object' and not as an actual object. This helps us to appreciate the subjective character of aesthetic judgement.

Considering the world of art as a world of 'found objects', Fairbairn suggests that the artist is good at discovering such objects, at isolating them, framing them and giving them permanence; and, that the role of the beholder is to discover these objects for him, or her, self. Fairbairn suggests, following Herbert Read, that an open mind is a prerequisite for this discovery and that in the discovery the beholder shares the experience of the artist and the satisfactions of aesthetic creation.

Fairbairn considers cases where aesthetic experience fails and asks why that might be. He focuses on the need for disguise and the extent to which the work of art may over- or under-symbolise its deeper significance. In the case of over-symbolisation the censorship of the artist's superego is too exacting and the beholder makes no discovery. In the case of under-symbolisation there is too little disguise, and this provokes a strong emotional reaction in any beholder whose superego is more exacting than the artist's, and who needs greater disguise of repressed urges under pressure of anxiety, so the beholder rejects the object with feelings of anger or disgust. Translating these findings into the discourse of form and content then, over-symbolisation – the over-elaboration of the disguise – can be seen as form without content, and under-symbolisation as content without form. Responses to exhibitions like the 'Sensations' exhibition at the Royal Academy in 1998 might be seen in this context.

Fairbairn considers the work of art as a restored object, and suggests that the duality of satisfaction underlying aesthetic experience corresponds to the duality of satisfaction provided by artistic activity, which provides a means of expression for the repressed urges of the artist, and enables his ego to pay a tribute to the supremacy of his superego: 'in so far as the work of art consists in a tribute paid by the artist's ego to his superego, it essentially represents a means of restitution, whereby his ego makes atonement to his superego for the destruction implied in the presence of repressed destructive impulses' (1938b: 178). For Fairbairn, the aesthetic appeal of a work of art for the beholder will depend upon its capacity to represent a restitution, that is when the object which presents itself is not simply a found object, but also a restored object. Over-symbolisation excludes the impression of destruction too rigorously and under-symbolisation produces too great a sense of destruction. Fairbairn concludes the paper with a section on aesthetic theory suggesting that, while what he calls perfectionist theories of aesthetics, represented by Aristotle, and expressionist theories of aesthetics, represented by Croce, might appear to be opposed, he argues, using tragedy as an example, that the need for order, symmetry and definiteness, and the need for the cathartic release of the emotions of pity and fear are both necessary. Therefore, unconscious destructive urges and a restored object are both necessary to aesthetics.

FAIRBAIRN ON MARION MILNER

In his critical notice on Marion Milner's *On Not Being Able to Paint*, Fairbairn gives a positive assessment of her work. In regard to sublimation (a point which he further develops in his critical notice on Kris) he says that it is refreshing to read a book on the psychological processes involved in art and never to come across the term 'sublimation'. He goes on to say 'sublimation is, of course, a concept which has its roots in impulse psychology; and it is difficult to find a place for it in a psychology of object relations' (Fairbairn 1950: 72). In regard to his overall response to the book he says that Marion Milner's 'observations from inside regarding the mental processes involved in painting appear to confirm some of the conclusions which I recorded in two contributions to the psychology of art in 1938 on the basis of an objective approach' (72).

FAIRBAIRN ON ERNST KRIS

In Fairbairn's critical notice on Kris's *Psychoanalytic Explorations in Art* he commends the author for being 'no less concerned with what psychoanalysis can learn within the field of cultural studies than with what it can teach' (Fairbairn 1953b: 169), but regrets the fact that Kris has not attempted a general theory of art. Fairbairn notes that Kris makes a comparison between dreams and art, suggesting that there is 'art-work' like there is 'dream-work', and draws attention to his own similar suggestion in the 1938 art papers.

Fairbairn identifies the basic concept underlying all of Kris's investigations, as being derived from Freud's thinking about wit: 'in the case of art the ego remains in control of the primary process whilst permitting a regression to the level at which this process functions. The theme of such controlled regression to the level of primary process may be regarded as providing the basic concept underlying all the investigations recorded by Kris in the present volume' (165). Fairbairn argues that Kris believes that it is characteristic of the artist that he should be able to gain easy access to id material without being overwhelmed by it; that the artist should be able to make rapid shifts from one level of psychic functioning to the other.

Fairbairn describes Kris's arguments concerning sublimation, and his attempt to clarify Freud's inconsistent use of the term, where Freud sometimes means the displacement of energy discharge from a socially unacceptable goal to an acceptable one, and sometimes means a transformation of the energy discharged. Fairbairn, however, uses this discussion to say more about the fact that the concept of sublimation presents considerable difficulties for those who:

> adopt a psychology of object-relations based upon the principle of dynamic structure. To those of this way of thinking, both the concept of the displacement of energy from a socially unacceptable to a socially acceptable goal and that of the transformation of energy itself assume a somewhat artificial complexion, since they imply an approach based upon a divorce of energy from structure. In terms of the principle of dynamic structure, the displacement of energy from a socially unacceptable to a socially acceptable goal would resolve itself, where the field of art is concerned, into a change in the relationships existing *between the artist and those objects who constitute society for him*; and similarly the transformation of energy would resolve itself into a complex change *(a) in the relationship of internally differentiated ego-structures not only*

> with internal objects but also with one another, and (b) in the relationships of the conscious ego-structure with external objects.
>
> (167; emphasis added)

This means that Kris's concept of 'regression to the level of primary process' needs to be given an object relations interpretation. This is developed in a later section of the chapter. Fairbairn goes on to look at the consequences, for the concepts of primary and secondary process, of adopting his mature theory of dynamic structure:

> According to the principle of dynamic structure, it is not a case of a structural ego being differentiated under the pressure of the impact of external reality out of an original id which is relatively formless, so much as of an id being a structure with primitive characteristics which is differentiated from an original (and relatively primitive) ego-structure under the influence of repression; and it can be seen that once such a differentiation has occurred, the repressed id-structure will retain primitive features (and acquire exaggerations of such features under the influence of repression), while that part of the ego which remains conscious and in touch with external reality will be free to develop under the influence of relationships with external objects ... The primary process will present itself as a characteristic feature of the activity of the repressed id-structure, and the secondary process as a characteristic feature of the activity of the conscious ego-structure; and the nature of artistic activity will then come to be described, not as an ego-controlled regression to the level of the primary process but rather as *an attempt to reconcile the primitive expression of a repressed id-structure with the requirements of a conscious ego-structure oriented towards external objects in a social milieu.*
>
> (167; emphasis added)

The Freudian distinction between primary and secondary process is understood by Fairbairn to represent the distinction between dynamic structures based upon internalised relationships, some of which have been dissociated and repressed during infancy and are therefore 'primitive', and the dynamic structure he calls the central ego which can learn from experience. This is discussed in greater detail later.

Fairbairn argues for the concept of artistic activity that he has already put forward in his papers on art – 'the reconciliation between the expression of the id-structure and the requirements of the conscious ego which it is the specific aim of the artist to establish is one accomplished through the specific activity of making (creating) things – and making them not primarily for utilitarian purposes, but . . . primarily "for fun" ' (168).

He goes on to argue that this conception of artistic activity finds a place for a scale of aesthetic values within it, absence of which has always been a weakness in psychoanalytic writings about art:

> the aesthetic failure of a work of art depends upon a comparative failure to effect the reconciliation to which reference has been made. Such failure may be brought about in either of two ways – either through a failure on the part of the artist to make the expression of the id-structure conform sufficiently to the requirements of the conscious ego . . . or through the requirements of the conscious ego proving so exacting as to preclude the expression of the id-structure from endowing the work of art with a sufficiently dynamic quality to render it convincing. . . . These two types of failure have been described . . . elsewhere as 'under-symbolisation' and 'over-symbolisation'.
>
> (168)

Fairbairn ends by suggesting that what differentiates art from other activities is to be sought in the fact that the processes involved in art 'are manifested within the field of creation – in the act of making things in so far as these things are made, not for utilitarian purposes, but for the sake of making them viz. in so far as they are made (so to speak) for fun' (169).

SUTHERLAND'S COMMENTS ON FAIRBAIRN'S ART PAPERS

In his biography of Fairbairn, Sutherland (1989) comments on the art papers in some detail. He believes that Fairbairn was too much influenced by Melanie Klein's theories at the time he wrote them. This influence was based mainly in Fairbairn's clinical experience of the reality of his patients' sadistic phantasies. Sutherland is critical of Klein: '[her] description of the depressive position has left us without an adequate account of what the new personalised self entails. Its creation and its subsequent creativity involved more specific understanding to be given of this process of restitution of a damaged object within a closed system' (52).

Sutherland is also critical of the notion of 'making things for fun' which Fairbairn continued to see as central even after he had replaced a pleasure-seeking psychology with an object-seeking psychology. Sutherland suggests that he laid 'insufficient stress on the artist's products as gifts in perpetuity to fellow men' (53) and that the satisfactions attendant upon technical mastery are also undervalued: 'although he includes all the experience of making the restitution from the agony of emptiness and despair, the achievement of the satisfying object from intensely exacting work is what gives the artist and the appreciation the excitement of hope and creation surmounting the destructiveness' (53).

Sutherland comments further that there is insufficient emphasis on the external reference for artistic activity. He cites Fairbairn's use of Herbert Read's notion of art as a 'solitary activity' and says that this 'detracts from this essential external reference in the "serious" elements of good art' (50). He also thinks there is an idealising tendency in that 'the destruction-restitution thesis without the manifest product of its transmutation into the sharable realities of the process within the individual mind leaves us too much in the familiar territory of the philosophers, poets, writers and religious thinkers, namely the antinomy of good and evil' (50), and that the real achievement of integration through the making of the object is also important: 'the artist shows that, however threatening the inner forces, they must be, and can be, faced and an integration achieved. This he does in the form given to the actual object he is driven to create' (51).

In a passage that is written from within the perspective of Fairbairn's psychology of dynamic structure and whose conclusions prefigure key aspects of the conclusions of this paper, Sutherland comments that 'the restitution from destruction at the personal level entails two tasks. First there has to be worked through a full experience of the concern and the despair about being able to *restore and preserve the good mother*, internally and externally. The second task is the reciprocal preservation of *the emergent self*' (52; emphasis added); the key point being to link the restoration of the destroyed object with the development of an integrated self. Having looked in some detail at the former already, I will now consider the latter from a Winnicottian point of view through Ken Wright's approach to art.

KEN WRIGHT'S THEORY OF ARTISTIC CREATIVITY

Ken Wright, in an unpublished 1995 paper, takes as his starting point what he calls 'a position statement by the Kleinian analyst, Hanna Segal'. His summary of Segal's position is as follows:

> In creating a work of art, the artist is not primarily engaged in a wish-fulfilling activity; he is working through significant inner conflicts and attempting to resolve them through the process of artistic creation. In order to do this, he does not escape from reality, inner or outer, but on the contrary, has to be deeply in touch with them. He also has to find a means of representing this reality in a truthful way, so that he may awaken in the observer a similar constellation of experience to that which exists in him while he is creating.

Wright argues that the requirement for truthful representation means that art is a symbolic activity and it is the symbolic nature of art that allows the viewer to share in the creative experience. He also notes that, by arguing that the 'significant form' of the art object symbolises an *unconscious* content, Segal avoids any clash between formalist and content-oriented approaches to art because these operate at a manifest level.

Wright says that he is in broad agreement with this approach and identifies the problem he has with Segal's argument as coming from its 'Kleinian twist'. According to Segal the artist is not just creating significant forms that give symbolic expression to elements of his inner life: 'He is re-creating objects which, in his inner world of phantasy, he has damaged or destroyed' (Wright). In short the key problem for Segal is the artist's destructiveness. Under this description the art-object is what Fairbairn called a 'restored object' and the making of the object is a reparative act.

For Segal (1990) then the significant form symbolised in a work of art is the reconstructed whole object, which was previously damaged or fragmented, and the whole of artistic activity is related to this 'core depressive conflict'. Wright finds this unconvincing and goes on to quote Segal further, as she opens up what seems to him to be a new theme: 'there is a longing to create an ideal state of mind and objects before what is felt as the havoc of the depressive position. Often the search is to regain a lost and unattainable ideal' (Wright 1995). In relation to this new theme Segal refers to the work of Adrian Stokes. She says that Stokes 'makes the . . . very convincing point that part of the difficulty in art is that it is to satisfy both the longing for *an ideal object and a self merged with it*, with the need to *restore* a whole object realistically perceived, *a separate mother not merged with the self*' (Segal 1990: 98; emphasis added).

Wright points out that Segal's final account of the creative process therefore includes 'the attempt to create and merge with an ideal, maternal object' which belongs to an earlier stage of development than the depressive position. He is convinced that the project of creativity has much more to do with the search for a lost and unattainable ideal than Segal allows and he spends the rest of the paper discussing an approach that takes this view seriously. This takes him back to an area of preverbal experience as seen through the 'eyes of Winnicott and a newer breed of psychoanalyst, who have observed mothers and their small babies interacting together, with fewer, or at least different preconceptions than Klein about what they should see'.

Wright asks what might be 'significant' to the baby and suggests that it is the mother's face, not her breast, that is the most 'significant form' in the infant's early experience. In particular he argues that it is the first and most important visual object in the infant's early experience and that 'a closer consideration of the mother's face and its role in infant experience, may help us to form some new ideas about the nature and function of creativity'.

After a careful and sensitive review of the relationship between the infant and its mother, or primary caregiver, and the role that the mother's face might play, he states:

Its changing and evanescent configurations, which eventually we come to think of as expressions, begin to acquire meanings that are linked, not only to those configurations, but also to relatively specific inner feeling states of the infant. This has led me to think of the mother's face as a kind of waystage in the infant's passage towards symbolic understanding. From this point of view, we can think of her face as a generator of protosymbols for the infant.

(1995)

This experience of the mother's face as a significant and expressive visual object underpins some elements of aesthetic experience for Wright, who makes the striking suggestion that 'when we look at pictures, we are still looking at this centrally important and loved object of infancy – the mother's face – and reading and being moved by its changing configurations', as Freud also says in his essay on 'Leonardo da Vinci'.

Wright goes on to compare faces and paintings and asks what it is that *paintings* do for people. In order to throw some light on this he first asks what *faces* do for people and refers directly to Winnicott's 1967 paper: 'Mirror role of mother and family in child development' (Winnicott 1971). Winnicott argues that the 'precursor of the mirror is the mother's face'. Wright suggests that the mother's expression provides a visual analogue of the baby's internal states and as such provides an embryonic 'objectification of subjectivity'. He then wonders if the artist 'uses the picture he is painting in ways that are similar to those in which the infant uses the mother's face', and suggests that viewers use paintings in much the same way – 'like a mirror that responds to the self'. He goes on to ask what it is that is 'picked up, contained and given back by the reflective forms of a painting', and suggests that we might think of a painting as a 'quasi-personal responding object'. Wright suggests that 'what we call "significant form" in a painting is form that picks up and resonates with aspects of the self. Its "inevitable sequences" are felt to be inevitable precisely because they resonate with and objectify, like the mother's response, what is already felt to be there in the self'. He clarifies what he means by self, by referring to the 'central affective core' of a person, and then, following Winnicott, goes on to consider what happens when the baby is angry and screaming and faced with a mother who cannot accept this aspect of the baby's self. Wright argues that it is unlikely that this aspect of the self will be mirrored and confirmed, but that it will be relegated into an area of 'bad' or unwanted selves, which are not integrated into the larger self, that is 'underpinned and contained within the mother's area of mirroring acceptance'. He suggests that this area of relegated selves might be part of what we mean by the unconscious. This model of a central self and unconscious subsidiary selves is consistent with Fairbairn's mature theory. These selves continue to exist but 'they are not under the control of the central ego'. Wright goes on to suggest that one of the projects of art is to create a new place to be for such repudiated and unmirrored elements of the self, and that one way in which this might be done is for the artist to create forms which mirror or echo these split-off selves. In short that the artist 'provides the maternal reflecting function which had been deficit' and in such a way that the 'wayward and "lost" elements of the self are able to be retrieved and gathered in within the project of the work of art, and given the place to be which they might have had, if the early maternal responses had been more flexible and accommodating'. The retrieval of lost elements of the self and their (re)integration into the central self is consistent with Padel's description of psychic growth in Fairbairn's mature theory.

For Segal it is the whole object that is being restored in creative activity, while for Wright it is lost aspects of the self that are being restored.

FAIRBAIRN'S THEORY OF ART IN THE LIGHT OF HIS MATURE THEORY OF DYNAMIC STRUCTURE

Fairbairn's theory of art modified by his mature theory, and interpreted according to Padel's theory of psychic growth can be seen to offer a theory that combines both Segal's and Wright's approaches. These appear as moments in such a theory. This entails a reconstruction of the self on a more realistic basis (the central ego becomes expanded by (re)integrating previously split-off aspects from subsidiary selves), and a modification of the ego ideal in the direction of a less limited, more whole, internal object (the ideal object is reconstituted on the basis of the increased realistic powers available as a consequence of the changes in the central ego).

If we return to Fairbairn's comments on Kris and in particular his reconstruction of the terms 'sublimation' and the 'primary' and 'secondary' processes, we can begin to rewrite Fairbairn's theory of art in terms of his theory of dynamic structure.

Sublimation – the change from socially unacceptable to socially acceptable goals within the field of art – involves a 'change in the relationship between the artist and those objects who constitute society for him' (Fairbairn 1953b: 165) and this is related to a complex change '(a) in the relationship of internally differentiated ego-structures not only with internal objects but also with one another, and (b) in the relationships of the conscious ego-structure with external objects' (165). In terms of the mature theory, the internal dynamic between the central ego and its ideal object and the libidinal ego/object and the anti-libidinal ego/object is directly related to the relationship between the central ego/ideal object and external reality. Changes in one will produce changes in the other.

In his discussion of the primary and secondary process Fairbairn continues to use a language of 'repressed id-structures' when he means the libidinal and anti-libidinal ego/object pairs. His 'conscious ego-structure' is the central ego and its associated ideal object. Primary process becomes 'the primitive expression of a repressed id-structure' (167), that is, of the libidinal and anti-libidinal ego/object, which are split-off early on in development and have all the hallmarks of early experience and affect. The secondary process is a manifestation of 'a conscious ego-structure oriented towards external objects in a social milieu' (167); that is, the central ego and its ideal object, which in Fairbairn's model of inner reality is reality-oriented.

Therefore the idea of 'regression to primary process thinking' becomes the activation of dynamic structures that are primitive because they have been unable to learn from experience, having been dissociated and repressed during infancy. Accessing and working over the content of these repressed structures is the source of psychic growth in Padel's understanding of Fairbairn's mature theory (the central self grows at the expense of the split-off and repressed subsidiary selves). Fairbairn was what Grotstein (1994a) has called a 'deficit theorist', that is changes in the environment are more likely to produce psychic change – change in the configuration of the dynamic structures that constitutes inner reality – than vice versa. However, the artist is, as Fairbairn stresses, a maker of objects par excellence, so there is a particularly intimate relationship between the attempts to make something and the real responses and limitations of external reality. It is through this intimate dialectic between the limitations of external reality and the malleability of dynamic structures that creativity and psychic growth manifest themselves. I want to suggest that at best *creativity and psychic growth are coeval*, that this is what we mean when we talk about great art, that somehow a work of art has managed to encapsulate, embody, or rehearse a moment of psychic growth in a way that is shareable.

In Fairbairn's theory of art the function of the superego is significant; it is to the superego that the ego pays tribute. In his mature theory the superego has become more complex: 'what Freud described as a "superego" is really a complex structure comprising (a) the ideal object or ego ideal, (b) the anti-libidinal ego, and (c) the rejecting (or anti-libidinal) object' (Fairbairn 1963: 224–5). Given the nature of the anti-libidinal ego/object it is clear that this is the source of the punitive version of the superego that needs to be ameliorated if psychic growth is to be possible. If we were to update Fairbairn's theory of art in the light of his mature theory we would have to replace the idea that the ego pays tribute to the superego by the notions that the anti-libidinal ego/object prevents aspects of the libidinal ego/object from becoming integrated into the central ego and that the central ego pays tribute to the ideal object. But what in this model is the ideal object? It is the repository of all positive values that have become associated with the acceptable part of the originally introjected object. In psychic growth the central ego and the ideal object become expanded by the integration of elements from the libidinal and anti-libidinal selves. The scope for thought and action, for aspirations and ideals, is expanded, and, given the nature of the ideal object, it is fair to say that the original object is partially reconstructed, made more whole than it was before. There is a move towards the ideal object becoming more like the original object before it was shorn of its over-exciting and over-rejecting aspects. So Padel's account of psychic growth, in one of its aspects, does involve the recreation of a more whole ideal object. This is directly comparable to the idea that Segal discusses and Wright uses as a starting point for his speculations: 'often the search is to regain a lost and unattainable ideal' (Segal 1990: 98).

The other side of Padel's account is dependent upon integrating aspects of the self from the libidinal and anti-libidinal selves, that is, from selves that have been relegated or denied; dissociated aspects of the self that form alternative loci for activity and perspective. It is by reclaiming aspects of these subsidiary selves that the central ego and its ideal object are able to grow. This aspect of the process is akin to the view that Wright puts forward. So, a Fairbairnian model of psychic growth, as developed by John Padel, can be argued to contain the theories of both Hannah Segal and Ken Wright as moments – moments that are inextricably linked and interdependent in Padel's account of psychic growth. *As the subsidiary selves become incorporated into the central ego and its ideal object so the self becomes more whole (reintegrated), and the ideal object becomes more like the original object at a new level of reality and realism.*

Padel's account of psychic growth within Fairbairn's mature model of mind allows us to reinterpret Fairbairn's art papers to produce a thoroughgoing object relations theory of creativity. This theory of creativity can be seen to contain within it both Kleinian and Winnicottian moments – restored objects and reintegrated selves.

A SIMILAR APPROACH

It is worth remarking here that a model which seems to be in many ways similar to that offered here was described by the late Ismond Rosen, psychoanalyst and artist, in his 1974 catalogue to an exhibition called 'Genesis'.[2] He was a member of the contemporary Freudian group and therefore uses classical Freudian terminology with an object relations subtext. His thoughts about the process of creativity, based on reflections upon his own practices as an artist, do seem to be similar to my interpretation of Fairbairn's model. I am unable to fully develop the comparisons with Rosen's work within this context because of constraints on space, but such a comparison might be a useful way of developing a clearer understanding of a potentially common model, currently obscured by different technical languages. In brief, Rosen argues through a threefold comparison between the book of Genesis, his experience of artistic creativity, and his psychoanalytic expertise, that 'Genesis is an account of creation, of the world, of art, and of the process of creativity itself; a testimony to the making of humanity, and the relationship to its maker, witnessed here by an artist who is also a psycho-analyst. The process of integration is the basis of creativity' (3). Rosen says there are three stages to creativity which he calls:

> 1. The First Mix, where the basic elements are produced ... 2. The Destructive Phase. Here the original elements are altered and undergo processes of loss and change ... 3. The Creative Phase of Reconstitutional Integration. As part of a creative 'jump', further elements are added, disparities are 'worked through' and integrated to form new qualitatively higher forms and ideas.
>
> (3)

Further on he describes the second destructive stage in relation to the creative artist in the following terms: 'one of the qualities which creative artists possess to a high degree is the capacity at times of dissatisfaction or change to regress within themselves in order to resolve underlying conflicts so as to be able to forge new integrations' (10). In the section of the paper catalogue which considers psychoanalytical ideas he writes:

> Clinical psycho-analysis and art-work share one major task: to make the unconscious conscious. In the baby, the bodily needs gain immediate conscious expression. It is only with later development of the ego that the child learns to wait, controls the drives, and tries to be good in order to remain loved by others. A half-way house is set up between the conscious and the unconscious, called the *preconscious*. This area is so called because we can by an effort of will make *preconscious* material become conscious. Available memory is stored in the *preconscious*, and so are the formed images from the unconscious, to which the artist may then have recourse ... A complicated inner set of relationships is therefore set up which dictates the movement of the traffic to and fro between the unconscious and awareness. Which unconscious wishes may be satisfied; what experiences or conflicts must be forgotten or repressed into the unconscious because they are painful or forbidden; and what manoeuvres the ego can make to produce compromises between irreconcilable inner or outer elements.
>
> (19; emphasis added)

Parallels with the developed model become evident with translation from the Freudian language to that used by Fairbairn. The importance of the preconscious is manifest.

PRECONSCIOUS MENTAL PROCESSES

I will now examine Ernst Kris's *Psychoanalytic Explorations in Art* (1953), in which the last chapter is devoted to 'Preconscious Mental Processes' described in classical Freudian terms but influenced by developments in ego psychology.[3] My reason for this focus on his descriptions of preconscious processes is to see if the proposed object relations-based model can be seen to support and explain a similar range of processes. Fairbairn, in his review of Kris's book, referred to the 'originality and impressiveness' of the section of the book containing the chapter on preconscious mental processes (Fairbairn 1953b: 164), adding that: 'his discussion of the function of the preconscious mental processes is extremely illuminating' (169). Thus despite Fairbairn's criticism of Kris's remaining within the energetic and economic model of the psyche, he thought the chapter was valuable.

Kris starts (even in 1953) by bemoaning the fact that 'in recent psychoanalytic writings preconscious mental processes are rarely mentioned' (Kris 1953: 303). He argues that this is to be regretted since the 'reciprocal relationship between the development of ego psychology and therapeutic technique ... [has led to] specific advances as to the handling of the relationship of preconscious to unconscious material in therapy ... this advice is to wait until what you wish to interpret is close to consciousness, until it is preconscious' (303). Kris sees the project of re-examining theoretical problems associated with preconscious mental processes as consonant with Freud's overall project for a 'psychoanalytic psychology, normal and abnormal' (304).

Kris accounts for the relative neglect of preconscious mental processes by reference to the history of psychoanalysis and the introduction of the structural model. He points out that the new structural concepts and the older topographical schema were never properly integrated. Kris notes that Freud's view of the preconscious as capable of becoming conscious easily is too simple and ignores other comments in his work. He selects for discussion three problems that address the complexity of the preconscious processes. The first concerns the ease or difficulty with which preconscious processes reach consciousness, and the differences between them. The second concerns the variety of preconscious mental processes that cover 'continua from purposeful reflection to fantasy and from logical formulation to dream-like imagery' (305) and how these differences might be accounted for. The third problem he identifies are the differences in reaction when preconscious material emerges into consciousness. In some cases it may not be noticed and in others it causes a strong emotional reaction. He asks how we can account for these differences.

Kris discusses the way in which Freud's characterisation of the preconscious changed, and argues that an explanation couched in terms of the 'nature of the prevalent psychic energy' (305) is preferable. In this model 'unconscious processes use mobile psychic energy; preconscious bound energy' (305). These degrees of mobility 'correspond to two types of discharge characterised as the primary and secondary process' (305). Kris then looks at the way that material from one topographical domain may move to another. So, in describing the movement from preconscious to unconscious he says 'a preconscious process from which the ego withdraws cathexis becomes subject to cathexis with id (mobile) energy and will be drawn into the primary process (the basic assumption of the psychoanalytic theory of dream formation)' (306).

In my proposed modification to Fairbairn's object relations model, this process would involve object relations material from either the (preconscious) libidinal or anti-libidinal internal objects being pushed or drawn into the associated (unconscious) internal object. Whether it is pushed or drawn and which of the internal objects it is (libidinal or anti-libidinal) is a potentially important matter and offers several different options for a description of the process Kris identifies while remaining consistent with his description.

Kris then goes on to describe 'the reverse (unconscious material becomes preconscious) [which] occurs when id derivatives are cathected with ego energy and become part of preconscious mental processes' (306). He gives four options for this process, only three of which involve the preconscious directly. In the first the id derivatives become part of preconscious mental processes 'at a considerable distance from the original impulse' (306). This means there is still considerable antipathy from the (preconscious) agent of repression. If this antipathy is lessened for any reason the preconscious mental process may be much closer to the original impulse and the unconscious wish less elaborately disguised. Although Kris treats these as two options it seems that they represent a continuum where the preconscious representation is closer to or further away from the id impulse depending upon the acceptability of that impulse to the (preconscious) agent of repression. The third option he specifies is that the id derivative 'may sometimes enter preconscious mental processes at a considerable price in terms of symptoms' (306). A fourth way in which id contents may reach consciousness is by its entering the perception system (*Pcpt*): 'they appear as percepts . . . [this is] the pathway of hallucination' (306). Kris contrasts this process with the normal process whereby 'preconscious material reaches consciousness by . . . the hypercathexis mediated by attention' (306). If we look at these processes from the point of view of my proposed object relations model it is clear that the repression of the (preconscious) libidinal and anti-libidinal internal objects is carried out by the ego ideal/ideal object, with the extra (indirect) repression of the libidinal ego/object coming from the anti-libidinal ego/object, according to Fairbairn's description. The degree of repression and therefore the degree of disguise that unconscious material will have to seek in order to be admitted to the preconscious will vary according to the relationship between the three preconscious internal objects. Again this gives us a wider variety of possible configurations of this process than are provided for by Kris. The way in which symptoms may be expressed is also dependent upon the detailed relationship between the preconscious internal objects. In the case of the material going directly to the perceptual system (*Pcpt*) and appearing as hallucination, this suggests that it is possible for material to escape the triangular relationship between preconscious internal objects and present itself to the perceptual system as if from the outside. This could be because there is a route around the repressing agent (ego ideal) or it could be because the repressing agent is suspended for some reason, as it is in sleep when a similar process occurs in relation to dreaming. Alternatively, it could be that this is an example of the projection of a preconscious internal object. It would be preferable from the point of view of the proposed model to assume that the activity of the ego ideal was altered or suspended. This appears to be Kris's conclusion when he discusses the process: 'this is the reason why we assume the working – at the passage into consciousness – of countercathectic energies that would prevent what is, to some extent, ego dystonic from entering full awareness' (306). It could be argued that this move from more or less explicit representation of the unconscious material through disguise, symptom and hallucination to 'acting out', creativity and play is a continuum dependent upon the degree of repression and the insistence (dynamism) of the unconscious.

In a section entitled 'Recognition, Recall and Integration' Kris looks at the ways in which ego-dystonic preconscious material might reach consciousness. Discussing the difficulties of conscious recall regarding memory, dream, thought or fantasy, he suggests that self-observation and reconstruction can be successful. He gives an example of a previously analysed woman reporting that her attention to, and enjoyment of, a concert was disturbed by thoughts which were alleviated when she doodled on the concert programme. Subsequent analysis of the doodles revealed that they contained symbolised reference to the matters that had been disturbing her concentration.

Kris suggests that recapitulating and reconstruction can work consciously but that it can also work at the preconscious level when only the results of the process reach awareness. He says that some analysts would assume that the 'patient's ego has preconsciously already established a unity of context, or re-established its control over an ego dystonic impulse or area of thought' (307) for the recall through free association to take place. This 'unity of context' is accounted for by Kris through the concept of the 'synthetic function of the ego' (308). Kris says that preconscious processes, under the control of the synthetic function of the ego, are safe against withdrawal of preconscious cathexis and repression and usually have effortless access to consciousness.

Kris makes a distinction between 'recognition' and 'recall', suggesting that recognition can be accomplished at a preconscious level, and that only when sufficient preconscious recognition has taken place, can conscious recall take place: 'the theoretical, psychoanalytic explanation of the relationship between recognition and recall is that the synthetic function of the ego, establishing a context, is in the case of recognition facilitated by the help of perception. . . . Recall then fills a gap, fits into a pattern' (309). Later he states the case more simply: 'it seems therefore reasonable to assume that facilitation of the ego's integrative or synthetic function by recognition is one of the dynamic factors leading to recall' (309).

Kris goes on to describe the process as it moves from recognition to recall and further to belief in the following terms:

> The relation of recognition to recall of the repressed can be tentatively described in these terms: since the 'original' situation has been recognised, previously not sufficiently invested id derivatives can be integrated into the pattern indicated by the reconstruction; this in turn strengthens the ego's position, permits a reduction of countercathexes and the gradual infiltration of further material – a result in the end not dissimilar to sudden-recall, in cases in which interpretation has led to the spectacular revival of repressed traumata. In both types of cases the full investment by the ego, the syntonicity of the event with superego and id strivings may lead to the feeling of certainty, to the change from 'I know of' to 'I believe'.
>
> (309–10)

If we try to relate this account to the proposed model we find something like the process that John Padel described as psychic growth, where material from the unconscious libidinal or anti-libidinal objects enters the preconscious and is acceptable to the ego ideal, but not sufficiently cogent until further unconscious material can be incorporated into the preconscious, at which point recall may occur and the originally unconscious material can be accepted into consciousness with structural consequences for the whole system. The synthetic function of the ego in Kris's description is represented in the proposed model by the flow of material from the unconscious to the preconscious and subsequently into consciousness. This means that the ego ideal is not being punitively repressive of the preconscious representation of unconscious material. It also means that the preconscious anti-libidinal ego is not being overly repressive of the libidinal ego and that the barriers between unconscious, preconscious and conscious are 'porous'. There is the possibility of material flowing through the system from the unconscious to consciousness. At this point it is necessary to remind ourselves that the proposed model is not just about allowing material to flow in one direction or another but is also centrally concerned with the transformation (development and destruction) of structures. In Padel's account the recovered material from the unconscious sub-selves allows the ego ideal and the central ego to be reconstructed on a more realistic basis. Structural transformations are involved as well as the flow of repressed material.

In a section called 'Discharge and Regression' Kris considers the flow of material from unconscious to conscious, and from conscious to unconscious.

He cites again his belief in the existence of two continua, 'one reaching from solving problems to dreamlike fantasy, and one reaching from logical cohesive verbal statements to dreamlike imagery. Both continua, I believe occur with some frequency in preconscious mental processes' (311). It is worth remarking that a structured preconscious of the sort contained in the proposed model provides a dynamic preconscious framework within which these continua might manifest themselves, with the ends of any continua being the dominance of *one* of the preconscious internal objects.

Kris returns to the concept of different kinds of energy. The ego as described earlier is characterised by bound energy, but he now introduces a distinction between two kinds of bound energy – one is neutralised energy the other is libidinal or aggressive energy. Relating the continua described above to the forms of energy discharged, Kris argues that:

> Fantastic, freely wandering thought processes tend to discharge more libido and aggression and less neutralised energy. In fantasy, the processes of the ego are largely in the service of the id. . . . In reflective thinking the contrary is likely. Reflective thinking, according to Freud (problem solving, as we would prefer to say), serves to a higher degree the autonomous ego interests. Discharge of libido and aggression is likely to be minimised, and that of neutralised energy to be of greater relevance.
>
> (311–12)

In terms of the proposed model, the distinction between kinds of energy maps onto the preconscious internal objects very neatly, and the difference between the processes depends upon the dominance of one or the other of these internal objects. So problem solving in the proposed model would be carried out by the ego ideal, while fantasy would be generated when the preconscious libidinal and/or anti-libidinal egos were dominant (implying that the related unconscious object was 'active').

Kris turns to a discussion of ego regression which he describes in the following terms:

> The very fact that . . . phenomena of ego regression are infinitely more frequent in fantasy than in deliberative preconscious processes suggest that in fantasy the discharge of libido and aggression may have in general a greater proximity to the id. . . . Topographically, ego regression (primitivisation of ego functions) occurs not only when the ego is weak – in sleep, in falling asleep, in fantasy, in intoxication, and in the psychoses – but also during many types of creative processes.
>
> (312)

In relation to the proposed model, this describes a state of the preconscious where the libidinal and anti-libidinal egos are making a significant contribution to the preconscious mental processes because the repressive aspect of the ego ideal is in (at least partial) abeyance.

Kris mentions two different phases of creation – an inspirational and an elaborational phase: 'the inspirational phase is characterised by the facility with which id impulses, or their closer derivatives, are received' (313). In terms of the proposed model the ego ideal is relatively passive or receptive to the preconscious libidinal and anti-libidinal material during the inspirational phase: 'during the elaborational phase, the countercathectic barrier may be reinforced, work proceeds slowly, cathexis is directed to other ego functions such as reality testing, formulation or general purposes of communication. Alternations between the two phases may be rapid, oscillating, or distributed over long stretches of time' (313). In terms of the proposed model the locus of control in the preconscious returns to the ego ideal. The creative process is characterised in this account by a shift in the locus of control between the preconscious objects. When the preconscious libidinal and anti-libidinal objects are dominant the ego ideal is quiescent and attention to the outside world is reduced.

In a final section called 'Reactions to Reaching Consciousness' Kris considers the relationship between the preconscious and the conscious, the 'second censorship' that operates in the preconscious. He considers what happens when individuals become conscious of their preconscious fantasies and notes that people tend not to feel responsible for their fantasies: 'tentatively, we assume that in preoccupation with fantasy the ego withdraws cathexis from some functions of the superego' (314). In relation to previous comments on the proposed model, I note that this is consistent with the description given above where it is assumed that fantasy implies some reduction in the repressive nature of the ego ideal and the preconscious anti-libidinal ego. Kris's comments have reproduced the distinction that (following Fairbairn) I have been employing between the ego ideal and the superego (the pre- and un-conscious anti-libidinal self). Kris also recognises a difference between the ego ideal and the superego and comments further: 'one gains the impression that while the ego ideal loses its importance for the individual, the punitive tendencies of the superego are enforced in some for whom self-punitive measures are part of the fantasy. In others the hypercathexis of the ego ideal is predominant while the function of critical self-observation seems reduced' (314). In terms of the proposed model the 'punitive tendencies of the superego' map on to the activity of the preconscious anti-libidinal ego. Thus the first description is of the (preconscious) anti-libidinal ego attacking the (preconscious) libidinal ego while the ego ideal is quiescent, and in the second the (preconscious) anti-libidinal ego is quiescent while the ego ideal and the (preconscious) libidinal ego are active.

Kris makes an interesting and important comment regarding the 'absolution from guilt for fantasy' when the fantasy is not one's own: 'this accounts for the role of the bard in primitive society and, in part, for the function of fiction, drama, etc. in our society' (314).

Kris goes on to consider the feeling of relief in relation to problem-solving activity which includes 'all areas of creativity' (315). He relates these feelings to 'functional pleasure' or what Freud (in 'Wit and its relation to the unconscious') describes as follows: 'when our psychic apparatus does not actually act in search of some urgently needed gratification we let this apparatus itself work for pleasure gain. *We attempt to gain pleasure from its very activity*' (quoted in Kris: 315; his emphasis). Kris identifies this activity as based on the discharge of neutralised energy which, in the proposed model, is identified as the activity of the ego ideal. Kris goes on to assert that 'an elaboration of this theory seemed to lead to improved understanding of aesthetic experience' (315), referring back to an earlier section of his book in which he formulates the following hypothesis:

> The shifts in cathexis of mental energy, which the work of art elicits or facilitates, are, we believe, pleasurable in themselves. From the release of passion under the protection of the aesthetic illusion to the highly complex process of re-creation under the artist's guidance, a series of processes of psychic discharge take place, which could be differentiated from each other by the varieties and degrees of neutralisation of the energy discharge. All these processes, however, are controlled by the ego, and the degree of completeness of neutralisation indicates the degree of ego autonomy.
> (63)

Relating this to the proposed model, the last sentence seems to suggest that the more complete the ego ideal the greater the autonomy of the individual. I suggest that the process of analysing aesthetic experience should be made easier by having a structured preconscious and that the process of differentiation between libidinal, aggressive and idealising components of the process could be more precisely made.

Kris mentions the fact that the solution of a problem can occur over several years, citing Freud's attempts to link symptom formation and the mechanism of dreaming. He then returns to the question of reactions to preconscious mental processes becoming conscious. In many cases, he repeats, there is no reaction; however, in some cases 'experiences appear in a special form, in which the feeling exists that awareness comes from the outside world' (317). Kris says that this is obviously true of hallucination as mentioned previously, but it is also true of revelation and inspiration, which we have also mentioned: 'in revelation or inspiration a preconscious thought is attributed to an outside agent from which it has been passively received' (317). Kris says that this feeling is common to creators of all kinds. Significantly he says that 'in the process of becoming conscious the preconsciously prepared thought is sexualised' (317). In relation to the proposed model it is the preconscious libidinal ego that is the seat of creativity in Fairbairn's theory. Kris's description of the process suggests that both the ego ideal and the preconscious antilibidinal ego are quiescent while the preconscious libidinal ego is active. Kris's elaboration of his account is interesting in this regard:

> Id energies suddenly combine with ego energies, mobile with bound and neutralised cathexes, to produce the unique experience of inspiration which is felt to reach consciousness from outside. Unconscious fantasies at work in some specific instances of these experiences can be reconstructed ... [and] are derived from the repressed fantasy of being impregnated and particularly of incorporating the paternal phallus.
>
> (317)

This reinforces the view that the process is libidinal in nature. I think that the sense of this material coming from outside can be accounted for in the proposed model by the lack of involvement of the ego ideal and the fact that the preconscious libidinal ego is incorporating and passing on material from the unconscious in a relatively unfettered way, that is the material is coming from outside the preconscious seat of the self.

This has not been an exhaustive investigation of the preconscious mental processes but I hope I have illustrated the ways in which the proposed model would be able to represent and explain these preconscious mental processes that Kris identifies and discusses.

A unified object relations theory of creativity might be possible but would also need to consider the views of Ehrenzweig (1967) and Milner (1987) on creativity whose component stages – projected schizoid fragments, the 'manic womb' and the integrative assimilation of previously rejected content in a socially acceptable form – have direct parallels with Padel's account of psychic growth within Fairbairn's mature psychology of dynamic structure. In particular the manic womb can be seen to rehearse the preconscious dynamic of the original move from the initial splitting of the original ego and its object into split-off ego object fragments and their transformation into the stable dynamic structure of the basic endopsychic position. This topic is also discussed in the next chapter where the manic womb is seen as the activity of a structured preconscious.

Chapter 6
The preconscious and psychic change in Fairbairn's model of mind

The development of Fairbairn's mature theory of endopsychic structure, which started in 1940 with his paper on schizoid phenomena, and finished in 1963 with his synopsis of the development of endopsychic structure was, in his own words, 'not the systematic elaboration of an already established point of view, but the progressive development of a line of thought' (1952a: 133). It could be argued that Fairbairn's early papers on dissociation, libido theory and the superego, made available to us now through the publication of Scharff and Fairbairn Birtles's invaluable two-volume collection (1994), prepared the ground for his mature theory, a point Rubens has made (1996). All of Fairbairn's papers between 1940 and 1963 contributed to the development of his theory, the fullest expression of which was probably his paper on endopsychic structure (1944). However, this was by no means his final word on the subject as the 1951 addendum to that paper, prepared for the publication of his only book in 1952, attests. Similarly the extended footnote in his paper on hysteria (1954), with its detailed discussion of ambivalence and the internalisation of good and bad objects, makes a significant contribution to the development of his mature structural theory, or 'psychology of dynamic structure' as he called it.

This means that the fully developed model is never completely stated in any one of Fairbairn's papers and subsequently there have been a number of papers, by people sympathetic to his work, suggesting modifications to his model (Rubens 1984; Greenberg 1991; Padel 1991; Mitchell 1994; Scharff and Fairbairn Birtles 1997; Grotstein 1998; Skolnick 1998). By looking at the way these thinkers have suggested the model be changed, I have come to appreciate its strengths. In general I have not been happy to suggest changes to Fairbairn's model while, in my view, its full potential has yet to be realised. However, through trying to understand and defend the model against these suggested changes, I have come to feel that there are some problems with the mature theory that do need to be addressed, in particular the process of psychic change and the nature of the unconscious in mature dependence. What follows is an attempt to produce a modified version of Fairbairn's model of endopsychic structure by considering his use of the topographical categories. Combining Fairbairn's structural model with Freud's structural model is impossible since they are based upon such very different underlying presuppositions about energy and structure:

> Freud's divorce of energy from structure represents a limitation imposed upon his thought by the general scientific atmosphere of his day ... From the standpoint of dynamic structure ... 'instinct' is *not the stimulus to* psychic activity, but itself consists in characteristic activity on the part of a psychical structure. Similarly, 'impulse' is not ... a kick in the pants administered out of the blue to a surprised, and somewhat pained, ego, but a psychical structure in action – a psychical structure doing something to something or somebody.
>
> (Fairbairn 1952a: 151)

But, since a satisfactory reconciliation between Freud's topographical model and his structural model has never been achieved, what I am suggesting is that a reconciliation between Freud's topographic model and a version of Fairbairn's structural model can be considered, and this is the principal aim of this chapter. My belief is that this new model is consistent with Fairbairn's original intentions, and with many of the changes suggested by others, and makes much clearer the process of psychic change that is essential to any psychology of dynamic structure. At the end of the chapter, I will mention a similar hypothesis from a Winnicottian perspective, which means the changes proposed here could allow for a productive exchange between object relations theorists as a whole.

FAIRBAIRN'S USE OF THE PRECONSCIOUS

Fairbairn included Freud's topographical categories – conscious (*Cs*), preconscious (*Pcs*) and unconscious (*Ucs*) (Sandler *et al.* 1997) – in his original diagram of endopsychic structure, but never discussed how these categories might be integrated into his mature theory. There is therefore good reason to suppose that Fairbairn did not see the topographical categories as being contradictory to his model in the way that he clearly saw, and explicitly rejected, Freud's libido theory. At the same time, comments regarding the preconscious do not appear with any regularity in his work and the model does not seem to have an important place for the category except in so far as the ideal object (ego ideal) only exists in the preconscious. Although there is no explicit reference in Fairbairn's work to the ego ideal being in the preconscious, and his diagram was never amended to locate it there, everything he wrote about the ego ideal after 1941 suggests that it was in the preconscious. In the lists of points he uses to define an object relations viewpoint (1954, 1963), he explicitly states that the ego ideal isn't repressed and that the superego comprises both the ideal object (ego ideal) and the repressed anti-libidinal ego and object. At the same time, he argues that the ego ideal becomes the repository of good relationships in the moral defence or defence of the superego (1943: 66) and that it is an internal object and the source of the desexualised and idealised imagos that the hysteric projects on to the analyst (1944: 136):

> When the exciting and rejecting objects are split off, there remains a nucleus of the original object shorn of its over-exciting and over-frustrating elements; and this nucleus then assumes the status of a desexualised and idealised object which is cathected and retained for itself by the central ego ... It will be noticed that the nuclear object in question is an accepted object for the central ego, and is thus not subjected to repression. This is the object which I now regard as providing the nucleus round which the super-ego, as I have come to conceive it, is built up; but, in view of its nature, it would appear appropriate to revive the term 'ego ideal' for its designation.
>
> (1952a: 178–9)

Fairbairn's final view of the superego was that it was actually made up of the (preconscious) ego ideal (which needs to become more realistic to achieve maturity) and the (unconscious) anti-libidinal ego and object (which need to be diminished in power and influence). This is the distinction between the 'positive' and the 'punitive' superego in psychoanalytic theory. In 1929, Fairbairn attended the international conference at Oxford where Ferenczi was also present. In 1928, Ferenczi had produced a paper describing the inner reality of a fully analysed patient in which the distinction between the ego ideal and the (punitive, unconscious) superego played a major role. Fairbairn notes in his papers the importance of the fully analysed patient as a topic of discussion at the 1929 conference (Scharff and Fairbairn Birtles 1994, vol. II: 454–61) and I think his idea of mature dependence was influenced by that discussion. I believe that Fairbairn came to know about Ferenczi's model and used it later, perhaps unconsciously, in his own mature theory. Roheim describes Ferenczi's argument thus:

> If we agree to call the destructive 'ethical' phase of our psyche the Super-ego and the libidinal phase the Ego-Ideal we might say, with reference to a recent paper of Ferenczi's, that analysis is finished when we have the pure Ego-Ideal without any traces of the Super-ego.
>
> (1930: 202)

Or, as Ferenczi wrote:

> In reality my objective was to destroy only that part of the super-ego which

had become unconscious and was therefore beyond the range of influence. I have no sort of objection to the retention of a number of positive and negative models in the preconscious of the ordinary individual. In any case he will no longer have to obey his preconscious super-ego so slavishly as he had previously to obey his unconscious parent imago.

(1928: 98)

This is totally consistent with Fairbairn's distinction between a (preconscious) ego ideal and the (repressed, unconscious) superego (anti-libidinal ego and object) and the model developed here.

In the original diagram, the central ego, shorn of its internal objects and split-off egos, has *Cs, Pcs* and *Ucs* components:

> as regards the relationship of the central ego to the other egos, our most important clue to its nature lies in the fact that, whereas the central ego must be regarded as comprising preconscious and conscious, as well as unconscious, elements, the other egos must equally be regarded as essentially unconscious.
>
> (Fairbairn 1952a: 104–5)

Macmurray (1939) describes one way in which a perfectly acceptable non-pathological unconscious, consistent with the central ego having an unconscious component, may come about from the progressive development of skills and habits which themselves underpin the development of more complex skills and habits, for example correcting a golf swing or tennis stroke, learning to write with your non-dominant hand, etc.

In Fairbairn's final view, the ideal object is a significant preconscious entity separate from, but associated with, the central ego. The central ego no longer has an explicit unconscious aspect. The (pathological) unconscious in this model is made up of the split-off libidinal and anti-libidinal selves. It is on the basis of this latter model that the idea of mature dependence and the disappearance of the (system) unconscious became associated (Rubens 1984; Mitchell 1994; Young 1998). The dissolution of the repressed sub-selves, as the major process of the move towards mature dependence, leads to their eventual disappearance and the emptying out of the (system) unconscious. In Fairbairn's model (Figure 6.1), the original ego is essentially reality oriented and preconscious. This ego becomes split and then subject to dissociation and repression because it is partly constituted by unacceptable object relationships – over-exciting and over-rejecting.

If we follow Fairbairn, as faithfully as we can, to see what his intention was regarding his model and the topographical categories, we find that he did not explicitly address the question of the relationship between *Ucs, Pcs* and *Cs* and his model of object relations. His diagram shows a central ego from whose *Pcs* the material for a dream he describes issued forth because of a

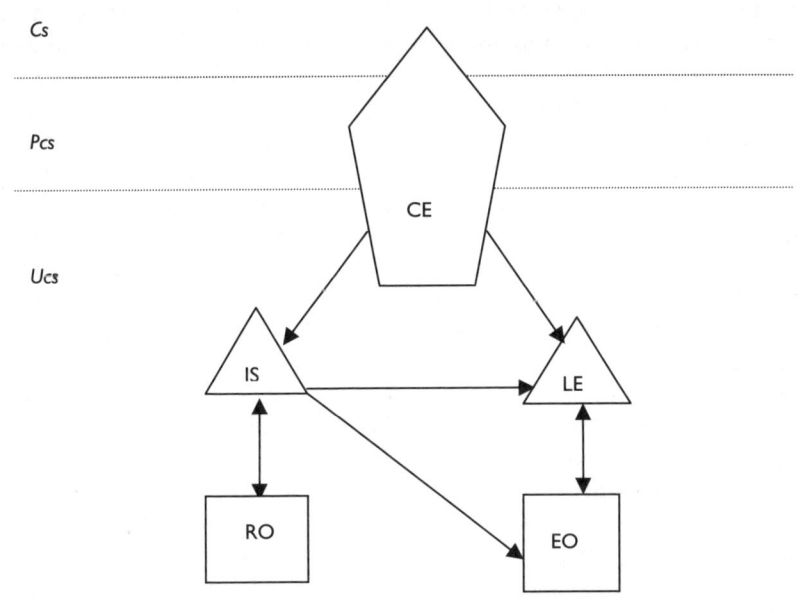

Figure 6.1 Fairbairn's original diagram. Reproduced from W.R.D. Fairbairn (1994) *Psychoanalytic Studies of the Personality* (p. 105). London: Routledge, with permission.

presumed configuration of inner structures – ego and object structures. We have in essence a *triangular relationship* between the central, libidinal and anti-libidinal selves. It is the conflict between these three structures and the way this waxes and wanes, in response to internal and external circumstances, that determines to some degree the *Pcs* and the *Ucs*. He says, in relation to the patient's dream, 'the dreamer's preconscious attitude towards her husband is ambivalent; and this is the attitude adopted by her central ego towards its external object, as well as towards the internalised representative of this object' (1952a: 104).

Fairbairn's 'difficulties' over where to place the 'good object' serve as an interesting clue to problems with an unconscious part of the central ego. Since Fairbairn (1943) suggested that the good object was only internalised for defensive purposes *after* the internalisation of bad objects into the unconscious, it follows that the logical place to internalise the good object would be the unconscious part of the central ego. But, to put the good object in the unconscious would contradict his argument about the (defensive) need to internalise bad objects but not good objects. Moreover, he explicitly says that the good object in the form of an ego ideal or ideal object was not repressed and was potentially available to consciousness, namely, was preconscious.

As a good Freudian, Fairbairn would have been aware of the fact that the system unconscious was unknowable except through the system's conscious and preconscious. A close reading reveals that Fairbairn sometimes seems to write as if he were describing the unconscious when in fact he is describing an assumed state of affairs internally (including the *Ucs*), that *Cs* contents, derived from *Pcs* contents, appears to indicate. Nevertheless the fact that his model is clearly related to Freud's model and is a thoroughgoing attempt to describe the whole system in object relations terms proves much more useful than any of these considerations. That is, Fairbairn's model has made its way in the world because of the introduction of a thoroughgoing object relations approach, rather than its offering a way of integrating the topographical categories within a structural model.

Fairbairn was only following Freud (1914) when he insisted upon the object relations basis of internalised experience. All internalised objects are really complex structures of associated object relationships (Padel 1985). As already noted, Fairbairn's mature model has a *conscious* (central) ego, a *preconscious* (ideal) object and two *unconscious* (libidinal and anti-libidinal) egos and associated unconscious objects. One question that might be asked is why can't there be preconscious libidinal and anti-libidinal dynamic structures? The relationship between the conscious ego and its ideal object is represented as if it was similar to the relationship between the other egos and their related objects, that is, the central ego is to the ideal object/ego ideal as the libidinal ego is to the libidinal object (LE is to EO in Figure 6.1) and the anti-libidinal ego is to the anti-libidinal object (IS is to RO in Figure 6.1), so it might follow that their objects would have a similar nature. If we go back to the origins of the basic endopsychic structure as described by Fairbairn, the three 'selves' are initially all constituted by relationships with differentiated objects. This initial internal situation, before defensive dissociation and repression are employed – split object, split ego – can be regarded as a preconscious precursor to the manic defence. The libidinal and anti-libidinal selves become repressed after they are split off from the central self, and at the same time the accepted object becomes its ideal object.

In conformity with what seem to have been Fairbairn's own intentions I will re-describe the constituents of Fairbairn's model as a central self, a libidinal self and an anti-libidinal self, where each is formed by the object relationships between a part of the ego and a complex object. In this way we might imagine Fairbairn's original five components being reduced to three. This then raises the question of the ideal object and the part it plays for the central self and its preconscious status. To keep it separate from the central self seems necessary as it is supposed to play an independent role mediating between the central self and the two repressed subsidiary selves.

The preconscious plays an important part in creativity (see Chapter 5) and can be seen as the manic-oceanic creative womb that Milner (1987) identifies as central to that process. In his review of Kris's *Psychoanalytic Explorations in Art*, Fairbairn concludes that:

> the reconciliation upon which the aesthetic value of a work of art depends would appear to be one characteristically effected at a preconscious level, although the artist's conscious contribution to the moulding of his creation must have an important influence upon its final form; and doubtless in the case of the greatest artists there is a happy combination between conscious and preconscious activity.
>
> (1953a: 430)

This statement both allows for, and gives considerable importance to, the preconscious. Within Fairbairn's model, the only preconscious entity is the ideal object or ego ideal. Perhaps at this juncture it is worth noting that the idea that the *ego ideal* and the *ideal object* are the same entity only makes sense if the dynamic structure so named has both egoic and object-like aspects, in other words, is a dynamic structure made from object relationships.

THE NATURE OF THE PRECONSCIOUS

I have taken the formulation of key features of the preconscious from 'The system preconscious' chapter of Sandler *et al.*'s (1997) work. Their overall definition of the preconscious is: 'the area of the mental apparatus in which instinctual wishes are examined, modified, permitted to proceed, or turned back ... a system that is descriptively speaking, unconscious' (85). This, as we shall see, only describes an aspect of the preconscious. We will need to look at the role of the preconscious in dealing with experience in and of the world, too, to get the whole picture.

Consistent with Fairbairn's view of dynamic structures being composed of object relations, Sandler *et al.* describe the content of each of Freud's topographical systems as being composed of object relations: 'thus a repressed sexual wish in the Unconscious would involve content representing both the object of the wish and the activity involved in relation to that object' (1997: 83).

When it comes to describing the way an instinctual wish enters the preconscious and the conscious, and the forms such representations take, Sandler *et al.* comment:

> In general, a derivative of an instinctual wish may be conscious or unconscious (in the descriptive sense), depending on its topographic location in the apparatus. It is not the original instinctual wish, but a substitute for it, one that can indirectly provide some degree of satisfaction of the instinctual wish from which it has been derived and which, in a sense, it conceals. Instinctual derivatives can take many forms,

including dreams, sublimatory activities, daydreams, neurotic symptoms, hallucinations, parapraxes, forms of 'acting out', creative productions, play activities, transference manifestations, and the like.

(83)

The wealth and variety of phenomena associated with the activity of the preconscious suggests that the preconscious itself might be structured and that there are very different routes that an 'instinctual wish' might take in moving from the *Ucs* to the *Cs*.

Sandler *et al.* argue that the preconscious develops gradually as a result of a person's experience and give an account of the ways in which the preconscious is formed by experience in the world:

> Preconscious contents include many diverse elements. In the first place there are those primary process derivatives of the instinctual wishes which are pressing forward for discharge and, by reason of their primary process transformation, have evaded the first level of censorship and have entered the Preconscious. . . . Secondly, the contents of the Preconscious include mental representations that have been formed as the result of past and present interaction with the external world. . . . Thirdly, we must include the products of preconscious imaginative (i.e. phantasy) and cognitive activity.
>
> (85)

In general, then, we find that the preconscious mediates between the inner and the outer world and is formed by its transactions with both: 'the Preconscious and its contents arise as a consequence of influence from two sides: from the depths of the mental apparatus (Unconscious) and from its surface. In addition, new ideational contents are constantly being formed within the Preconscious itself' (85–6).

The preconscious is a place where integration can take place in conformity with reality but without entering consciousness:

> In the work of the Preconscious, a great deal of integration and synthesis occurs. . . . The 'necessities', 'demands' and 'limitations' imposed by the real external world . . . are taken into account. . . . The Preconscious may make use of its capacity to delay and control the peremptory instinctual wishes arising from the Unconscious that have penetrated into the Preconscious. *This implies that the Preconscious* has the capacity to examine and scrutinise its own contents without these having to enter the Conscious.
>
> (86)

The world of the preconscious is, properly speaking, a symbolic world with access to language, a creative world of problem-solving and decision-making:

'much of the activity of the Preconscious can be subsumed under the heading of *thinking*, and a substantial amount of problem-solving and decision-making is accomplished within the system' (86); also, 'it is important to note that the Preconscious is regarded as being able to make use of *verbal symbolism*' (89); and:

> whereas the Unconscious is regarded as following the pleasure principle, the Preconscious is influenced by what is known as the reality principle. This refers to the taking into account the realities of the external world ... in assessing the consequences of his action.
> (89)

The reality principle is a major aspect of the preconscious, especially in regard to its role as a second level of censorship between the *Pcs* and the *Cs*:

> Immediate gratification of the instinctual wishes or their derivatives is delayed or abandoned if this threatens the self-preservation needs of the individual or his moral and ethical principles. The reality principle plays a major part in the operation of the 'second censorship' between the Preconscious and the Conscious, but it can be considered to be the dominant 'principle' in the functioning of the Preconscious as a whole.
> (89)

The importance of the preconscious as an invaluable core of the most essential aspects of our selves is stressed:

> The Preconscious is said to function predominantly according to the *secondary process*, which is, developmentally speaking, the outcome of the influence of the external world on the mental apparatus. This impingement brings about such characteristics as the notion of causality, logic, a sense of time, and an intolerance of ambiguity and contradictory elements. Most important, in the course of development, the Preconscious becomes, together with the Conscious, that part of the mental apparatus in which language can be used as an efficient tool for the manipulation of mental content. The acquisition of verbal symbols for things and for abstract ideas goes parallel with the differentiation between the Unconscious and the Preconscious. Words can be used to harness and to attenuate the force of instinctual wishes.
> (89–90)

While considering the preconscious I want to look briefly at Freud's description of the movement of experience between the *Cs, Pcs* and *Ucs* and vice versa, and at the different levels of censorship between *Ucs* and *Pcs*, and

Pcs and *Cs*. I think these must be seen as operating in both directions. So the preconscious allows material from the *Ucs* to enter the *Pcs*, and it filters *Pcs* material into the *Ucs* too. Similarly, the *Pcs* allows material to enter *Cs*, and filters *Cs* material into the *Pcs*. Thus, the homogeneous *Pcs* of Freud's theory is carrying out sophisticated filtering and transforming procedures at the boundaries with both the *Cs* and the *Ucs*. This seems to me to raise the question of *whether the Pcs might be structured* to deal with these different activities. This does not seem to have been part of psychoanalytic thinking on the preconscious during the period when the topographical model was dominant, despite many examples of the heterogeneous functions attributed to the preconscious.

As Freud notes:

> On the one hand we find that derivatives of the *Ucs* become conscious as substitutive formations and symptoms – generally, it is true, after having undergone great distortion as compared with the unconscious, though often retaining many characteristics which call for repression. On the other hand, we find that many preconscious formations remain unconscious, though we should have expected that, from their nature, they might very well have become conscious. Probably in the latter case the stronger attraction of the *Ucs* is asserting itself. We are led to look for the more important distinction as lying, not between the conscious and the preconscious, but between the preconscious and the unconscious. The *Ucs* is turned back on the frontier of the *Pcs* by the censorship, but the derivatives of the *Ucs* can circumvent this censorship, achieve a high degree of organisation and reach a certain intensity of cathexis in the *Pcs*. When, however, this intensity is exceeded and they try to force themselves into consciousness, they are recognised as derivatives of the *Ucs* and are repressed afresh at the new frontier of censorship, between the *Pcs* and the *Cs*. Thus the first of these censorships is exercised *against the Ucs itself*, and the second *against its Pcs derivatives*. One might suppose that in the course of individual development the censorship had taken a step forward.
>
> In psychoanalytic treatment the existence of the *second censorship*, located between the systems Pcs and Cs, is *proved beyond question*. We require the patient to form numerous derivatives of the *Ucs*, we make him pledge himself to overcome the objections of the censorship to these preconscious formations becoming conscious, and by overthrowing this censorship, we open up the way to abrogating the repression accomplished by the earlier one. To this let us add that the existence of the censorship between the *Pcs* and the *Cs* teaches us that becoming conscious is no mere act of perception, but is probably a hypercathexis, a further advance in the psychical organisation.
>
> (1915: 193; emphasis added)

This last sentence is relevant to issues of psychic change addressed in the next section.

CRITICISMS OF FAIRBAIRN'S MODEL AND SUGGESTIONS FOR IMPROVEMENT

John Padel (1991, 1994) addresses the problem of how psychic growth takes place within a Fairbairnian framework (see Chapter 2). Padel makes an invaluable contribution to our understanding of Fairbairn by paying close attention to a description of the way in which psychic change may come about with particular reference to the analytic situation.

Padel's account argues that in order for psychic change to take place the subsidiary selves, or aspects of them, have to be able to be transformed (as described in the next section) from the unconscious to the preconscious where they, or rather representations of object relations, can then make their way into consciousness where they can be worked through, such a change being one of psychic growth or integration. Similarly, the passage of new experiences into consciousness and then, if repressed, through the preconscious to the unconscious, seems to be a similar process though working in the opposite direction, and could lead to some forms of undesirable psychic change of a regressive or disintegrative nature.

Padel's comments, upon the process of sorting day residues during sleep, seem entirely consistent with Freud's account:

> What actually happens in dream-formation is a very remarkable and quite unforeseen turn of events. The process begins in the *Pcs* and reinforced in the *Ucs*, pursues a backward course, through *Ucs* to perception, which is pressing upon consciousness. This *regression* is the third phase of the dream-formation. For the sake of clarity we will repeat the two earlier ones: the reinforcement of the *Pcs* day's residues by the *Ucs*, and the setting up of the dream-wish.
>
> (Freud 1917: 227)

As part of this research, I searched for references to the preconscious and found that there is a dearth of them. Kris (1950) was already aware of this and, given that the topological theory was the theoretical system that Freud spent most time working within, expresses similar regrets to those expressed by Greenberg about the apparent dropping of the concept from contemporary psychoanalytic thinking. Greenberg (1991) believes that the relational view has gone too far and ignores some very real aspects of the drive/structure model, in particular the topographical distinctions between the *Ucs*, the *Pcs* and the *Cs*.

Mitchell (1994: 81) has expressed the opinion that Fairbairn's model, as developed in his 1944 paper on endopsychic structure, was unnecessarily complicated and over-formal. He prefers the implicit model of Fairbairn's 1943 paper where the internalisation of the good object as a preconscious ego ideal was carried out as a defence against the already internalised and unconscious bad objects.

In a recent paper, Grotstein suggests a modification to Fairbairn's model that comes out of his discussion, from a Kleinian perspective, of the patient's dream through which Fairbairn developed his model of endopsychic structure. This suggestion is isolated and unconnected to any other detailed discussion of this problem in Grotstein's work that I know of. It falls far short of a concrete modification to the model, though it suggests far-reaching changes along the lines of the change to the model proposed here. Grotstein says:

> I believe that Fairbairn may well have come around eventually to postulating a normal endopsychic structure but one situated topographically in the preconscious rather than the unconscious – because of his injunction, with which I am in agreement, that good objects do not need to be internalised (except for defensive purposes), only unsatisfying ones. The system preconscious would be the reservoir for the legacy or memory of satisfying experiences with reliable objects as opposed to the unconscious, which is the reservoir for the concrete internalisations of unreliable but needed objects that putatively need to be controlled and processed dissociatively.
>
> (1998: 79–80)

In a similar vein, Scharff and Fairbairn Birtles (1997), in a review article of Fairbairn's contribution to psychoanalytic theory, suggest that there should be a modification to Fairbairn's model of endopsychic structure so that the subsidiary selves, as well as being unconscious, should also appear within the central ego as conscious entities.

Meanwhile, Rubens, in a series of carefully argued papers (1984, 1994, 1996, 1998), has suggested that 'structure is pathology' in Fairbairn's model, and that this can only be overcome by what he calls 'non-structuring internalisations', that is, the internalisation of good object relations into the ego ideal. While agreeing that Fairbairn believed there was some growth through non-structuring internalisation, it is also true that he thought the development of the ego ideal was significant, and this is at least a quasi-structural development based upon internalisation, depending upon your view of the preconscious as a structural division within the endopsychic structure. Rubens accepts that Fairbairn thought that mature dependence depended upon not just backgrounding unconscious structures but also on externalising and dissolving them. Only John Padel seems to have included this process in his suggested explication of the dynamics of Fairbairn's model.

FAIRBAIRN'S MODEL MODIFIED IN RELATION TO THE TOPOGRAPHICAL CATEGORIES

My own contribution is a modification to Fairbairn's model of inner reality based upon the development of the role of the preconscious. The resulting model might be seen as the incorporation of the topographical categories within Fairbairn's model of endopsychic structure to produce a new model of inner reality. I would argue that this model is consistent with many of the suggestions for modification of Fairbairn's model but quite different from any of the concrete proposals heretofore.

For me the best place to start is with the work of John Padel. As noted earlier, Padel suggests that psychic change and psychic growth in particular come about by the transformation of the split-off, repressed libidinal and anti-libidinal object relations from unconscious to conscious, that is, their (re-)incorporation into the central ego. Similarly, he suggests that unacceptable aspects of day-to-day object relations are split off and directed to these split-off, repressed sub-selves appropriately on a regular basis during sleep. There is thus a two-way process in this model where, in a repressive move, conscious experience is being turned into unconscious (split-off, dissociated) experience associated with either the libidinal or anti-libidinal self, and, in an integrative move, where (object relations) aspects of these repressed, split-off selves are being brought to consciousness and reincorporated into the central self. Padel does not employ the preconscious consistently but in Freud's topographical theory these transitions would always be via the (system) preconscious. Fairbairn acknowledges the existence of the preconscious by placing the ego ideal or ideal object there. When Padel talks about the repressed selves not being absolutely split off from the central ego, or not being equally repressed, he is implying that some aspects of these selves can become conscious or potentially conscious, that is, they are preconscious. A full description of the processes Padel describes, without using the concept of the preconscious, would show conscious experience being transformed into unconscious material without mediation. It seems to me much more reasonable, given that the preconscious is a part of Fairbairn's model, to see it playing a mediating role between the central ego and the unconscious libidinal and anti-libidinal selves. Given that there are two levels of censorship and that the ego ideal is most closely associated with the second level between the *Pcs* and the *Cs*, it seems reasonable to suggest that there are *Pcs* representatives of the libidinal and the anti-libidinal selves.

Rubens, as we have seen, suggests, correctly in my view, that in Fairbairn's theory structure is pathology, and that psychic growth, in a developmental sense, takes place by means of non-structuring internalisations. Accepting that structure is pathology *and* having no way to ameliorate this process other than the development of non-structuring internalisations (cf. Mitchell and the internalisation of the good object as a defence against bad internal objects) seems to me to be a counsel of despair. I therefore suggest that Padel's notion that these structural elements, 'like the Zuider Zee', can be drained and reclaimed as productive aspects of the central self is an attractive and convincing hypothesis, producing a more realistic ideal self (ego ideal plus ideal object) and a central self with more (realistic) powers. My suggestion, which might perhaps provide a common basis for these different approaches to agree upon, is that Fairbairn's original model is modified so that the *topographical* distinctions between the *Ucs*, the *Pcs* and the *Cs* are incorporated into the model consistently. Each of the selves represented should be regarded as comprising object relations. Thus, we have a *Cs* central self with a *Pcs* ideal self as per Fairbairn's original diagram, but now we have a *Pcs* and a *Ucs* libidinal self and a *Pcs* and a *Ucs* anti-libidinal self.

The proposed model contains Grotstein's suggestion of preconscious libidinal and anti-libidinal selves as well as an ideal self. This model, in having potentially conscious libidinal and anti-libidinal selves in the preconscious, would also be consistent with Scharff and Fairbairn Birtles' suggestion for a modification of Fairbairn's model. This incorporation of a *structured preconscious*, as a modification within the model, allows for all the many features of the preconscious that Sandler *et al.* (1997) specify. It means that experience of the world can make its way from the *Cs* via the *Pcs* and into the *Ucs* and vice versa.

As noted earlier, Greenberg suggests that Freud's drive theory has been too much ignored by object relations theory and should be reconsidered. The model I have proposed here, by recombining a structural model with the topographical categories, goes some way towards doing just that. Mitchell's preference for a more dynamic defensive preconscious aspect of the model also seems to be supported here without giving up the complexity of the endopsychic structure.

The Kleinian view too might find some support in this model, where descriptively unconscious phantasy is at the heart of the major preconscious process of organising the integration/disintegration of the psyche, and a triangular (Oedipal) relationship, between the ideal, the libidinal and the anti-libidinal selves at a preconscious level, determines the level of integration.

THE CENTRALITY OF THE PRECONSCIOUS

Some comment needs to be made about the central ego, the unconscious sub-selves and the distinction between ego and object in Fairbairn's model. Like Padel, I see the central ego as the locus of real activity in the world. The unconscious subsidiary selves I see as being the repository of unprocessed and uncontained experience from childhood (Wright 1991). As to Fairbairn's use of the terms 'ego' and 'object' to differentiate between two different aspects of the sub-selves, I do not see any fundamental problem. In the

Preconscious and psychic changes in Fairbairn's model 129

Cs

Pcs

Ucs

Central self – becomes more integrated and realistic with psychic growth

Ideal self – becomes more realistic with psychic growth

Preconscious aspects of libidinal and anti-libidinal selves

Libidinal self   Anti-libidinal self

Unconscious libidinal and anti-libidinal sub-selves become depleted through psychic growth

All selves comprise object relationships

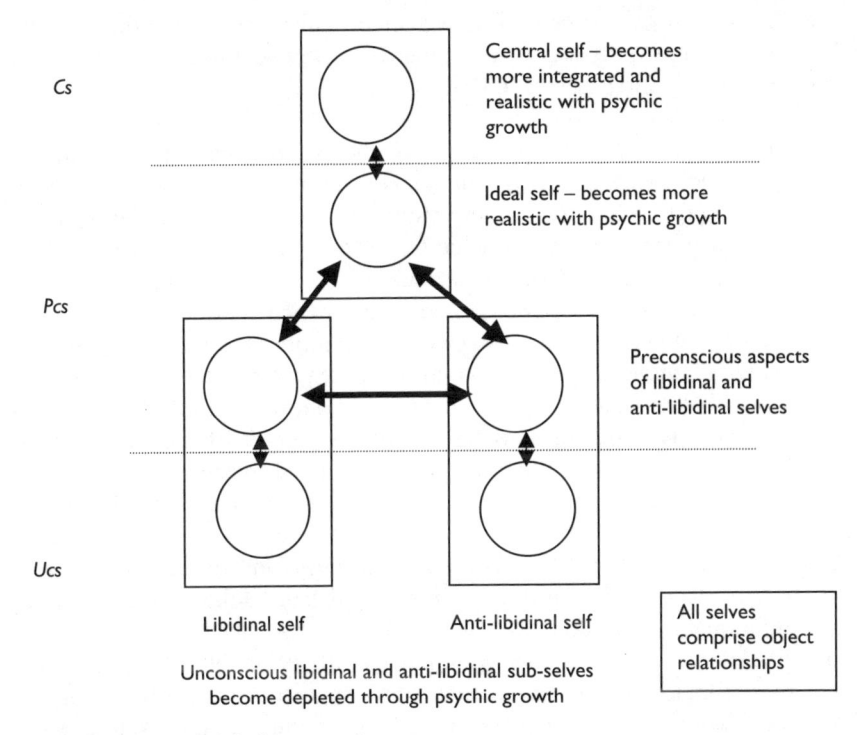

Figure 6.2 A new model of inner reality.

modified model the libidinal links cross boundaries between the *Pcs* and the *Ucs*, and the *Pcs* and the *Cs*, and the *Pcs* has now become the central symbolic and Oedipal (triangular)[1] area of the model, and the place where aggressive links now all reside; it seems reasonable to think of this area as the seat of the self. The ideal self and the preconscious libidinal and anti-libidinal selves are all connected libidinally to dynamic structures outside their domain and may therefore be seen as the more egoic aspects of each of them. Let us remind ourselves of part of Freud's comment, quoted earlier, 'the existence of the censorship between the *Pcs* and the *Cs* teaches us that becoming conscious is no mere act of perception, but is probably a hypercathexis, a further advance in the psychical organisation' (1915: 193). I am suggesting that it is the establishment of this *triadic preconscious ensemble of* relationships between these dynamic structures, or self-objects (Kohut 1971), that mediates this advance in psychical organisation.

In passing it is worth commenting on the distinctions between the conscious central ego, the triad of preconscious formations – ideal, libidinal and anti-libidinal selves – and the dyad of unconscious libidinal and anti-libidinal selves. The number of elements at each level being of some significance – one-person, three-person and two-person psychologies respectively. John

Padel has drawn attention to this aspect of Fairbairn's diagram and the relations between its dynamic structures that depend upon the distinction between two- and three-person relationships:

> What he labels indirect repression is really the basic, two-person relationship, which because of its intimacy is for many people so precarious ... On the other hand the three-person situation not only contains the threats of the Oedipal relationship but seems to make the achievement of two-person intimacy impossible. Each of these two types of relationship is a most effective suppressor of the other one. Fairbairn felt that the five structures shown in his diagram gave much more explanatory scope than the two of classical theory – ego and superego. I not only find that true but now believe that it is so valuable because it shows both the repressed two-person relationship and the internal structure of the three-person relationship and shows them dynamically related to each other.
>
> (1991: 606–7)

I believe that locating the three-person relationship within the preconscious actually represents Padel's interpretation of Fairbairn's diagram better than the original diagram itself.

Balint (1958) points out that Rickman (1950, 1951, 1957) has identified three psychologies of the mind, each of them associated with a number. Balint, a contemporary of Fairbairn, goes on to characterise each of these areas in the following way:

> the best known among these three areas is characterised by the number '3', and may be called *the area of the Oedipus conflict* ... The whole area is characterized by the fact that everything that happens in it involves in addition to the subject at least two more objects ... the second area ... is *the area of the basic fault*, characterized by the number '2', which means that in it two, and only two, people are involved. Their relationship, however, is not that obtaining between two adults, it is more primitive ... [finally] we have *the area of creation* which is characterized by the number '1'. There is no outside object involved; consequently there is no object-relationship and no transference. That is why our knowledge of these processes is so scanty and uncertain.
>
> (1958: 338–9)

The coincidence of these distinctive areas of the mind as described by Balint and the distinctive, topographically consistent, areas of the proposed model give reason to hope that it may have captured some of Balint's thinking. When Balint discusses the origins of these structures in developmental terms he comes to the following tentative conclusions:

it is thinkable that the earliest level might be that of primary love and with it the level of the basic fault, out of which ... the level of the Oedipus conflict develops by differentiation ... the level of creation by simplification.

(339)

This would not be at odds with the proposed model in any radical way.

WINNICOTT, POTENTIAL SPACE AND THE PRECONSCIOUS

In the course of my researches I came across a paper by Civin and Lombardi (1990) which looks at many of the problems I have been addressing, but from a Winnicottian perspective. Broadly speaking, I believe that the view they have developed is consistent with my main thrust. In their summary, they explain the reasons for choosing their approach and point to the possibility for synthesis between models based upon the primacy of the mediating zone they identify with both the Freudian preconscious and the Winnicottian concept of potential space:

> Greenberg and Mitchell (1983) have suggested that the drive/structure and the relational/structure model are mutually exclusive models of psychic life. We regard their contribution as an invaluable one, which makes explicit the fundamental divergences in psychoanalytic theory. We have examined a derivative tendency in the field, for drive and relational theorists alike, to present psychic life as a dichotomy between inner experience and outer experience.
>
> We see a tendency to equate the drive model with unconscious motivation, and to the primacy of internal experience. There seems to be an equivalent tendency to equate the relational model with conscious perception and motivation, and to the primacy of external experience. We are advocating, for drive and relational theorists alike, greater focus on the *process* of intermediation between internal and external in the psychic life of the individual.
>
> Within the context of the drive model, precedent for such a focus is found in Freud's conception of the preconscious, an essential third dimension whose function was to mediate between the conscious and the unconscious. Within the context of the relational model, Winnicott's notion of potential space serves as a bridge between interior experience and external reality in the life of the individual.
>
> Finally we have argued that by constructing three-part models of psychic life, these theorists have laid the groundwork for a synthetic theory. Though for Freud the drive state is primary, and for Winnicott

the relationship between the infant and its environment (mother) is primary, each theorist posits an intermediate zone that fulfils a similar function in the psychic life of the individual. Whether we choose to call that zone the preconscious or potential space, its function is to translate bidirectionally between the infinitely dimensioned realm of interior, or unconscious, experience and the time- and space-bound realm of external, or conscious, experience.

By highlighting the parallel constructs, we are not claiming to have created a synthesis between the theories. Our claim is that the eventual road to synthesis appears to reside in the direction of a movement away from the dichotomy between the primacy of inner or outer experience, and towards the common meeting ground of the primacy of an intermediating function.

(1990: 583–4)

The model I proposed above, based upon Fairbairn's model of endopsychic structure but using the topographical distinction between conscious, preconscious and unconscious to group the different dynamic structures, offers a richly structured intermediate (preconscious) area made up of a triad of dynamic structures. These three structures represent alternative selves – ideal, libidinal and anti-libidinal. It is the relations between and within these structures that mediate the flow between the conscious and the unconscious world. This triadic structure in the preconscious is a prerequisite for mediating both symbolic and Oedipal relations. It is also equivalent to the original schizoid position within Fairbairn's theory and a good candidate for the creative manic womb of Milner and Ehrenzweig.

Part II

Chapter 7
Fairbairn, Macmurray and Suttie: towards a personal relations theory

John D. Sutherland (1993) called for a comprehensive theory of the self. To take up this challenge, I think we need to go back to the work of Fairbairn, Macmurray and Suttie, with Fairbairn's psychology of dynamic structure at the centre. I think it will help us to pursue this project if we give the distinctive body of work from this group of Scots a unique name. Object relations theory is appropriate, but it has become a catchall phrase that can be seen to include Kleinians, contemporary Freudians, a variety of independents at the very least, and maybe self-psychologists and intersubjectivists too, many of whom share little in the way of fundamental ideas with Fairbairn, whom I take to be the exemplar of the personal relations viewpoint. So I propose 'personal relations theory' – a term invented by Fairbairn but never used by him. It was in Sutherland's synoptic last paper, 'The autonomous self' (1993), that I first read that Fairbairn wanted to call his unique development of object relations theory 'personal relations theory'. I had been looking at the parallels between the thinking of Fairbairn and Macmurray, and had read Andrew Collier's *Being and Worth* (1999), which commends Macmurray's Spinozist view that rationality and irrationality are qualities of emotion, a view on reason and emotion that is similar to Antonio Damasio's (2003). In response to Collier's book, Wesley Shumar's (1999) review in *Alethia* (relaunched as the *Journal of Critical Realism*) suggests that Macmurray's work might form a theoretical basis for the object relations approach to psychoanalysis. One person that provides a link between Macmurray and Fairbairn is their Scottish contemporary, Ian D. Suttie, who was still active at the time when both men were formulating their later thinking. Macmurray explicitly acknowledged Suttie's influence on him, and Sutherland (1989) acknowledged Suttie's influence on Fairbairn. At a conference on Fairbairn in New York a few years ago, Allan Harrow (1998) of the Scottish Institute of Human Relations drew attention to the connections between Sutherland, Fairbairn and Suttie, mentioning Macmurray in passing. Harrow also noted the religious dimension to the theories of all these men: they all argue that there is an innate capacity for empathy (as do Sutherland and Trevarthen) and that in our early infancy we depend totally upon an all-powerful, all-knowing and loving personal other who has the power of life and death over us. Suttie and Fairbairn believe that separation anxiety is the major problem we face as we grow up. Fairbairn holds that our original object is constitutive, to some degree, of our ego ideal. Taken together, the ideas of Suttie, Fairbairn and Macmurray could furnish us with a felt relation to the world that is akin to the positive notion of a loving personal god. As a secularist I have some difficulties with the religious dimension to this body of thought, but I appreciate that it provides a personal relations account of the widespread belief in God or gods, without implying anything about the actual existence of gods. It would also be consistent with Freud's view that the ego ideal is significant in the formation of social groupings and Fairbairn's view that the good object can be internalised into the ego ideal as a defensive measure after the development of the basic endopsychic structure.

In 1935, in his introduction to *The Origins of Love and Hate*, Suttie wrote presciently:

> English psychologists, who remain unattached to any 'school', suffer a great disadvantage in lack of cooperation or even of common understanding. Further (largely as a consequence of this), they suffer in prestige and publicity and are stigmatised by psycho-analysts as half-hearted, eclectic and individualistic plagiarists of the Freudian discoveries. Neither their criticisms of psycho-analysis nor their own positive views had sufficient unity to lend each other support or to serve as a basis for further cooperative development.
>
> (Suttie 1960: 4)

Sadly, this might be seen to apply to the fate of all the men I have cited: Suttie, tragically, because he died within a few days of his book's publication; Fairbairn because he remained an independent thinker in Scotland, far away from London, the centre of psychoanalytic development in the UK; and Macmurray because of his communitarian and action-based philosophy. Yet the three men are connected by their shared cultural roots. In a recent essay on Macmurray, Trevarthen (2002) locates the origins of the views that he and Macmurray share in the Scottish Enlightenment. Indeed, I think it is the legacy of the productive confrontation between idealism and common-sense thinking in eighteenth-century Scotland, from which, by the 1930s, these three distinctively different thinkers, two educated at Glasgow and one at Edinburgh, came to develop strikingly similar ideas concerning the nature, origins and development of the self.

What I am hoping to do is to use something from all three men – Fairbairn, Macmurray and Suttie – to sketch in the characteristics of a personal relations theory approach. I have been struck by the way in which each of the three develop similar ideas in similar terms. Maybe by bringing together their individual strengths and combining them as part of a personal relations theory, their own singular contributions will also come into greater and more positive relief.

FAIRBAIRN

David Scharff and Ellinor Fairbairn Birtles (1997) have already pointed out the degree to which Fairbairn's thought has been appropriated by a number of strands within contemporary psychoanalysis without that appropriation being properly acknowledged. At the level of university education in the UK, in the various new psychoanalytic studies courses that have developed over the past decade or two, Fairbairn is sadly under-represented relative to his real importance in the development of psychoanalytic theory. Object relations has become almost synonymous with Klein in many people's minds and few other thinkers are properly recognised, Winnicott being the exception perhaps. However, as we know from synoptic studies of the development of object relations thinking, neither Klein nor Winnicott ever achieved the level of clarity or consistency that Fairbairn, with his training in philosophy, was able to achieve (Mitchell and Greenberg 1983; Hughes 1989).

MACMURRAY: THE PRIMACY OF ACTION

One of the distinguishing characteristics of Macmurray's philosophy is the primacy of action. As Bevir and O'Brien (1999) put it: 'In modern philosophy, the self appears first of all in a contemplative realm, withdrawing from action to attain certain knowledge of itself and thus the world. Macmurray, in contrast, privileges action over thought. Action is the fullest expression of our human nature because it involves both mind and body whereas thought involves mind alone' (Bevir and O'Brien 1999: 3). It should perhaps be pointed out that action is, at the very least, felt action. As Macmurray says, 'The infant's original consciousness, even as regards its sensory elements, must be feeling and feeling at its most primitive and undiscriminated level ... the most we have a right to assert ... is an original capacity to distinguish in feeling between comfort and discomfort. We postulate therefore; an original feeling consciousness with a discrimination between positive and negative phases' (Macmurray 1995b: 57). The baby then employs the only means open to communicate a feeling of comfort or discomfort to the mother. This recalls Fairbairn's account of infantile dependence and the pristine ego and Suttie's conclusion that, 'We need only suppose the child is born with a mind and instincts *adapted to infancy*; or, in other words, so disposed as to profit by parental nature.... Instead of an armament of instincts ... it is born with a simple attachment-to-mother who is the sole source of food and protection' (Suttie 1960: 12). The infant is born

' "adapted" ... to being unadapted', as Macmurray puts it (Macmurray 1995b: 48). Trevarthen noted that Macmurray's Gifford Lectures published in the late 1960s 'were read with gratitude by a group of observers of infancy ... who felt that they had independently discovered innate human abilities of a kind that had escaped attention by the authorities of behavioural and cognitive development in children' (2002: 82). This group also included Daniel Stern. Published in the early 1950s, Fairbairn's book, which met with a hostile reception, may have been simply too early to trigger a similar reaction of recognition. After all, the research of John Bowlby on separation and loss and his development of attachment theory were significantly influenced by both Suttie and Fairbairn. According to Trevarthen: 'Modern naturalistic research has brought proof that infants are born as human beings who express personal powers of consciousness. Macmurray's view of human nature has been confirmed and extended. ... Their researches give support to a rich common-sense understanding of the "personal powers" born in humans and developing rapidly in the young child. Our assessment of Macmurray's theory of the infant mind to the mother's care and teaching opens the way to an examination of what this psychology implies morally and politically' (Trevarthen 2002: 105). All of this echoes ideas common to Fairbairn and Suttie and raises questions concerning the moral and political dimensions of this viewpoint. Is this 'a land fit for *mature dependence*'?

Bevir and O'Brien argue that:

> Macmurray ... defends a thick concept of the self as embedded in interpersonal relations: 'The Self is constituted by its relations to the Other' – 'it has its being in its relationships' [Macmurray 1995b, p. 17]. This dependence upon others appears most forcefully in the relationship of the child to the mother ... Such dependence 'the mother–child relation' represents 'the basic form of human existence', that is 'a "You and I" with a common life' (Macmurray 1998, p. 60) ... it is inherently communal.
>
> (Bevir and O'Brien 1999: 2)

This is a view common to all of them.

So far we have an active self which is innately geared to suckling and to making and sustaining relationships with a personal other. The overriding importance of the success of this earliest of relationships is stressed by Suttie, Fairbairn and Macmurray. According to Fairbairn, it is failure in this early relationship that lies at the heart of all psychopathology. Sutherland and Trevarthen on the basis of recent infant research argue that the infant is more active in making and sustaining this crucial relationship than Fairbairn, Suttie and Macmurray realised, but this is a minor difference rather than an absolute disagreement, and all accept the foundational nature of this early relationship.

MACMURRAY'S DISILLUSIONMENT AND FAIRBAIRN'S TRIPARTITE STRUCTURE

What happens when this earliest relationship fails in one way or another, as it inevitably must, when, in Fairbairn's terms, it becomes unsatisfactory to some degree? For Fairbairn, this is the point at which the basic endopsychic structure is formed in order to be able to sustain the necessary relationship with mother. When Macmurray comes to deal with this process he chooses a phenomenon that he may have encountered in Winnicott, the process of *disillusionment*, the refusal of the mother to continue doing things that she judges the child is now ready and able to do for itself. This is clearly a benign situation and thus simpler to analyse than the random shortcomings of everyday life that lead to unsatisfactory situations which generate the basic endopsychic structure. However, there is a striking parallel between Macmurray's analysis of the possible consequences of disillusionment and Fairbairn's tripartite endopsychic structure. Macmurray suggests one positive and two negative possible outcomes to any attempted disillusionment characterised by the dominance of one or other of two motives, love and fear. Macmurray derives these basic motivations from Suttie and they need to be carefully considered against Fairbairn's choice of love and aggression as the underlying motive forces in any attempt to properly order a personal relations theory. For Suttie and Macmurray, fear produces aggression and hatred as a response to having love threatened or withdrawn. I think it would be fair to say that the libidinal and anti-libidinal subsidiary selves of Fairbairn's theory of dynamic structures that form to bind aggression are based upon responses to fear. So the gap between these different formulations is not substantial.

In Macmurray's account of the negative response to disillusionment, based upon the continued existence of fear, we see something very similar to the development of Fairbairn's subsidiary libidinal and anti-libidinal selves. One response is characterised by Macmurray as being 'good', or over-compliant and the other as 'bad', or aggressive and rebellious:

> Both types of attitude – submissive and aggressive – are negative, and therefore involve unreality. They carry over the illusion of the negative phase of withdrawal into the return to active relationship. They motivate a behaviour in relationship which is contradictory and therefore self-defeating. For the inherent objective – the reality of the relationship – is the full mutuality of fellowship in a common life, the only way in which the individual can realise himself in person. But both the dispositions are egocentric, and motivate action that is for the sake of oneself, and not for the sake of the Other, which is therefore self-interested. Such action is implicitly a refusal of mutuality, and an effort to constrain the other to do what we want. By conforming submissively to his wishes we put him under an obligation to care for us. By aggressive behaviour we seek to

make him afraid not to care for us. In both cases we are cheating: If it succeeds in its intention it produces the appearance of mutuality, but not the reality. It can produce, at most, a reciprocity of co-operation which simulates, even while it excludes, the personal unity which it seeks to achieve.

(Macmurray 1995b: 105)

See Chapter 8 for an extended discussion of these parallels.

FAIRBAIRN'S SUBSIDIARY SELVES AND TRANSITIONAL TECHNIQUES

We all start out oriented towards reality and are deflected from that by our experiences of the world and others. The attempt to achieve mature dependence is the attempt to achieve a real relation to others and to see things clearly as they are. Our subsidiary selves operate exactly like these negative motivations based upon past personal relations and prevent our acting realistically or really sharing our world. This naturally raises the issue of how one can overcome these negative aspects of the developing relationship between self and the world, which leads into the wider world of self and other. This is the world of Fairbairn's transitional techniques. Their terminus for some is in the achievement of mature dependency, which on this account has a substantial social and political dimension. For Padel (1991) the motor of psychic growth is bringing to consciousness personal relations from the subsidiary selves and working for their transformation, so that the powers of the central self are enhanced at the expense of the subsidiary selves.

SUTTIE: SOCIOCULTURAL INFLUENCES ON THE SELF

Suttie is particularly strong in his recognition and understanding of the contingent nature of the social world. Apart from his grounding in biology, which leads to his trenchant criticism of the death instinct and instinct theory in general, he seems to me to be the first to develop the view that the Oedipus complex is a social and not a psychological situation, as Fairbairn later put it. Suttie says: 'The Oedipus Complex, being largely contingent on particular modes of rearing and forms of family structure, culture and racial character must vary within wide limits' (1960: 5). In a wider context he also notes that 'Freud and Adler . . . naively regard as "human nature" or "instincts", traits and dispositions which may turn out to be the product in subtle ways of certain factors in *our particular culture*' (7). Suttie even suggests that a properly matriarchal culture may not require repression at all given that it is the renunciation of the mother under patriarchy that is the motor of repression in Freud. This is a radical perspective indeed and would repay further investigation. Like Suttie, Fairbairn and Macmurray both recognise the contingent nature of our social existence, which accounts for the existential aspects of their thinking. Indeed it can be regarded as foundational to the view that this is a tragic rather than a fallen universe.

TOWARDS A PERSONAL RELATIONS THEORY

The personal relations theory that I am proposing is based in the work of these three Scottish thinkers, Fairbairn, Macmurray and Suttie, and takes account of the recent work on human development and infant research identified by Sutherland and spelt out in some detail by Trevarthen. It recognises that we are active, reality-oriented, personal and social beings from the start, instinctively geared to suckling and to forming and sustaining relationships. It argues that we can only develop to our fullest if we are part of a joyful and loving dyad in our earliest relationship. It asserts that our overall motivations are love and fear and that it is fear that generates splitting and repression within inner reality. Finally it stresses that our fulfilment is in personal relationships within a community, and that the form of our social and political reality is contingent, but the great obstacle is fear. Each new life is a new possibility for love to blossom into mature dependence, organising and sustaining a common world for the benefit of all.

A REALIST SCIENTIFIC APPROACH TO PSYCHOANALYSIS (SEE CHAPTER 8)

One approach to the human sciences that can allow for the possibility that psychoanalysis is a human science and provide us with a means of developing an integrated view of object relations psychoanalytic thinking is critical realism, as has been argued by David Will (1980, 1986) in a series of papers in the early and middle 1980s. A critical realist view of psychoanalysis as a human science could provide us with the means to reconcile the view we have of psychoanalysis as an academic discipline and the developing relationship with the neurological sciences. Recent developments within critical realism (Collier 1999) have brought the work of the philosopher John Macmurray to the fore. I argue that there is a strong parallel between Macmurray and Fairbairn which could and should be developed into a coherent theoretical underpinning for object relations theory. I believe that Fairbairn's theory is well suited as the hub around which an attempt to integrate psychoanalytic thinking might take place by producing a unified theory of object relations – what I am calling personal relations theory.

SUTTIE, ATTACHMENT THEORY AND THE POLITICS OF PERSONAL RELATIONS THEORY (SEE CHAPTER 9)

Attachment theory, with its connections to normal scientific research and its overlap and connections with ethology, the study of animal emotions, developmental psychology, etc., offers the possibility of a scientific practice, allied to long-term biological and evolutionary studies of animal behaviour and emotion in general, that are now being augmented by neuro-psychological models, with putative theories of mind bearing some relation to psychoanalysis (neuro-psychoanalysis). The main problem with attachment theory is that it is not a psychoanalytic theory at all since the unconscious is generally regarded as being totally biological in origin, attachment being a biological process of bonding akin to the ethological mechanism of imprinting in geese and ducks.

However, it does have psychoanalytic roots, and this change of designation has enabled it to produce an impressive body of work. Since depth psychology or psychoanalysis generally means long-term relationships with relatively few individuals it does not lend itself readily to the sort of experimental paradigm that attachment theory has been able to embrace and develop. However, there can be no doubt that the underlying motivation is broadly consistent with psychoanalysis – the experiences we have in childhood, and with our original attachment figures, affect the way we subsequently experience the world and produce long-lasting effects on the ways in which we can act on and experience the world.

What I would like to see is a much closer collaboration among psychoanalysis, developmental psychology, ethology and attachment theory so that the findings from the more empirical disciplines can be developed further. I believe that this is happening within some institutions, but that this discourse sometimes loses sight of its invaluable psychoanalytic roots. In Chapter 9, I therefore rehearse Bowlby's affinity with Suttie and Fairbairn and his acceptance of a multiple-self model and then look at some contemporary work on developing the rapprochement between attachment theory and psychoanalysis from within this perspective. It is the absence of a multiple-self model and the substitution of cognitive or biological explanations of one sort or another for this multiple self-model that I think needs to be carefully looked at. I then look at the political dimensions of both attachment theory and personal relations theory.

Chapter 8

Fairbairn and Macmurray: psychoanalytic studies and critical realism

Psychoanalytic studies, as an academic discipline, is a relatively new subject and one that is still not clearly defined in terms of its overall intentions or aims. There have been psychoanalytic studies courses established in the UK for about fifteen years, all exclusively at Master's level or above. One tension within psychoanalytic studies seems to me to reside in offering training for a career as a therapist (or as an adjunct to a therapeutic practice) and being a 'proper' academic discipline. I do not think this tension has been resolved. While some of the psychoanalytic studies courses were developed originally as a support system for therapeutic training, they are now having to face up to becoming an established academic discipline alongside other much longer-established areas like literature, philosophy, history or sociology (all of these subjects currently having some involvement with psychoanalytic thinking, usually of a Lacanian complexion). Many of the British psychoanalytic studies courses are based around the dominant theories of practising analysts, which, since the 'Controversial Discussions' (King and Steiner 1991), have been made up of three separate strands roughly characterised as Freudian, Kleinian and Independent – amongst whose number would be found Balint, Fairbairn and Winnicott, for example. So, actually existing psychoanalytic practice is itself multi-vocal, in terms of its theoretical affiliations, though the largest number of British practising analysts probably belong to the Independent group. In addition, some postgraduate courses in psychoanalytic studies are strongly Lacanian, and the University of Essex has both Jungian professors and a strong Jungian-based set of courses. Meanwhile the predominant psychoanalytic influence elsewhere in the University remains Lacanian. In object relations psychoanalysis much of the work that has gone on has been concerned with problems of therapeutic practice rather than with the problems of theory and the application of theory to other problems like the interpretation of texts or the nature of human reality. The British psychoanalytical profession is incapable of speaking with one voice on these matters because of the continuing schisms between different factions within it. Still less is it able to develop and support an alternative unified theory of object relations psychoanalysis to counterpose to the Lacanian model that has been enthusiastically taken up within other disciplines. At the same time scepticism in the form of poststructuralist, deconstructionist and relativist theories, commonly lumped together under the umbrella term postmodernism, has meant that the development of a scientifically based approach to psychoanalysis is deeply compromised in many people's eyes. Thus, we have an academic climate in which the development of psychoanalytic studies as a scientific subject is deeply compromised by the hegemony of a profoundly sceptical and anti-realist set of theories. There is also a tension, internal to psychoanalysis, which in my experience makes it more difficult for non-clinical academic contributions to debates to find a reception than those based upon clinical material. This might be called the problem of legitimising non-clinically based academic approaches to the area.

The view of critical realism that informs this chapter is based upon Roy Bhaskar's works, *A Realist Theory of Science* (1978) and *The Possibility of Naturalism* (1989), and it is from this context that I turn to the question of whether critical realism can make any difference to psychoanalytic studies. One part of that answer has already been given through the work of David Will, Andrew Collier and Michael Rustin (Rustin 1991: 115–44) all of whom have argued, successfully in my view, that psychoanalysis can be treated as a scientific subject. I will look briefly at this in a moment. Another part of the answer could be based upon a theory of object relations psychoanalysis under a critical realist perspective that might then be able to engage adequately with its Lacanian counterparts within a literature and philosophy that is comfortable in its essentially philosophical apprehension of Lacan's work. If one of the purposes of critical realism is to underlabour for the sciences then underlabouring for the science of persons might well be an extremely important role it can play. Above all I regard the scientific feasibility of arguing from a realist, action-based approach to the human mind as intrinsic to Fairbairn's own assumptions.

In this regard I want to suggest that critical realist Andrew Collier's recent book *Being and Worth* does offer the possibility of a grounding theory for object relations psychoanalysis, as was suggested by Wesley Shumar in his review of the book in *Alethia* (1999). More than that, however, I want to argue that Collier's use of Macmurray brings to the fore aspects of objects and objectivity that are uniquely paralleled in the object relations theory of Ronald Fairbairn, a point I will seek to demonstrate. In a similar vein, I will try to show that Collier's general characterisation of psychoanalytic theory, though Freudian in origin, fits the object relations theory of Fairbairn best. Further, I will suggest that Fairbairn's theory can be interpreted as an attempt to derive a psychoanalytic theory from a view of objects that is consistent with Macmurray's and hence consistent with critical realism. Fairbairn's daughter Ellinor Fairbairn Birtles[1] says that Fairbairn and Macmurray did know each other from the mid-1930s onwards and that they came from a similar philosophical background and arrived at a similar conception of human relations. She argues that Macmurray's Gifford Lectures, later published as *The Self as Agent* (1995a) and *Persons in Relation* (1995b), outline essentially similar positions to those developed by Fairbairn (Fairbairn Birtles). I will argue that Macmurray's thought in the Gifford Lectures are complementary to Fairbairn's psychology of dynamic structure.

DAVID WILL, CRITICAL REALISM AND PSYCHOANALYSIS AS A SCIENCE

Whilst it may generally be regarded as unfashionable to concern oneself with the scientific status of psychoanalysis, nevertheless during the 1980s David Will, a Scottish psychiatrist and psychoanalyst, wrote a number of papers developing the idea that within a critical realist philosophy of science it is possible to defend the idea that psychoanalysis is a science and to suggest what the consequences are for research in this area (1980, 1986). His work has been described by Andrew Collier in his book *Critical Realism*, and Collier adopts Will's definition of the sort of psychoanalytic theory a critical realist philosophy of science would require:

> The pressure of positivism is to attribute all the individual's vicissitudes to the environment, while hermeneutics (like biological reductionism) attributes everything to the individual's inner endowment. *Psychoanalysis must avoid both these pitfalls and propound an epigenetic theory of development, that is, one which recognizes the interaction of a real environment with a really existing inner world of fantasy, including misperceptions of the environment.* Here, as in the case of socio-linguistics, critical realism's notion of stratification and multiple determination serves as a corrective to one-sided explanations.
>
> (1994: 224)

Will's defence of psychoanalysis as a science is based on Roy Bhaskar's work in the philosophy of science. Will argues against the Popperian view of science as generating falsifiable hypotheses and uses Bhaskar's arguments concerning empirical realism to reveal its inadequacy for those sciences concerned with open systems. He then describes Bhaskar's view of science based upon transcendental or critical realism and develops parallels between the way it describes science as proceeding and a similar process within psychoanalytic thinking. He summarises Bhaskar's 'three-phase scheme of development of all scientific activity' as follows:[2]

> *Phase one.* The first empirical stage ... the transcendental realist interprets this as the identification of a real invariance resulting from the manifest operation of a generative mechanism.

Phase two. Plausible generative mechanisms are imagined which could account for the phenomena in question.

Phase three. The reality of the generative mechanisms imagined in phase two is subject to empirical testing.

(Will 1980: 203)

Will's suggestion for the equivalent set of procedures within a psychoanalytic frame is given by Table 8.1. His subsequent comment, which is also included, is of particular interest since it refers to the level of argument I am engaging in here.

Table 8.1 Psychoanalytic thinking and scientific activity

Stratum 1	Seductive behaviour of a female hysteric in relation to a male analyst explained by	
Stratum 2	Repetition of previous experiences (theory of transference) explained by	Mechanism 1
Stratum 3	Projection of unconscious material explained by	Mechanism 2
Stratum 4	(conflicting theories of the nature of the unconscious)	(Mechanism 3)

It should be noted that this example also indicates that psychoanalysis is not a closed system of fixed beliefs and that, indeed, it is at this most basic level that major conflicting theories (e.g. Freudian, Kleinian, Fairbairnian and Lacanian) do disagree most fundamentally. The relative value of these conflicting theories must be empirically tested in terms of their explanatory power.

(Will 1980: 207–8)

Will argues that, since the human sciences are characterised by open systems and the criteria for theories is explanatory, 'the clinical situation itself provides the setting for scientific work in psychoanalysis and psychotherapy. It is in this setting that explanatory hypotheses are generated *and* it is in this setting that they will be tested' (209). This view is consistent with Fairbairn's view developed in 1952 where he argues that 'the psychoanalytic technique itself constitutes a valid experimental method' (1952b) and 'the psychoanalytic method has largely ceased to be a historical method involving reconstruction of the patient's past, and has largely become a method for investigating the influences of (characteristically unconscious) situations and relationships in inner reality upon contemporary experience and behaviour' (110). In this paper Fairbairn stresses the explanatory nature of science and argues for the importance of the generative mechanisms outlined above: 'we are now in a position to see that a true estimate of the scientific status of psychoanalysis from an experimental standpoint can only be reached after the full significance of the concepts of "transference" and "inner reality" has been appreciated' (109). Now, it may be that Fairbairn was arguing for closure within the clinical setting, given his approving quotation of Ezriel, who says that the analytic session can be seen to satisfy the experimental requirement for 'the observation of *here and now* phenomena in situations which allow us to test whether a number of defined conditions will produce a certain predicted event' (110). But I suggest that Fairbairn, like Will, has 'argued that the experimental nature of the psychoanalytic process itself be acknowledged ... [and] that the way by which psychoanalytic hypotheses are tested is by virtue of their explanatory power' (Will 1980: 209). It should be noted that Fairbairn in his paper on the aims of therapy (1958) stressed the *whole relationship* between the analyst and his patient as people, not just the transference relationship in which many of these phenomena become manifest.

Will ends his 1980 paper on 'Psychoanalysis as a human science' by proposing certain urgent research projects. These are: (a) the development of an adequate theory of the effectivity of psychoanalysis; (b) the construction of an adequate history of the development of psychoanalytic theory; (c) a scientific attempt to choose between conflicting theories; and finally (d) the development of adequate critiques of psychoanalytic hypotheses. Given his view on the importance of clinical matters for the generation and testing of theory, the non-clinical student of psychoanalytic studies might well find guidance as to what sort of research to engage upon from this list.

In his 1986 paper 'Psychoanalysis and the new philosophy of science', Will takes up aspects of (c) and (d) above and seeks to find a way of arbitrating some of the controversies between different schools within the psychoanalytic movement. In the course of this he makes three explicit criticisms of Fairbairn's theory which I feel I need to address.

Will's first criticism of Fairbairn relates to the notion of the *contingency* of the symbol in Freud's theory. He argues that 'it is only because of the contingency of the symbol in dreams that displacement, condensation and overdetermination can occur. None of these processes would be possible if there was a non-contingent, bi-univocal, one-to-one correspondence between the symbol and what it symbolizes' (1986: 168). He goes on to argue that Fairbairn's work:

> is premised on denial of the *contingency of the object* of libido. (Libido being seen as object-seeking rather then pleasure-seeking.) This leads in turn to a progressive denial of the contingency of the symbol. (If libido is 'innately' directed towards certain objects, then there must be 'innate' symbols.) This leads Fairbairn to view dream interpretation in a reductionist way, which leads him to claim that all human characters appearing in a dream are seen as inevitably representing aspects of the dreamer's split ego.
>
> (169)

In regard to the first point, in Fairbairn's theory the original object of the original self is contingent and shares to some extent or another innate aspects of loving, warmth, safety, nourishment – essentially animal requirements for survival and attachment. The relationship between the newborn and its contingent caregiver, who might be the infant's biological mother but does not have to be, then starts to develop. So the contingency remains, as the *real relationship* between an infant and its caregiver and the vicissitudes of that relationship as it expands to include relationships with significant others. As we know from attachment research, infants can be differently attached to different significant others. The innate symbols, so called, are for Fairbairn minimal in content and oriented towards survival and attachment, that is, object-directed relations and dependency. Will's argument suggests a much stronger set of built-in symbols than this and infers that this is what leads Fairbairn to argue that dreams are ' "shorts" . . . of situations existing in inner reality' (1952a: 99).

In Freud's conception of inner reality, after the development of the structural theory, there are three complex structures, an ego, an id and a superego, which are all to some extent unconscious. In Fairbairn's model of inner reality there are six complex and dynamic structures – three ego-related and three object-related – so that the dream is not confined to a mapping onto ego-structures alone, as is stated by Will. There are three pairs of ego–object dyads that are libidinally bonded to each other, two of which are described as unconscious by Fairbairn, though others have argued that they are not always completely unconscious all of the time (for example, Padel). Each of these dynamic structures is built upon internalised relationships, with significant others initially, the two unconscious dyads being based upon over-exciting and over-frustrating aspects of relationships with others which are repressed. Fairbairn makes three different interpretations of the patient's dream in his endopsychic paper, only the last of which argues that the people in this particular dream do map onto each of the complex dynamic structures that constitute the inner world for Fairbairn, and this in the context of deriving his own model of inner reality. To be 'shorts' of inner reality does not mean that every dream has to be analysed at this level, or that every aspect of the structure of the inner world will necessarily be represented in the dream. Will's argument here seems to be overstating the case and drawing linked conclusions that are not warranted by Fairbairn's theory. Fairbairn, in his paper on hysterical states (1954), gives several examples of the way in which he uses dreams as representations of inner reality in therapy for the purpose of making the patient aware of the degree to which he or she[3] is split, in order to help reduce such splitting to a minimum. This is, in his view, the main aim of therapy along with turning the closed system of inner reality into an open system in relation to the external world (1958: 83–4). We should also note that dream interpretation does not have the same place it had in therapeutic practice in Freud's day, the interest being focussed more on the here-and-now aspects of relationships in the consulting room.

Will's second criticism of Fairbairn concerns his assertion as to the secondary nature of aggression. For Fairbairn, libidinal relations with the world are the underlying dynamics of the infant's relationships with the world around him or her, and aggression only arises initially as a response to a real frustration by the environment. This is similar to Will's formulation that 'infantile rage was always a response to real frustration by the environment' (1986: 170). However, in any specific example of infantile rage, Fairbairn would be looking for the cause in either the relationship with the outer world or the relationships within the inner world. After the first weeks the inner world is already of sufficient complexity that psychological factors cannot be ruled out as the reasons for the baby's anger or aggression: 'I take the view that the earliest psychopathological symptoms to manifest themselves are hysterical in character; and I interpret the screaming fits of the infant in this sense' (Fairbairn 1952a: 130). Fairbairn accepted that there is both a libidinal and an aggressive relationship to the world that are separate and not commutative. He believed that the aggressive relationship is instituted by situations of frustration and deprivation and installed in the dynamics of inner reality and the dynamic structures of which it is composed, and is not part of some innate predisposition like that postulated by Freud and Klein. Like Macmurray (1997: 56), Fairbairn believed that aggression is born of fear, but that the basic human orientation is love.

The third explicit criticism of Fairbairn by Will concerns the 'reductionism whereby all psychopathology stems at root from schizoid splits occasioned by real traumatic experience at the hands of an inadequate mother' (1986: 171). It might be more in keeping with Fairbairn's own tone to say that splitting does occur in early infancy as a result of unsatisfying experiences with caregivers in a situation where the need to preserve the relationship with the caregiver is paramount. These failures are not seen as in any sense the deliberate or malicious achievement of an 'inadequate mother'. We know that there are vindictive, cruel and destructive people who do have children and do abuse them, and Fairbairn knows this too, for he dealt with abused children in the 1930s (Scharff and Fairbairn Birtles 1994, vol. II: 159–82). Will's formulation of this criticism is set in a context where he says that he does not want to see the infant as either the victim or the villain. He conceives of the development of the individual 'as an interplay between nature and nurture, between innate characteristics and the effects of the environment' (1986: 170–1). As Grotstein (Grotstein and Rinsley 1994: 85) and Mitchell (Grotstein and Rinsley 1994: 141) have argued, Fairbairn sees the child as essentially (psychologically) innocent. It enters the world unburdened by innate rage or envy or the possession of a death-instinct, but with the innate goal of object-relating with a warm and loving, supportive and nourishing other upon whom it is totally dependent. If that process goes well, the degree of splitting is minimal and the person can develop to live a full life within the bounds of their culture's ideas of such, and may from a position of mature dependence work within that culture to creatively develop and expand such notions. I think Will lacks specificity regarding the level and nature of the innate characteristics that he assumes. He mentions Lacan in favourable terms and there is something of Lacan's argument against object relations in the criticisms he makes. As Collier has noted, Lacan's formulation of the nature of desire as unfulfillable makes his theory anti-therapeutic (1999: 51).

It is crucial to recognise that the notion of the unconscious in Freud and Fairbairn are different, reflecting as they do their different concepts of endopsychic structure. As Fairbairn comments regarding the therapeutic situation: *'the contrast between past and present (like that between unconscious and conscious) has come to be largely subordinated to the contrast between inner reality and outer reality'* (1952b: 127; emphasis in original). Freud's 'system unconscious' is a complex dynamic set of impulses of a libidinal or aggressive nature seeking some sort of expression. Fairbairn's unconscious is two distinct sub-selves, one libidinal (over-exciting) and the other anti-libidinal (over-rejecting), both of which comprise a set of unpleasant object relationships that have been dissociated and then repressed. In my interpretation of Fairbairn's theory, his 'system unconscious', as opposed to the descriptively unconscious (that is, the preconscious, which also includes the ego ideal), is a social product. That is, Fairbairn's 'system unconscious' does not exist before splitting takes place and can, in theory, be reintegrated into what would then be a mind characterised by just the conscious and the preconscious (descriptively unconscious) domains. I believe that Fairbairn's original dynamic pristine ego, with its libidinal relation towards others in the world, is a mainly preconscious (essentially bodily) self upon which conscious structures are built and from which unconscious structures, based upon split-off internalised relationships with others, are made. In this description, innate characteristics are preconscious (descriptively unconscious), not (system) unconscious. The reasons for believing that this is a valid interpretation of Fairbairn's work are discussed below, but Fairbairn himself always stressed that splitting inevitably occurred within human society and that it is never finally resolved. In other words, short of an ideal society there would always be a system unconscious.

FAIRBAIRN AND MACMURRAY

Having tried to defend Fairbairn's theory against Will's criticism, let me now turn to showing the ways in which Fairbairn's theory has strong parallels with Macmurray's theory of objects and objectivity as it is represented by Andrew Collier in *Being and Worth* (1999). The sense of familiarity I felt with Collier's exposition of Macmurray's philosophy was due, not only to having read one of Macmurray's books (*Reason and Emotion*, 1935) in the 1960s, but because Macmurray's view of the object, as represented by Collier, reminded me most forcefully of Fairbairn's object relations theory. Despite both having lectured at the University of Edinburgh, there is no evidence that Fairbairn and Macmurray met. However, as we have seen, Ellinor Fairbairn Birtles says that they definitely knew each other from the mid-1930s onwards and that Macmurray drew parallel conclusions to those reached by Fairbairn in his mature object relations theory (Fairbairn Birtles 1997).

The parallels I am concentrating on here, and hope to demonstrate, are for the most part between Macmurray's work of the early to middle 1930s and Fairbairn's work of the early to middle 1940s collected and published in 1952 as *Psychoanalytic Studies of the Personality*. I want to show that there are parallels between Macmurray's view of the object, objectivity and the person as an active being first and foremost, and Fairbairn's view of persons as object-directed, object-related and object-dependent in the object relations theory he developed. The parallels I am considering initially are not, in general, at the level of detailed psychoanalytic theories *per se*, though I will argue later that such do exist between Macmurray's later work, namely *Persons in Relation* (1995b), and Fairbairn's mature object relations theory. What is more fundamental perhaps are the underlying assumptions about the nature of persons, their relation to objects and the relation between reason and emotion, which seem to me to be very similar. If it can be successfully argued that Fairbairn's object relations theory is consistent with a particular philosophical theory that is itself consistent with critical realism, then the possibility of developing critical realist arguments in support of an object relations psychoanalysis would be more easily acceptable to academic departments which are more comfortable with the philosophical arguments than the clinically based arguments of object relations psychoanalysis.

The opening pages of Fairbairn's paper on endopsychic structure (1944) state clearly Fairbairn's position that 'libido is primarily object-seeking' and '[it is in] disturbances in the object relationships of the developing ego that we must look for the ultimate origins of all psychopathological conditions'. This latter assertion depends upon the notion of 'internalised objects' based upon Freud's concept of the superego as an endopsychic structure originating in the internalisations of objects. It was one of Fairbairn's major criticisms of Freud that he never thought through the consequences for the structural model of the differences between the ego, the id and the superego in terms of internalised objects on the basis of a no longer sustainable distinction between energy and structure rooted in nineteenth-century physics. Fairbairn claims that powerful notions like the repetition compulsion and the death instinct are better regarded as the consequences of the internalisation of, and continuing libidinal relationships with, bad internal objects (1952a: 78), and that the notion of 'phantasy' is better understood as relationships between internal objects (King and Steiner 1991: 358–60).

In terms of an overall schema of development, Fairbairn rejects Abraham's and Freud's notions of psychosexual development and suggests there are three developmental phases: infantile dependence; a transitional phase; and mature dependence. For Fairbairn the newborn infant is object-seeking and object-dependent but active and libidinally related to the external object. The original ego is described as 'pristine', suggesting, as Grotstein has written, a psychological innocence regarding the external world. As relationships with caregivers develop there are inevitably some unsatisfactory aspects to them, which prompt the infant to internalise aspects of the world, in particular significant objects, in order to, in some degree, control them or their effects upon him: 'he accordingly follows the only path open to him and, since outer reality seems unyielding, he does his best to transfer the traumatic factor in the situation to the field of inner reality, within which he feels situations to be more under his own control' (1952a: 110). I will return to the passage this is extracted from, since it can be seen to parallel some of Macmurray's fundamental ideas about the origins and need for thinking, and the nature of the circumstances that give rise to this need. This process of internalisation of relationships between self and other, and the need to split off aspects of these in order to protect the relationship with the significant other upon whom one is totally dependent, gives rise to a structured inner reality. This is the phase Fairbairn calls infantile dependence.

Once the infant has a structured inner reality alongside its embeddedness in external reality, it is the working out of the relationships between inner and outer reality and the way this is handled that constitute the second or transitional stage for Fairbairn. I have described the structure of inner reality and the relationship of this structure with the categories of conscious, preconscious and unconscious in previous chapters. Suffice it to say that Fairbairn sees the structure of inner reality and the relationships between inner and outer reality as determining the differences between psychosis and neurosis, the specific nature of the main categories of psychoneurotic symptoms, the nature of narcissism and the reality behind phantasy.

Fairbairn's infant starts out with a realistic perspective on the world, but through relations with others and the consequent development of a complex inner reality can become lost in maintaining relationships with internal objects. However, through experience of 'good enough' relationships, education, therapy, etc., the possibility exists for 'returning' all those unconscious internalised objects to the external world and adopting once again a realistic approach to the world at a new level of complexity and competence. This final stage of development, which Fairbairn calls mature dependence, stresses the essentially social nature, that is, external object-related orientation, of human beings and argues that their relationships to external objects do not have to be distorted by relationships with unconscious internal objects. Therefore all good and bad objects can be returned to a proper realistic place in the external world. My own researches suggest that Fairbairn thought that the child is initially, for the most part, descriptively unconscious, that is, preconscious, and by the point at which mature dependency is reached the system unconscious (the inner reality of unconscious internalised objects) has been effectively undone; that is, unconscious internal objects have been effectively dissolved and the conscious/preconscious person again is free to relate realistically to the world around them in so far as their times and ideologies will allow. As noted earlier the maturely dependent person is also best equipped to effectively challenge and creatively engage with their times and ideologies.

The point of this description of Fairbairn's theory has been to indicate the thoroughgoing nature of his object relations theory and his underlying realism, and to illustrate how this relates to Macmurray's philosophy in his 1933 work, *Interpreting the Universe*, and his 1935 work *Reason and Emotion* (from which the bulk of Collier's commentary is drawn).

MACMURRAY AND FAIRBAIRN

Collier describes the way various thinkers have approached the question of reason and emotion and argues for a model derived from Spinoza, which he describes as follows:

> The faculties of the soul are reduced to one: emotion. Rather than reason being a separate faculty, rationality or irrationality are qualities of emotions. This moral psychology provides the twofold foundation for Spinoza's ethics: nothing can overcome an emotion except another emotion; but emotions can be more or less rational insofar as they are based on more or less (cognitive) ideas – and it is sometimes possible to transform irrational emotions into rational emotions by passing from inadequate to (more) adequate ideas.
>
> (1999: 16)

This might well be a crucial point in the development and legitimation of an object relations psychoanalysis, and it is in connection with just this point that Macmurray is introduced into the argument. The following remarks by Fairbairn can also be used to reinforce this idea: 'physical development is characterized, not by the gradual integration of a number of separately functioning organs, but by the gradual differentiation of a unified functioning structure; and it would seem reasonable to assume that mental development is characterized by a similar process' (1956a: 53).

Let us consider, then, some of the fundamental similarities between Fairbairn and Macmurray. In *Conditions of Freedom* Macmurray writes concerning the personal and the sharing of a common life:

It is, indeed, the erroneous postulate of any thoroughgoing individualism. It assumes that the human individual is an independent, self-contained entity with a personal life of his own which he may or may not purpose to share with others. In fact, it is the sharing of a common life which constitutes individual personality. We become persons in community in virtue of our relations to others. Human life is *inherently* a common life.

(1997: 37)

Fairbairn, in his 1956 paper in the *British Journal of the Philosophy of Science* (1956a) involving a critical evaluation of certain basic psychoanalytical concepts, writes:

Psychological hedonism has for long appeared to the writer to provide an unsatisfactory basis for psychoanalytical theory because it relegates object-relationships to a secondary place. Indeed, it involves the implicit assumption that man is not by nature a social animal . . . as Aristotle described him . . . and that accordingly social behaviour is an acquired characteristic. This assumption would appear to be in complete contradiction of the facts of animal psychology.

(1956a: 52)

A second fundamental similarity between Fairbairn and Macmurray is the assumption of an active person engaging the world in practical and realistic activity. Macmurray writes:

Life is essentially concrete activity. Thought involves the temporary suspension of concrete activity. It holds up the action of life. We *stop* and think. What is it, then, that brings about this stoppage of the normal processes of life activity? . . . The primary cause is some recognized failure in concrete activity. We stop to think because our undeliberated action has gone wrong, or because the immediate motives, which normally determine the direction of action, have failed.

(1933: 18)

The following paragraph is also of some significance, as I hope to show:

There are many other ways, of course, in which the stoppage of action can be brought about. But all of them are in the nature of breakdowns in the primary processes of spontaneous activity; and all of them give rise to the state of mind in which thought begins, a state of hesitation. Thought begins in doubt. It is only when either naturally or artificially we are in two minds, when we are faced with a question to which there may be two answers, that reflection becomes possible. This state of doubt, with the questions in which it formulates itself, arises always, directly or indirectly, from some hitch in the process of living, or rather from the consciousness of such a hitch. This consciousness involves both a feeling of dissatisfaction and the recognition of an unsatisfactory situation.

(19)

Fairbairn's declaration of an original dynamic, object-directed and realistic, unitary ego or self is totally consistent with Macmurray's view of life as concrete activity. In his paper on endopsychic structure Fairbairn writes: 'characteristically the child's sense of reality is of low degree compared with that of the adult; but he is none the less actuated by a reality sense from the beginning, even if he is all too liable, in the face of frustration, to stray into tension-relieving sidetracks' (1944: 141).

When we turn to Fairbairn's account of the origins of endopsychic structure in the early experience of the infant, we will again see strong parallels with Macmurray's idea of thinking as interrupted concrete activity. Note in particular Macmurray's idea that thinking involves being in two minds (two perspectives) and compare this with Fairbairn's own original contribution on the splitting of the ego, originating, as Freud described, in the internalisation of the nursing couple, either of whom the infant could identify with. In a footnote to his paper on the nature of hysterical states, Fairbairn produces his final formulation of the way that endopsychic structure originates:

> In my opinion it would be a pointless procedure on the part of the infant to introject the maternal object if his relationship to his actual mother were completely satisfying, both within the emotional sphere and within the more specific sphere of the suckling situation . . . it is only in so far as the infant's relationship with his mother falls short of being completely satisfying that he can have any conceivable motivation for introjecting the maternal object . . . (1) . . . the differentiation of objects into categories to which the terms 'good' and 'bad' can be applied arises only after the original (pre-ambivalent) object has been introjected, and (2) . . . this differentiation is effected through splitting of an internalized object, which is, in the first instance, neither 'good' nor 'bad', but 'in some measure unsatisfying' and which only becomes truly 'ambivalent' after its introjection. . . . I describe introjection of the unsatisfying object as *a defence* – 'the first defence adopted by the original ego'. This implies, of course, that I do not regard introjection of the object as the inevitable expression of an infant's instinctive incorporative needs. . . . Nor can the process of introjection of the object (viz. the process whereby a *mental structure* representing an external object becomes established within the psyche) be regarded simply as a manifestation of that general perpetuation of experience which is described as 'memory'.

(1954: 107n)

The origins of this hiatus in an 'unsatisfactory' situation is another compelling parallel between the two men's thinking.

For Fairbairn, the free flow of libidinal activity by the original self is interrupted by some unsatisfying aspects of his or her relationship to the mother or primary caregiver. This leads to a unique psychological process called introjection in which a representation of a personal relationship with the external object is created as a mental structure within inner reality. This internal object is subsequently split into three, based upon the nature of the relationships with the significant others it derives from. There is, then, a libidinal object based upon over-exciting relationships with the caregiver, an anti-libidinal object based upon over-frustrating or rejecting relationships with the caregiver, and an ideal object based upon the acceptable relationships with the caregiver. Each of these objects is libidinally bound to aspects of the original self, which becomes split as the object is split. In order to preserve the relationship with the caregiver the disturbing over-exciting and/or frustrating relationships are split off and repressed. Thus three selves may be conceptualised based upon these three different sets of relationships. Each of the subsidiary selves represents powers that are unavailable to the central self because they are split off and repressed. That is, it represents a diminution of the powers available to the person unless the splitting can be undone. This is Fairbairn's object relations equivalent of the Freudian structural model.

It is worth noting here that Collier's development of the Augustinian notion that evil is a privation of being finds echoes in Fairbairn's concept that pathology is the diminution of powers based upon attachment to bad internal objects and that, when these attachments have been worked through and overcome, the stage of mature dependence is characterised by an attitude of *giving*, and both the accepted and rejected objects are *exteriorised*. Mature dependence is also characterised by a 'capacity on the part of a differentiated individual for co-operative relationships with differentiated objects' (1952a: 145). This links with Macmurray's notion of objectivity and its goal, which is to 'stand in conscious relation to that which is recognized as not ourselves' (1933: 72), which is itself linked to morality in *Reason and Emotion* where Macmurray says, 'morality demands that we should act "in the light of eternity", that is, in terms of things as they really are and of people as they really are, and not in terms of our subjective inclinations and private sympathies' (1935: 23). Fairbairn's notion of mature dependency as the equivalent of Freud's genetic character is then intrinsically moral and realistic. As Ellinor Fairbairn Birtles comments in an unpublished source (1997), comparing Macmurray to Fairbairn, ' "each sees the other as he really is" is the precondition for "mature dependence" '. She also notes the similarities in their 'educational and intellectual' background, and a common assumption they make that human beings are both social and political beings, which she identifies as an assumption of Scottish as opposed to English culture.

PERSONS IN RELATION: THE RHYTHM OF WITHDRAWAL AND RETURN

In order to show how Macmurray's and Fairbairn's theories regarding psychoanalytic theory relate, I am going to look in detail at Macmurray's account of disillusion from the chapter in *Persons in Relation* (1995b) called 'The rhythm of withdrawal and return'. I will suggest a way in which this work and Fairbairn's can be seen as complementary by using Bhaskar's 'three phase scheme of development of all scientific activity'.

In this chapter we find Macmurray considering the ways in which the early treatment of the child can lead to specific patterned differences of response to the world. The fact that he derives three different patterns that I will argue are consonant with Fairbairn's tripartite division of inner reality, is of particular interest. The context within which these different 'selves' develop is very specifically concerned with what Winnicott called 'disillusion' – the gradual introduction, by the mother, of (increasingly complex) elements of reality into the infant's life. By contrast Fairbairn's account of the development of the structures of inner reality depends upon a disillusionment that is contingent and not part of a benign attempt to help the infant master aspects of the world in a timely fashion.

Macmurray initially considers the ways in which the infant becomes accommodated to the patterns of presence and absence of the mother and develops compensatory processes for enduring her absence in the form of phantasy:

> So the infant's expectation is grounded in imagination; and his waiting is filled with the symbolic satisfaction of his desire in phantasy; the images he forms and the feelings of anticipatory pleasure which accompany them persist through the period of waiting, and coalesce, as it were, with the actual satisfaction when it comes. This exercising of the power of phantasy is the first stage in the development of reflection, and the success of anticipation and satisfaction – with the same images accompanying both – institutes the primary distinction between imagining and perceiving.
>
> (1995b: 88)

He also considers the consequences for the infant of its needs for the mother not being met:

> But the unexpected may happen; the prediction may not be verified. Then the basis of confidence and security is broken. If the response to his cry is too long delayed, or if the mother's effort to relieve his distress is unsuccessful, then the negative motive is no longer subordinated to a positive, confident expectation. It becomes dominant, and finds expression in a

paroxysm of rage and terror, and what power of phantasy the child has acquired will lend itself to the symbolic representation of danger.

(88)

This leads him onto a consideration of the infant's possible responses to benign disillusionment:

> In the early stage of our life this reversal of the natural dominance of the positive motive is occasional and accidental. It foreshadows however a periodic reversal which is necessary and inevitable in passing from one stage to the next. If a child is to grow up, he must learn, stage by stage, to do for himself what has up to that time been done for him by the mother. But at all the crucial points, at least, the decision rests with the mother, and therefore it must take the form of a deliberate refusal on her part to continue to show the child those expressions of her care for him that he expects. This refusal is, of course, itself an expression of the mother's care for him.
>
> (88–9)

By considering the mother/primary caregiver in a positive mode, Macmurray can concentrate on the possible responses of the child without having to consider the caregiver's motives. This process represents in many ways a quintessential problem of relationship for Macmurray. This process of experiencing a problem within a relationship, of seeking to understand it and find a way of restoring the relationship, is an underlying part of this common pattern of withdrawal and return; part, too, of Macmurray's understanding of the development to maturity we all make, and the distinctions between appearance and reality, the real and the unreal, good and evil, beautiful and ugly, true and false that arise within this process:

> The distinction of Self and Other is present from the beginning, since the infant, being dependent totally upon the mother, must wait upon the other person for the satisfaction of his needs. There is a necessary time lag between the consciousness of need and its satisfaction. But so long as the expectation is not disappointed, so long as there is regularity in the recurrence of the supply of his needs, there is no crisis which concentrates attention upon himself by compelling him to make a demand instead of merely waiting passively. At most there is a point in personal development, which may vary considerably from child to child, at which the contrast between Self and Other is finally established as a pervasive attitude in action and reflection.
>
> (96)

From the initial conflict between the infant's needs and expectations and the caregiver's benign disillusionment, Macmurray shows how the basis of morality is developed:

> The moral struggle is primarily a struggle between persons. It is only secondarily, though also necessarily, a struggle within the individual. For the motivation of the individual, and the consciousness which it contains, has reference to the Other. He needs the Other in order to be himself; and his awareness is an awareness of the Other. Consequently, if his relation to the Other becomes negative, the conflict is reflected in himself. He must maintain the relation even in rejecting it: he cannot escape from it except by escaping from himself. His relation to the Other becomes ambivalent. He is divided in himself, fearing and therefore hating what he loves, turned against himself because he is against the Other. From this conflict of agents are derived all the characteristic dichotomies in terms of which human life must be lived, and in it they are contained. With their emergence in consciousness, as distinctions between real and unreal, right and wrong, good and evil, true and false, action becomes necessary and human life becomes problematic. We are compelled to distinguish and to choose. These reflections ... reveal the form of the basic problem itself. ... From the standpoint of the individual it is the problem of overcoming fear.
>
> (98)

It is fear that stands behind hatred and jealousy and the problem is how can we overcome fear and learn to trust and love the Other.

In using disillusionment as an example, Macmurray argues that there are three alternative ways in which the infant might respond. One, the positive outcome, is that the infant might learn to do what it was capable of doing for itself and come to understand that this was intended by the mother it loves:

> If the return from the negative phase is to be completely successful it is necessary that the dominance of the negative motive be completely overcome, and that the positive relation to the mother be fully re-established, in spite of her continuing refusal to satisfy his demand. It is the conditions and implications of such a successful overcoming of fear that concern our study ... they consist in recognizing the illusions involved in the negative phase, and as a consequence the disappearance of the conflict of wills. ... To recognize as unreal what has been taken as real is to reverse a valuation, and value ... is primarily felt. ... What is required for the recognition of unreality is a change in feeling ... coupled with a memory of the earlier attitude.
>
> (99)

This leads to a fundamental insight into the nature of the world:

> 'Mother appeared to be against me, but she wasn't really'.... 'I thought Mother was bad but she wasn't. She was good. It was I who was bad.' This provides the formal basis of moral experience. The second implication provides the formal basis of intellectual experience – the distinction between true and false. The child recognizes in action, if not yet in reflection, that his expectation was based upon too limited an experience.... Thus the disappointment of expectation based upon the experience of an invariant sequence in the behaviour of the Other, the experience of being in error.... Whether the child succeeds or fails in overcoming the negation in his relation to the mother, he must recognize that his expectation has been falsified.
>
> (100)[4]

So, a successful disillusionment is a prototypical example of a process of growth towards maturity, the recognition of a difference between appearance and reality, a recognition of error and therefore truth and falsity; in short, it is exemplary of psychic growth. However, every attempt at benign disillusionment does not lead to psychic growth:

> The return from the negative is not, then, necessarily achieved in its completeness, or satisfactorily. If it were, the original positive relation of mother and child would be re-established fully at a higher level; a level at which the child has learned to trust the mother in spite of appearances, and at which he has something to contribute of his own initiative to the common life.... It may be achieved, or nearly achieved, upon occasion, but on the whole and on balance the most we can hope for is a qualified success.... Even with the best of mothers this can only be so in the main and never absolutely and continuously. So far as she falls short of this perfection of love, so far as the child's feeling that she is against him is not an illusion; and by so much she must fail to overcome his negative attitude and to reinstate a fully positive relation.
>
> (101)

So Macmurray turns to consider 'the formal result of this general failure to overcome completely the negative motivation which sustains the phase of withdrawal, and consequently the illusions and contradictions which are inseparable from it' (100).

The overall consequence is that the relation with the Other is established upon a mixed motive:

> It contains an element of fear which is not integrated within the positive motivation of the return to action, but suppressed.... But no action can

have contradictory intentions.... It can, however, have contradictory motives, one of which is suppressed, and therefore 'unconscious'. And since our actions contain a negative element which is in the same sense 'unconscious', the unconscious motive may find expression in action, so that we find that what we have done is not what we intended.

(102)

The process of developing a moral dimension to activity should be compared to Fairbairn's account of the 'moral defence' (1952a: 65), which is diametrically opposed to the benign example of disillusionment given here. In Fairbairn's example the parental motivation is negative and the child, in order to preserve the notion that its external object is good, falsely attributes the badness of the situation to itself. We also need to remind ourselves of Davidson's 1978 work on irrationality (1982) and the degree to which this is the result of split-off sub-selves acting with their own motivation. The negative relations with the Other described by Macmurray have here become tantamount to split-off aspects of the person. This at least provides us with a starting place for arguing that the split-off sub-selves of Fairbairn's model are echoed in the divisions Macmurray introduces into the infant self as a consequence of being unable to complete the process of withdrawal and return at a higher level of integration:

> For simplicity's sake let us return to the child, and consider only the extreme possibilities.... If ... he accedes to his mother's demands because he must, and against his will, the tension of contradiction is not resolved. He remains egocentric and on the defensive; he conforms in behaviour to what is expected of him, but, as it were, as a matter of policy. In that case, he cannot find satisfaction in the new forms of co-operation, and they remain for him unreal.... The contradiction between the imagined satisfaction and the unsatisfactory actual persist.... If this condition becomes habitual ... it will institute a permanent dualism between the ideal and the actual.... Here, then, is an account of the genesis of dualism as a habit of mind.
>
> (1995b: 102–3)

It is interesting to note that, when Winnicott reflected (1989: 582), at the end of his life, on Fairbairn's work, and the criticisms that he had made of it, it was Fairbairn's insistence upon the importance of feeling real that Winnicott cited as one of the most significant of Fairbairn's contributions.

In a passage that brings to mind Winnicott's concept of impingement and the distinction between the true and the false selves, Macmurray describes one of the 'two courses open' to the 'child who has been forced back into co-operative activity without a resolution of the conflict':

> He remains egocentric, and the objective of his behaviour is security, through self-defence. What he cannot do, so long as his fear is not overcome and dissipated, is to give himself freely to his mother in the fellowship of mutual affection without constraint ... he will conform obediently and even eagerly to the pattern of behaviour expected of him. He will become a 'good' boy and by his 'goodness' he will seek to placate the mother whose enmity he fears. In compensation for this submission he will create for himself a secret life of phantasy where his own wishes are granted. And this life of the imagination in an imaginary world will be for him his *real* life in the *real* world – the world of ideas. His life in the actual world will remain unreal.
>
> (1995b: 103)

This course can be seen to share similarities with Fairbairn's notion of the libidinal self.

However, the child may take another course and seek to impose his own will upon his mother:

> He may become a 'bad' boy, rebellious and aggressive, seeking to gain by force or cunning what is not freely given to him. In that case he will carry the conflict of wills into the world of actuality, and seek power over the Other. He will use his imagination to discover and exploit the weaknesses of those on whom he is dependent, and to devise techniques for getting his own way. . . . *His* real life is the practical life, the life of action as the use of power to secure his own ends by his own efforts. The life of the imagination is unreal in itself, and has value for him only as a means to success in the practical life.
>
> (103–4)

The results then of this failure to overcome the negative motivation is to produce 'an individual who is either characteristically submissive or characteristically aggressive in his active relations with the Other' (104).

It takes little imagination to see the characteristically aggressive and manipulative self as one version of the anti-libidinal self, which Fairbairn initially called the internal saboteur. Perhaps this is a key to a further parallel between the two, that these internal sub-selves reflect and are based upon residues of object relationships that have been dissociated and repressed and that this tripartite structure that forms the basic version of Fairbairn's inner reality is formed precisely from the sorts of relationship that Macmurray distinguishes here.

DISILLUSION AND THE PSYCHOLOGY OF DYNAMIC STRUCTURE

If we consider Macmurray's object relations account of the process of disillusion as equivalent to phase one of Bhaskar's three-phase schema of scientific activity, then I would argue that Fairbairn's object relations theory of dynamic structure provides us with generative mechanisms that adequately account for the invariants Macmurray identifies and is equivalent to phase two of Bhaskar's schema. Phase three of the schema, the testing of Fairbairn's theory, is less well developed than I would like because of his lack of a school and is also a site for struggle and discussion since it does involve a further level of theoretical and practical work on the nature of the unconscious within psychoanalysis itself.

As we have seen, Macmurray discusses the consequences of the object relationship between the baby and its mother when the mother, rather than satisfying the child's expectations over a particular matter, judges that the child can achieve this specific goal itself and thus leaves them to it deliberately but with love.

He considers three possible responses to this. The first is one in which the child manages to overcome whatever problems there are and achieves its goal and in the process realises that its mother was acting benignly. Thus the child has extended its powers, has a more realistic view of itself and mother and is restored to mutuality with mother.

This is the positive outcome, and is a case of psychic growth in Fairbairn's terms.

In the two other outcomes considered by Macmurray there are negative consequences. Full mutuality with mother isn't restored, and there is a continuing impediment to that full restoration. It is also the case that the powers of the child have not been enhanced since, even if it did manage to achieve the goal itself, its relationship with mother has been changed.

Macmurray identifies two different ways that the relationship changes, both relating to power relations. In one, the infant submits to the mother's superior power and its need for her support, and in the other the infant challenges that power. In the terms Macmurray uses, the infant becomes a 'good' boy or a 'bad' boy.

Since these are unlikely to be global and enduring transformations of the child as opposed to tendencies which, if the circumstances are repeated often enough, may lead to long-term attitudes and character traits of the sort described by Macmurray, what sort of mechanisms might we imagine that could deliver these results?

Fairbairn's theory is based upon the idea that the original object, the external other (mother or caregiver) with whom the infant makes the first relationship, where relationship is the paramount need, does become internalised when that relationship becomes unsatisfactory to some degree. (This precedes the time when conscious disillusionment might take place.) Furthermore, that internal object gets split into three, one positive and two negative, as a consequence of early experiences of the vicissitudes of human relationship. Aspects of the infant's ego are attached to the separate parts of this split internal object, that is, the ego becomes split. This is the basic endopsychic structure, constructed from the earliest relationship, where splitting is used for defensive purposes, that is, to maintain the relationship with the carer upon whom the infant depends totally.

If we look at the process of disillusion with this model in mind, then, when the mother refuses to do something because she believes the infant can do it for themselves, there are three possible responses based upon the basic endopsychic structure. If the infant is already well looked after and confident, that is, the central self is generally well developed and the libidinal and anti-libidinal selves are considerably less well developed, then, assuming the mother's judgement is realistic and the infant is more or less ready to make the leap, the chances are that the infant will manage the task, and its central self and its powers, and its confidence in and love for mother, will be enhanced and it will grow psychically and really. This is Macmurray's positive response and Fairbairn's idea of psychic growth.

If one or other of the internalised bad objects – the libidinal or anti-libidinal objects – based upon over-exciting or over-rejecting object relations is sufficiently developed because of the way the child has been treated to date, then this is going to colour the way the object relationship is seen when mother attempts to disillusion the child. If it is the over-exciting aspect that has been developed then passivity might be expected, if the over-rejecting aspect then aggression might be expected as a response. Certainly it is likely that, unless mother is already sensitive to the levels of frustration the child can manage – and the chances are that she is not if one or other of these is already well developed – then she is likely to reinforce one or other of these internalised bad objects and thus encourage the defensive splitting of powers and the withdrawal into compensatory phantasy or acting out:

> These two modes of behaviour are ambivalent. They have the same motive and the same ultimate objective – fear for oneself in relation to the Other, and the defence of oneself from the other ... the two type forms are ... better regarded as extreme limits between which fall the actual dispositions of human beings.
>
> (Macmurray 1995b: 104)

In a statement that seems to me to encapsulate many essential aspects of the object relations approach developed by Fairbairn, Macmurray writes:

> both types of attitude – submissive and aggressive – are negative, and therefore involve unreality. They carry over the illusion of the negative

phase of withdrawal into the return to active relationship. They motivate a behaviour in relationship which is contradictory, and, therefore, self-defeating. For the inherent objective – the reality of the relationship – is the full mutuality of fellowship in a common life, in which alone the individual can realize himself as a person. But both the dispositions are egocentric, and motivate action, which is for the sake of oneself, and not for the sake of the Other; which is therefore self-interested. Such action is implicitly a refusal of mutuality, and an effort to constrain the Other to do what we want. By conforming submissively to his wishes we put him under an obligation to care for us. By aggressive behaviour we seek to make him afraid not to care for us. In both cases we are cheating. . . . If it succeeds in its intention it produces the appearance of mutuality, not the reality. It can produce, at most, a reciprocity of co-operation which simulates, even while it excludes, the personal unity which it seeks to achieve.
(105)

However, there is hope, since these responses have been learned, and:

In principle what has been learned can be unlearned; and empirical experience offers us many examples of the transformation of character, sometimes by a gradual change, sometimes by a sudden and dramatic conversion. The rhythm of withdrawal and return does not cease with the achievement of organic maturity; it is the personal form of the life of personal relationship. The transition from the withdrawal to the return repeats itself indefinitely, and each time it is made there is a possibility that it should be made successfully.
(105)

I think that this might profitably be compared with Bion's idea that the oscillation between the paranoid-schizoid and the depressive positions (P/S<->D) is endemic to human relationship and personal being. Here Macmurray offers the possibility that the sort of personal and social integration that constitutes maturity, in terms that both Fairbairn and Macmurray share, is a real possibility.

COLLIER AND FAIRBAIRN

Collier discusses Macmurray's view of reason and emotion and quotes approvingly Macmurray's view that 'reason is the capacity to behave in terms of the nature of the object' (1935: 19) and that 'in feeling emotions we feel the things to which the emotions refer. And therefore we can feel rightly or wrongly' (25).

Collier is defending the Spinozist position that emotions involve beliefs, and that is why they can be right or wrong. He then goes on to consider a psychoanalytical account of the process which, in his example, derives from Macmurray, and concerns a fear of mice: 'a psychoanalyst might say that mice are unconsciously believed to be dangerous, or more likely, unconsciously identified with something that is believed to be dangerous' (1999: 24). He follows this with a discussion of therapy:

> The practical importance of the question whether emotions are right or wrong *analogously with* beliefs or *because they involve* beliefs becomes clear when we ask how to put right irrational emotions ... the psychoanalytic account however allows us to deal with the problem in a cognitive way: by becoming aware of their unconscious identification of a mouse with a penis (or whatever), one comes to be able to order one's actions on the basis of well-founded beliefs. This is not a *purely* cognitive process: the emotions associated with the unconscious belief must be abreacted. But the becoming-conscious of the belief is what sets off the abreaction.
>
> (24)

This now becomes a matter of psychoanalytic theory as much as of philosophy and I am going to briefly look at Collier's own description of inner reality based in Freud's structural theory and compare and contrast it with Davidson's 1978 view, developed in his paper 'Paradoxes of irrationality' (1982), before returning to Fairbairn and the way he might describe such changes in the case of psychic growth.

In a discussion of Freud's structural theory and the ways in which it has been reduced to a binary head/heart or culture/nature dualism, Collier describes how Freud's three-agency structural theory has been misinterpreted by Timpanaro and Lacan (Collier 1999: 50). He goes on to describe the structural theory as he sees it: 'ego, superego and id are all psychological entities, not biological or social ones, though all these are produced in the first instance by the interaction of a biological organism with a socially structured world' (50). An essential part of Fairbairn's critique of Freud was that Freud had failed to adequately develop his conception of these structures as psychological entities, the exception being the superego. Perhaps part of the rationale for the elision of the superego in the theories Collier criticises is that the ego and the id are insufficiently developed as psychological entities and are of a different nature to the superego, which is both Klein's and Fairbairn's original model of an internal object.

In 'Paradoxes of irrationality', Davidson adopts a similar view of Freud's model to Collier. Both Davidson and Collier introduce corrections to Freud's model to sustain the claim that these are three agentive psychological entities (dynamic structures). Davidson suggests that these three agencies are all person-like entities, where a person is defined as a coherent set of beliefs and desires. While he does not actually argue about the exact number of such agencies that are necessary to define a person, he does suggest that conflict between these person-like entities, where overall control of the person's activity can move from one to the other and they can be unconscious, could adequately account for irrational thought, behaviour and emotion.

The amendments to Freud's structural model that both Collier and Davidson make, implicitly or explicitly, seem to me to transform that model to one that Fairbairn explicitly describes in the following terms: 'these internal objects should be regarded as having an organized structure, an identity of their own, an endopsychic existence and an activity as real within the inner world as those of any objects in the outer world' (King and Steiner 1991: 359). That is, the modified model of Freud's structural theory, produced by Collier and Davidson, is consonant with Fairbairn's own alternative structural model.

If we look, then, at the way in which the process of psychic change has been dealt with in Fairbairn's theory, the following description by John Padel explains in object relations terms how this takes place:

> The subsidiary ego–object relationships cannot be lacking in complexity (witness the way in which we come to know them in so many different guises in dreams); nor can they be absolutely split off from the Central Ego.... If analytical therapy works it does so by making more exchanges available between the Central Ego and its subsidiaries, which allows the whole personality more possibilities of exchange with other people in the outside world.... The Central Ego may to some extent grow by internalizing fresh relationships from the outside world, but these are likely to be shorn of their unacceptable and new aspects which get sorted and filed into the categories 'libidinal' and 'anti-libidinal'.... The growth of the Central Ego must ... take place by working over and accepting elements from the repressed structures ... the therapist shows understanding of the three-person situation presented by the patient ... to that extent the therapist is accepting what is brought but also differentiating the libidinal and anti-libidinal elements in it which have made the patient reject the whole libidinal–anti-libidinal relationship.... The repressed relationships in it, libidinal and anti-libidinal, cannot be equally bad – or equally repressed – at the same time: the libidinal is 'bad' when it threatens basic stability, which the anti-libidinal ensures; the anti-libidinal is 'bad' when it prevents or inhibits the basic enjoyment which gives meaning to living. So each of these rejected relationships will need to be looked at from the point of view of the other one, the therapist showing that the patient is putting him in the role now of seducer or disturber, now of the disapprover or inhibitor. Finally the previously

rejected libidinal–anti-libidinal relationship may be reviewed for its reality based badness or desirability.

(1991: 608–9)

The powers that were split-off and repressed into the subsidiary selves are retrieved and reintegrated into the repertoire of the now more realistic central self and the degree of splitting is reduced coincident with an increase in the capacity for objectivity of the central self and its now more realistic ideal object/ego ideal.

I have argued that there is a distinctive thread of Scottish object relations thinking that could be developed by critically comparing the work of Ian D. Suttie, Ronald Fairbairn and John Macmurray. This work probably has its roots in the Scottish Enlightenment. This perspective, which I call Personal Relations Theory, a term suggested by Fairbairn but never used, in order to distinguish it from object relations theory, which is more immediately associated with Klein than Fairbairn, could, I believe, provide the basis for a psychoanalytic theory that is consistent with critical realism.

As a final comment I would like to draw attention to the importance that Roy Bhaskar has placed upon the idea of unconditional love in his discussion of ethics where he says, 'we may yet win through to a world in which we can live in a stance of unconditional love for ourselves and each other and for every other being (or for that matter non-being) in our environment' (2000: 18). The reason this is important for me is that at the beginning of Fairbairn's development of his mature theory (in the early to middle 1940s), his 1940 paper on 'Schizoid factors in the personality' argues that the worst thing that can happen to a newborn infant short of death is to come to feel, '(a) that he is not really loved for himself as a person by his mother, and (b) that his own love for his mother is not really valued and accepted by her' (1952a: 17). This trauma is at the seat of all subsequent schizoid manifestations in the person's thought and experience. Unconditional love, on the other hand, is an essential component in the care of children and in the prevention of pathological splitting whose long-term consequences can be so devastating to our ways of thinking and being.

Chapter 9

The politics of attachment theory and personal relations theory: Fairbairn, Suttie and Bowlby

By the mid-1990s attachment theory was a well-developed and successful, scientifically based, research programme into *forms of attachment* – their distribution across the population and the variety of their forms – and, *reflective functioning* – the ability to achieve a consistent and coherent narrative about your own life, self and experiences with significant others. In *The Politics of Uncertainty* (Marris 1996) and *The Politics of Attachment* (Kroemer and Roberts 1996) these developed findings were used to look at the consequences for national politics and the development of the welfare state. The overall conclusions, that secure attachments make for a happier and more productive civil society, is beginning to be recognised in the measures that the UK government is taking to protect children, in particular, from poverty and deprivation. In 1996, in her introduction to *The Politics of Attachment*, Patricia Hewitt[1] wrote, 'The free marketeers forgot something which Adam Smith himself never forgot: that markets depend upon non-market institutions, on trust, on relationships between people and within communities, on norms of good behaviour, on social capital. Destroy that and not only do you damage efficiency, you also destroy the conditions for a good life' (Kroemer and Roberts 1996).

In regard to attachment theory I will be arguing that Bowlby was directly and fundamentally influenced by both Suttie and Fairbairn and that, as we have already seen, infant development researchers like Trevarthen (2002) and Stern (1985), whose work is often cited in support of Bowlby, were directly influenced by Macmurray whose work is also strongly related to both Suttie and Fairbairn. As such it is perhaps curious that when attachment theory is discussed in relation to national politics by psychoanalytically oriented commentators (Holmes 1996; Rustin 1996) the connection with the work of Suttie, Fairbairn and Macmurray isn't acknowledged. Perhaps worse is the failure to mention Fairbairn or Suttie in connection with the development of 'British object relations' and apparently to incorporate Bowlby into an essentially Kleinian tradition (Rustin 1996). Bowlby himself is a much better guide to his own antecedents and affiliations in his foreword to *The Origins of Love and Hate*, where he writes '[Suttie, Ferenczi, Hermann and the Balints] . . .

saw the infant as striving from the first to relate to his mother, and his future mental health as turning on the success or failure of this first relationship. Thus was the object relations version of psychoanalysis born' (Bowlby 1988a: xvi). Regarding another deep-running debate in psychoanalysis concerning the role of 'real-life events and situations', Bowlby gives a further brief account of the development of object relations psychoanalysis as he sees it:

> Influenced in varying degrees by the initiative of the Hungarian analysts, the main advocates of the object relations paradigm have been Melanie Klein and a number of native-born Britons given to independent thinking, of whom Ronald Fairbairn and Donald Winnicott are the best known. In addition to Ian Suttie, another in the group is Harry Guntrip and I count myself yet another. In North America Harry Stack Sullivan and Heinz Kohut are the best known representatives. With the notable exception of Melanie Klein, all those named have held explicitly that most differences in individual development that are of consequence to mental health are to be traced either to differences in the way children are treated by their parents or else to separations from or losses of parent-figures to whom the children have become attached.
> (Bowlby 1988a: xvi)

While Holmes in his book on attachment theory (1993) acknowledges the influences of Suttie and Fairbairn on Bowlby, in his contribution to *The Politics of Attachment* (Holmes 1996) he quotes Winnicott: 'Thus adults and infants are programmed to bond to one another for survival's sake', paraphrasing Suttie's much earlier conclusion, which is rehearsed by Bowlby in his foreword, 'Instead of an armament of instincts latent or otherwise . . . [the child] is born with a simple attachment-to-mother who is the sole source of food and protection . . . the need for mother is primarily presented to the child mind as a need for company and as a discomfort in isolation' (1988a: xvii).

The first part of this chapter shows how Fairbairn's model of mind and Bowlby's internal working models of mother might be reconciled and provides a personal relations view of both forms of attachment and reflective functioning. From there the use of object relations theory as political theory will be considered. Central to this process will be an attempt to show the relevance of Fairbairn's idea of mature dependence for personal relations theory as political theory.

SINGLE OR MULTIPLE SELVES: FAIRBAIRN AND ATTACHMENT THEORY

There is a history of tension between attachment theory and psychoanalysis even if, or perhaps because, the principal proponent of attachment theory in the late 1950s was John Bowlby, a practising analyst. Bowlby always saw attachment theory as a variety of object relations theory (Bretherton 1998: 132) and continued to practise as a psychoanalyst throughout his professional life (Steele and Steele 1998a: 96). Bowlby's ideas on attachment theory led to what one commentator (Slade 2000: 1148) has called his 'virtual expulsion' from the British Psychoanalytic Society. However, empirically based work on attachment theory by developmental psychologists, and the introduction of new concepts and tools into the research by Mary Ainsworth and Mary Main, among others, has meant that there is a rich body of scientific work concerning the early development of children and their relationship with significant others that could be of great benefit to psychoanalysis as a supplement to both its theory and practice. Recently there has been a call for a rapprochement between attachment theory and psychoanalysis (Steele and Steele 1998a). This call recognises the overlapping concerns of the two disciplines and asks for some consideration of the implications for psychoanalysis of the development of this scientific work over the past 40 plus years.

I am interested in this rapprochement because I believe that Bowlby's theory is closer to Fairbairn's 'psychology of dynamic structure' than to any other psychoanalytic theory,[2] and that this parallel is inadequately understood by some of the people discussing this rapprochement. Bowlby himself always recognised the similarity of perspective between himself and Fairbairn, as I will demonstrate later. Because Fairbairn's model is not widely understood, however, the deeper parallels have for the most part gone unnoticed. Indeed, so little known is his work in some quarters that in recent discussions Cassidy could argue that 'The object relations theorists were able to acknowledge the importance of early relationships with significant people while at the same time maintaining a place for Freud's drive theory' (Cassidy 1998: 121). This is not true of Fairbairn or Suttie, who explicitly opposed Freud's drive theory long before Bowlby formulated attachment theory. Similarly Lyons-Ruth can maintain that 'Previous object relations theorists had been deferential to the need to emphasise the distortions of intrapsychic fantasy and too respectful of the need to develop more fully the theoretical implications of a break with drive theory. While many contemplated the cliff, only Bowlby made the leap' (1998: 128). Again, not true, as Fairbairn and Suttie not only opposed drive theory but also opposed Klein's insistence upon innate aggressive and envious tendencies, as we have seen in previous chapters. The fact that Steele and Steele, in their call for rapprochement, only consider Anna Freud, Melanie Klein and Margaret Mahler is unwitting testimony to the success with which the Freudian and Kleinian wings of the British Psychoanalytic Society have kept major aspects of the Independents' legacy from a wider public, and is a further justification for attempting to draw attention to Fairbairn and Suttie's work.

When Fairbairn does get considered explicitly, and his influence on, or parallels with, Bowlby are discussed, as is the case of Inge Bretherton (1987,

1998), his full model is not used. Only a high level characterisation of Fairbairn's model is used, and it is differences at this level that are considered. Important as these may be, the appropriate level of comparison, as far as I am concerned, would involve, at the very least, a discussion of the relationship between the internal working model of mother, one of the fundamental mechanisms of attachment theory, and the multiple dynamic structures of Fairbairn which resolve themselves into three alternative selves, each based upon object relationships with mother or principal caregiver. It is only when a comparison at this level has been carried out that the deep parallels between the two approaches – Bowlby's and Fairbairn's – can be seen. It is in this light too that Main's essay on multiple models (1991) considering Bowlby's own call for multiple internal working models of mother (1973: 203–9) can begin to suggest a different model to that of a single internal working model of mother and thus be compared to Fairbairn's multiple-self model. As Main herself notes, Bowlby sees multiple internal working models of mother, some of which are unconscious, as directly parallel to the notion of an inner reality with a dynamic unconscious: 'the hypothesis of multiple models, one of which is highly influential but relatively or completely unconscious, is no more than a version, in different terms, of Freud's hypothesis of a dynamic unconscious' (Bowlby 1973: 205). In Chapter 3 I considered the work of Donald Davidson on pathologies of irrationality in which he argues for the partitioning of the mind into self-consistent person-like entities with coherent beliefs and desires in a model which is based in Freud's structural theory but, as I argue, closer in tone to Fairbairn's own structural theory.

In *A Secure Base* Bowlby points to the similarity between an internal working model of mother and an internal object and to the ways in which, with multiple internal working models of mother, the processes of splitting and internal dynamics can manifest themselves (1988b: 120n). Main's paper suggests reasons why multiple internal working models of mother or primary caregiver might arise and the way that this might provide insight into the insecure-avoidant form of attachment. Steele and Steele (1998a) argue that Klein has provided us with an account of the internal world of the insecure-disorganised infant. If we were to adopt a similar approach, it may be argued that Fairbairn's multiple-self model is a good account of the internal world of the insecure-avoidant and/or the insecure-ambivalent child. Should this sort of argument be pursued we would have a variety of different attachment patterns, each associated with a different psychoanalytic theory, and the existing and manifest contradictions between these psychoanalytic theories would militate against any coherent psychoanalytic model of attachment behaviour as a whole. I believe that there is an alternative to this and in order to illustrate it I will use the diagram of an internal working model of mother (see Figure 9.1), as developed by Inge Bretherton (1987), as part of a representation of an inner reality like that described by Fairbairn, already familiar from earlier chapters. In other words there will be three internal working models of

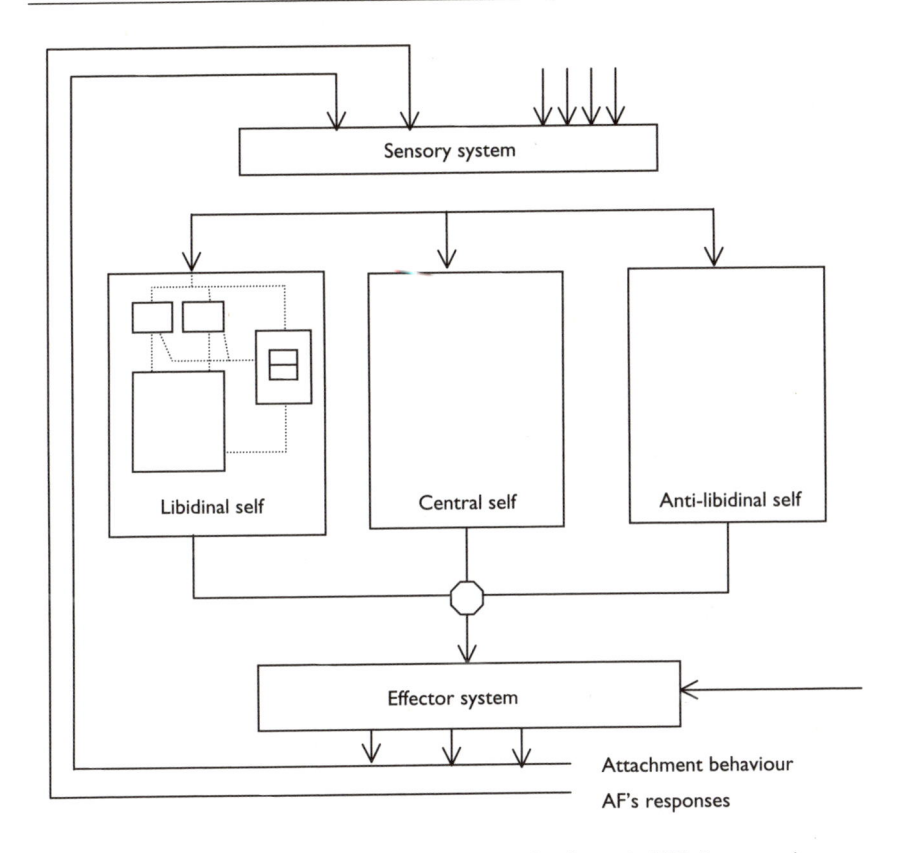

Attachment and personal relations theories 173

A diagram of multiple internal working models based on Bretherton's 1987 diagram and organised in a similar way to Fairbairn's model of inner reality divided into three separate selves each based upon a working model of mother.

Figure 9.1 Bretherton's (1987) model modified to emulate Fairbairn's model of inner reality.

mother operating in parallel and outputting their results onto the same effector space or vector.

Input via the senses goes to all the internal working models and each independently, and in parallel, decides what action to take. Each working model outputs signals to the effectors as and when it feels it is necessary. If each of these internal working models of mother was of equal power and importance but based upon significantly different expectations and responses due to previous patterns of object relationships then you might get a stream of contradictory signals to the effectors that would produce apparently contradictory behaviours. This would be more like the pattern of disorganised attachment behaviour. If the central self, based upon good object relations, was well established and the relative strength of the subsidiary selves was low, then the frequency and likelihood of contributions from the less well established subsidiary selves interfering with the central self's ability for secure attachment would be small. Insecure-avoidant and insecure-ambivalent patterns might arise if one or other of the subsidiary selves, based upon over-exciting or over-rejecting object relations, was both well established and triggered by circumstances. The suggestion here is that there is no need to dichotomise coherent and incoherent responses into single *or* multiple working model theories.

Fairbairn's theory suggests that some degree of splitting is inevitable, and the attachment behaviours that are clearly documented and explored may all be the product of a model of multiple internal working models, where, because of prior object relationships, the different internal working models are differently developed and more or less well repressed. Splitting of the self is a matter of degree, and Fairbairn's theory of development suggests that the internal working model of mother and significant caregivers laid down in early childhood can be undone later by making the split-off selves conscious and producing a central self of greater coherence by reintegrating the split-off object relationships into that central self. This also seems to me to coincide with the idea that developmental psychologists have suggested, of developing better models of others as part of the necessary development of the child. In this case, however, it isn't just a matter of developing specific skills but a process of reordering essentially primitive working models of self and (m)other into a coherent view of things. Psychic growth in this model means that the central self grows *at the expense* of the subsidiary selves. It is also worth mentioning that each of these putative selves offers a locus of control that can give rise to precisely the forms of narrative, coherent or incoherent, explored using the Adult Attachment Interview (AAI) (George *et al.* 1985).

Steele and Steele argue that there is 'no unified perspective which may be called the contemporary psychoanalytic form' (1998b: 138–9), but I am suggesting here that there is considerable overlap between Bowlby and Fairbairn, investigation of which could perhaps provide such a perspective. The following is a short list of some of the most striking parallels between the two theories:

1 against drive theory and for a relational theory
2 notion of self and other based upon the internalisation of object relations with real mother or primary caregiver
3 importance of real-world relationships and experience
4 defensive splitting of self and repression of alternative sub-selves in order to preserve good relations with primary caregiver
5 internal structure based upon multiple internal models of relations with mother or primary caregiver
6 lifelong importance of early object relations with significant others
7 development as a matter of reinterpreting and reintegrating previously rejected (primitive) object relations based sub-selves into central self.

The single central and important difference between Fairbairn and Bowlby is that Bowlby saw attachment as a biological process or mechanism while Fairbairn opposed Freud's drive theory and any other biologically based theory on the grounds that it was not a psychological and personal explanation, that is, it was not at an appropriate level for the subject matter under investigation – a person. This is a view he shared with John Macmurray who, in *Persons in Relation*, puts forward a developmental schema that might well provide useful common ground to both approaches (see Chapter 8). Of particular interest in the light of the arguments about the importance of fear in the development of the insecure-disorganised pattern (Hesse and Main 2000) is Macmurray's argument that hatred is a derived and not a fundamental aspect of human beings' motivation (1995b), which he identifies as love and fear. This has striking parallels with Fairbairn's argument concerning the derived nature of aggression and is in both cases diametrically opposed to the Kleinian account of these issues.

FAIRBAIRN AND BOWLBY

There is no doubt that attachment theory was influenced by Fairbairn's object relations theory. John Bowlby acknowledges as much in the founding text of attachment theory, his three-volume work *Attachment and Loss* (1969–80). In the second volume, *Separation*, Bowlby explicitly acknowledges the similarities between his own position and Fairbairn's. In relation to the idea that aggression is a response to frustration he writes, 'The position consistently adopted by the present writer . . . is close to Fairbairn's' (256). And in regard to the general concept that psychopathology is directly related to separation anxiety he writes that, 'Fairbairn's main theoretical position . . . is in all other respects consistent with the theory of frustrated attachment advanced here' (397), the differences being 'peripheral' to Fairbairn's main theory. In relation to Fairbairn's developmental schema of the move from infantile to mature dependency, Bowlby notes that his theoretical position of a 'secure base and strong family support' as essential to maturity 'has much in common with positions adopted by a number of other psychoanalysts, especially those who give substantial weight to the influence of the environment on development' (360). His first example is Fairbairn and he quotes approvingly Fairbairn's (1952a) argument that ' "any theory of ego-development that is to be satisfactory must be conceived in terms of relationships with objects" . . . [and] that during an individual's development "an original state of infantile dependence . . . is abandoned in favour of a state of adult or mature dependence" ' (360–1).

Attachment theory is an intra-personal theory; it is about the dependence of people upon each other and the ways that their ability to cope with the world realistically and creatively can be disturbed and damaged by a disruption of their attachments to significant others. These patterns of attachment are established during infancy but operate throughout life. There is reference to an intra-psychic component in the form of internalised working models of mother and infant but this remains underdeveloped. Fairbairn's theory also stresses the crucial importance of significant others, our object-directedness, which he calls dependence, and the importance of dependence throughout life. But, he also has a well-developed model of inner reality with internalised working models of mother and child as part of the endopsychic structure he argues is common to us all. There is a direct relationship between endopsychic structure and dependence and the move from infantile to mature dependence involves changes in endopsychic structure.

FAIRBAIRN'S PSYCHOLOGY OF DYNAMIC STRUCTURE AND ATTACHMENT BEHAVIOUR

I will be arguing that the different forms of attachment can be seen to be specific configurations and economies of a dynamic endopsychic structure. This provides a unifying overview of these phenomena within personal relations theory which are accounted for within attachment theory by an essentially biological concept of attachment and internal working models of mother or the primary caregiver.

In his late work, *A Secure Base*, Bowlby (1988b) still refers to the concept of 'working models of self and other' as the underlying mechanism and structure of inner reality that would provide an explanatory framework for the different patterns of attachment. Fairbairn's psychology of dynamic structure is founded upon the idea that the central ego and its ideal object, the anti-libidinal ego and its (rejecting) object and the libidinal ego and its (exciting) object are all based upon internalised relationships of self to mother or primary caregiver, with appropriate affective colouring. And given the primacy of the emotional in these approaches it would be truer to say they are situated emotional relationships; that, in short, splitting makes these dynamic structures into three different working models of the (emotional) relationship with mother.[3]

Attachment theory and associated research have discovered that different forms of attachment to different significant others is possible. For example, the infant might be attached differently to mother and father. As discussed in Chapter 2, within Fairbairn's theory this is both accounted for, and enabled by, a process in which the child is actively discriminating, and internalises and organises aspects of its relationships with significant others, among these three internal structures. Fairbairn describes this most clearly in his discussion of the Oedipus situation, which he sees as a social situation. Here the many and varied internalised relationships with mother, father and others are sorted and organised between the different selves (central, libidinal and anti-libidinal) and the resulting configuration can mimic the conventional Oedipus situation (1944) but is also capable of producing a variety of other configurations. In this way the gender identification of the child is related to both patterns of attachment and the child's own active choice amongst alternative ways of being that is, however, socially constrained.

In my view Fairbairn's psychology of dynamic structure is a strong candidate for a clear and coherent model of inner reality based upon 'working models of self and others'. This theory then should have something to say about the underlying mechanisms producing the observationally determined variety of patterns of attachment. In Fairbairn's view the degree to which the pristine ego (self) becomes split into central, libidinal and anti-libidinal selves is directly related to the early relationship with mother or primary caregiver. Since splitting in this case is not just a splitting of the object into acceptable (good) or over-exciting or over-rejecting (bad) aspects but also a splitting and repressing of aspects of the ego too, the degree of splitting will also reflect the degree of pathology, in the sense of powers (resources, abilities) no longer available to the infant because repressed. All structure generating splitting is a diminution of the powers available to the self (central). Splitting here is a defensive move to protect and sustain the crucial relationship with the primary caregiver.

Within the category of secure attachment one could argue that the degree of splitting, the harshness of the splitting, the degree to which the repressed libidinal and anti-libidinal selves are active, is minimal. The central self is dominant and available and determines the overall response of the child to the situation without any undue interference from the subsidiary selves. (It is worth noting here that this is close to the original activity of the pristine ego in that it is directed towards an outer object on which it is also dependent.) This process is always going to be subject to wider cultural constraints and does not represent an absolute since it is possible that in some cultures even the normal protest of a securely attached infant could be regarded as pathological and social mores could be different. The differences between a culture in which crying was (a) good for the baby, (b) bad for the baby or (c) a potential communication from the baby, would produce quite different ways of handling the situation (and the baby). So, in a non-absolutist way, secure attachment would be the equivalent of a low degree of splitting in the endopsychic structure.

What then of the other forms of attachment that have been described; can they too be represented using Fairbairn's model of endopsychic structure? I would argue that they can, since a higher degree of splitting between the different structures reflects a greater degree of inconsistency, or difference, in the ways the child has been responded to, and consequently a greater degree of autonomy to the split-off selves, so that one or other, or both, might be activated by the 'Strange Situation'.

The underlying model for the libidinal self is over-exciting relationships and the underlying model for the anti-libidinal self is over-rejecting relationships, so different sorts of behaviours would be produced by one or other of these dynamic structures becoming ascendant in response to a real-world situation. Anxiously attached infants exhibit a variety of forms of behaviour that in attachment theory are classified as avoidant or ambivalent. In avoidant attachment the infant treats mother's behaviour as a rejection and then itself mirrors this behaviour by rejecting mother upon her return. In ambivalently attached children there is an oscillation between behaviour that is similar to secure attachment and behaviour that is similar to avoidant attachment. This suggests that there are different degrees of splitting between the avoidant and the ambivalently attached child, depending upon the degree to which the anti-libidinal self has been developed through relationships with the caregiver, the avoidant child being more used to feeling rejected and consequently more likely to reject the caregiver in order to avoid the risk of being rejected again.

In the case of disorganised attachment which has also been recognised as a category of behavioural response to the 'Strange Situation', the infant doesn't respond consistently to separation but produces a variety of different responses to the situation, some of which appear bizarre. This sort of response suggests that there is no clear dominance of any one of the dynamic structures of inner reality. This could mean that the endopsychic structure is more radically split than in the other cases and that the locus of action is being transferred between the three selves to some degree or another. This can be compared to the manic phase that precedes the establishment of the basic endopsychic structure discussed earlier in the book. However, it could also be argued that the so-called bizarre behaviour of the disorganised infant is the product of the ascendancy of the libidinal (over-exciting) self and that the technique adopted is a form of exciting behaviour where one can forget one's anxiety by distracting oneself from it.

At this point it would be useful to consider Gergely and Watson's (1996) work on bio-social feedback and affect-mirroring to see if aspects of their research into emotion regulation might be used to give some clearer description of the types of relationship with the primary caregiver that could be argued to form the core of the dynamic structures of Fairbairn's psychology. It is the creation of the basic endopsychic structure through the splitting and repression of subsidiary selves that is the major mechanism of emotion regulation at this stage of development in Fairbairn's theory, following an initial period of primary identification and incorporation. In Gergely and Watson's paper the notions of mirroring (Winnicott 1971) and containing (Bion 1962) are described as 'affect-mirroring' and the process is described in such a way that particular forms of affect-mirroring can lead to both the calming of a distressed infant and an increase in that infant's sense of self-control over its own emotions. The processes of 'contingency detection' and 'maximisation' elegantly account for such results and could be posited as the processes of the core relationship internalised by the central self.

Gergely and Watson also identify two pathologies of affect-mirroring, one in which distorted or inconsistent mirroring takes place, and the other in which mirroring is absent and the caregiver responds with a display of their own emotion. In both these cases one can see how the response of the caregiver could be interpreted as a rejection or a frustration. Not being seen for who one is or being responded to by the other in an angry, depressed or a distracted way, a way that is not interactive, would create the core feeling of frustration and rejection that is characteristic of the anti-libidinal self. Linking this back to an interpretation of attachment behaviours in terms of Fairbairn's model, we could argue that good enough affect-mirroring (infantile dependence in Fairbairn's terms[4]) will encourage healthy development of the central self and that pathologies of affect-mirroring will encourage development of the anti-libidinal self. Drawing on Fairbairn's model and assuming that the absence of mirroring is more frustrating and rejecting than not being mirrored realistically, we might speculate that the difference between ambivalent and avoidant attachment could be at least partly accounted for by the degree to which absence or unpredictability of mirroring is prevalent in early experiences of the caregiver: detachment, unwillingness, or inability to mirror, signifying potential pathology in the caregiver. The Adult Attachment Interview identifies the form of attachment that the parent or potential parent of a child has from the coherence or otherwise of the narrative they are able to provide of their own lives and attachment figures. Long-term studies suggest that the unborn child's future attachment patterns at one year are predictable from the expectant parent's AAI responses, and that inter-generational transmission of attachment patterns takes place predominantly through attachment to mother despite the fact that different forms of attachment can develop in relation to different attachment figures, for example mother and father. It is in this way, it is argued, that attachment patterns, secure and insecure, are passed on from parent to child.

When it comes to the development of the libidinal self, with the notion of over-exciting relationships at its core, it is interesting to note that Gergely and Watson describe another strategy of emotion regulation called 'distraction-soothing' that would seem to be a candidate for the core relationship of the libidinal ego. When distraction-soothing is a predominant form of engagement, some form of exciting or shocking impingement upon the infant is used to try and distract them from their current concerns. This apparently works to some degree but also increases the sense of impingement on the infant by outside forces and when taken to extremes might be consistent with disorganised attachment and its associated bizarre behaviour.

I suggest that it is useful to think about the connections between such strategies for emotion regulation and the dynamic structures associated with Fairbairn's model of endopsychic structure and ways these might be used to account for different categories of attachment. In particular the strategy of distraction-soothing does seem to be a precursor to both manic ways of dealing with conflict and the development of aspects of creative activity where apparently unconnected categories or contexts are invoked and juxtaposed for the creation of new insights, humour or play. It is important to stress that under normal circumstances these different strategies of emotion regulation do not in and of themselves inevitably lead to splitting; it is a degree of repetition, predominance and severity that is likely to contribute to that. The sort of disturbed behaviour that produces disorganised attachment is severe and traumatic; a black parody of distraction-soothing as described by Gergely and Watson. Some of the phenomenology of experience within extreme sports seems to fit this model: the presence of a force that is much more powerful than yourself, that picks you up and could dash you down and kill you, but which, as in the case of the child thrown into the air and then caught, produces fear followed by a rush of good feeling at having survived such a potentially life-threatening situation.

THE POLITICS OF ATTACHMENT AND PERSONAL RELATIONS THEORY

Having demonstrated how, within personal relations theory, a psychoanalytic interpretation of both attachment and reflexive function are possible, it is now time to consider what in this light they might mean. Rustin (2001) has argued that both the Strange Situation and the Adult Attachment Interview (AAI) are powerful and legitimate scientific tools, but given the personal relations theory interpretation of them, what is it that they are measuring?

I believe that what the Strange Situation and the AAI measure is the degree of splitting in the inner reality of the person, what other strands within object relations psychoanalysis might call the degree of integration. Underlying this interpretation is the view that secure attachment is a precursor to, in the case of the infant, or an indicator of, in the case of the adult, mature dependence, or more accurately the capacity for mature dependence since, as I will argue, mature dependence is a social and communal relationship of people to each other which, in any particular social formation, may not be readily available. It should be noted that secure attachment is independent of family form, social class and national or cultural origins or location.

What then of the 'politics of attachment'? In works that address the question directly (Marris 1996; Kroemer and Roberts 1996) the clear subtext is related to 'security' and 'uncertainty'. This seems to be prompted in the main by Bowlby's characterisation of 'a secure base' as it is expanded to include all of the institutions of society. However, the UK remains a class-divided society where the gap between rich and poor is still widening. In her introduction to *The Politics of Attachment* Patricia Hewitt writes:

The neo-liberal account of individuals – rational, self-interested, atomized – also turns out to be less than the whole story. The left has always had a different, more optimistic view of human nature, knowing people to be selfless as well as selfish, altruistic as well as self-interested. The rich tradition of developmental psychology and attachment theory – particularly well developed in this country since the 1950s – brings to an impoverished political debate the fundamental insight that we are, each of us, necessarily social beings, individuals created through relationships with others. The need for attachment, for an identity rooted in belonging, is about as far from 'no such thing as society' as it is possible to be.

(Kroemer and Roberts 1996)

However, the provisions of even the most forward-looking British politicians hardly match existing social welfare measures already in place in Scandinavian countries. The reorientation of the British state towards the model of a Scandinavian state could be supported, in part at least, on the basis of arguments from attachment theory and personal relations theory, but there is little evidence that this is on the government's agenda.

That there is still room, and the need, to make such changes is at least partially supported by recent studies. Anecdotally, Philip Pullman, whose 'Dark Materials' trilogy was joint winner of the third Astrid Lindgren Memorial Award in 2005, is quoted as contrasting the Swedish and UK governments, saying that the Swedish government 'genuinely stands up for children and the world of the child, and children's rights in every sense' (Edemariam 2005). George Monbiot (2005), in a recent comparison of the performance of the Swedish and the British economies, quotes *The Economist* which refers to the UK as a 'pioneer of neoliberalism' and Sweden as 'one of the last outposts of distributionism'. He reports that by conventional measures of economic success like GDP per capita, current account balance and inflation, Sweden, pursuing 'policies designed to narrow the inequality of conditions between social classes', using measures described by *The Economist* as 'punitive taxes' and 'grandiose programs of public spending', appears to have ensured its 'economic competitiveness while ensuring that the poor obtain a higher proportion of national income'. In Sweden, according to the UN, the richest 10 per cent earn 6.2 times as much money as the poorest 10 per cent; in the UK that ratio is 13.8. However, it is in terms of human welfare that the quality of life in Sweden is most clearly superior to that in the UK: 'According to the quality of life measure published by *The Economist* . . . Sweden ranks third in the world, the UK eleventh, Sweden has the world's third highest life expectancy, the UK the twenty-ninth. In Sweden there are 74 telephone lines and 62 computers per hundred people; in the UK just 59 and 41.' Monbiot reports that the UN's Human Development Report for 2004 shows that in Sweden 6.3 per cent of the population live below the poverty line for developed nations ($11 a day) whereas in the UK the figure is 15.7 per cent. In Sweden 7.5 per cent of the population are functionally illiterate, just over a third of the UK's figure of 21.8 per cent. He adds that in the UK, according to a separate study, you are three times as likely to stay in the economic class into which you were born than you are in Sweden. In another recent study by the Geneva-based World Economic Forum (Ward 2005) the UK ranks eighth in a global league table of countries measured according to the gender gap between women and men: 'In a study of 58 countries, assessing patterns of inequality in areas including economic status, political empowerment, health and education, Britain is pipped only by the four Scandinavian countries – with Sweden at the top of the chart – and by Iceland, New Zealand and Canada.' However, these figures are skewed by Margaret Thatcher's 11-year premiership and based primarily on the UK's success in educating girls to secondary and higher education levels. When it comes to economic opportunity, 'a measure based largely on access to the labour market through maternity rights and availability of government-provided childcare', the UK is 41st behind countries including India and Colombia. This is based upon 1998 figures so does not include recent improvements to Britain's maternity pay and leave. However, the UK 'comes 21st in the category of economic participation, measuring the proportion of women in the labour force and the gender pay gap, which is still 18 percentage points adrift in Britain 30 years after the Equal Pay Act'. Britain also only ranks 28th on the scale of female health and well-being, 'a category including teenage pregnancy as well as maternal and infant mortality rates and the effectiveness of government efforts to reduce inequality'. All of which is further support for the argument that there is considerable work to be done on transforming the UK social order if we are to produce the sort of object relationships appropriate for secure attachment.

Other general aspects of the social order that have been referred to by people using attachment research as their guide are the creation of community and changes to local democratic control, addressing poverty and the differences in material wealth, and securing a more caring and sensitive society with a transformed moral base. If a society was ordered to maximise secure attachment it would be both more secure and more certain and predictable than today's society, but is this the most important lesson that we can learn from attachment theory?[5]

OBJECT RELATIONS PSYCHOANALYSIS AS POLITICAL THEORY

In a recent paper, relevant to the whole thrust of this book, Gal Gerson (2004a) has identified the analysts and thinkers I have been proposing as the main representatives of personal relations theory, as members of a coherent object relations theory, different from but related to Melanie Klein, whose underlying psychoanalytic theory can be usefully considered as a putative political theory. This group comprises Suttie and Fairbairn as well as Bowlby and Winnicott but does not include Macmurray, who is not an analyst. Gerson clearly differentiates this group as a whole from Klein on three counts, all of which will already be familiar. These are first, 'the primacy of sociability' – the fact that for these authors 'relationship is the personalities axiom' and that 'the quest for recognition . . . is constitutive of the self's structure'. Second, as has been stressed several times before, it is the child's real relationships with their real carers, without whom they could not survive, that determines the nature of inner reality. In general 'in both theory and treatment, this vision of psychoanalysis takes on a stronger social aspect, turning from the isolated patient to the environment' (774). The third difference Gerson identifies is 'The relation between integration and the environment' for which he uses Winnicott's model of the mother mirroring the infant. As has already been discussed, the whole process of the relationship between mother or primary caregiver and infant is the basis for the splitting of the pristine self and the development of the basic endopsychic structure in Fairbairn's theory. In the previous chapter I discussed how this relates to both Suttie and Winnicott by looking at the parallels between Fairbairn and Macmurray. Earlier in this chapter the process of splitting and the degree to which it was necessary was related to ways of handling the infant, amongst which would be mirroring. As we saw in Chapter 5 on creativity there are strong parallels between Winnicott's view of mirroring and the internal reality Fairbairn describes.

For a flavour of Gerson's complex argument I will quote from his abstract of the paper:

> Object relations psychoanalysis . . . perceives dependence as the natural state of all humans . . . [and] . . . perceives humans in their original state as already grouped and driven by an urge to associate. Company (rather than private property or political participation) stands out as the basic right, and all the other rights follow on it as instruments for fulfilling it. The primacy of care lends itself to the justification of distributive measures meant to bolster family cohesion and individual confidence at the expense of the open market. The theory is therefore compatible with the premises of the social-democratic welfare state.
>
> (769)

As we shall see, this last sentence is also regarded by Gerson as representing one of the theory's limitations, but first let us look at his argument, from the object relations theory shared by Bowlby, Suttie, Fairbairn and Winnicott to the political theory Gerson develops.

Gerson considers the state of nature theories of Locke, Hobbes and Rousseau in some detail in order to be able to show how this object relations view differs from these. Gerson starts from the shared starting point of infantile dependence – 'the individual in the state of nature ... [is] ... primarily sociable rather than fearful or hungry' (777), 'in the state of nature there is no well-defined [social] individual yet' (777) – to argue that this differentiates the object relations view from other 'state of nature' political theories, in particular Hobbes and Rousseau.

Gerson goes on to consider the question of individual rights, and what rights might necessarily follow from the view that 'object relations psychoanalysis perceives humans as structured by the search for company as soon as they are born' (780). Here Gerson specifically argues for a difference between this object relations theory and that of Locke:

> The psychoanalysts' state of nature is populated with infants who seek proximity to others rather than property or privacy. Biblical God plays no role here, but evolution does by driving infants to attach themselves to parents for their survival. Attachment is universal and belongs to the species survival. The *pattern* of attachment, on the other hand, is not a natural course that is identical in all cases. It is a specific process that moulds each individual into a unique personality. The formation of the adult personality belongs to society and history rather than to nature.
>
> (781)

Gerson argues that this approach reverses Locke's liberalism: 'In Locke's account, the individual is the starting point, political society forms through adults' decisions to enter the social contract, and politics is structured by rules set by this choice; in object relations, society is the premise and individuality its product' (781).

In his discussion of the development of separateness and agency from the relationship with the primary caregiver, Gerson uses Winnicottian disillusion, which was examined in relation to the parallels between Fairbairn and Macmurray in the previous chapter. Gerson argues that in the object relations theory he is discussing – what I have been referring to as personal relations theory – 'Attachment ... precedes other motivations such as material gain and explorative curiosity, sexuality and aesthetic pursuit ... to become fully human and capable of agency it is first necessary to be held by a specific other ... object relations starts with community and proceeds towards the distinct individual' (784); a view that I hope by now can be seen as totally consistent with the personal relations theory of Suttie, Fairbairn and Macmurray.

Gerson argues that when it comes to individual right, since the infant self is pristine, it is the environment within which the infant grows and develops that is crucial: 'the subject of right is the family environment that makes personal integration possible' (785). He goes on to argue that the object relations view of rights concerns 'what one has in common with others rather than what one holds back from others' (785), and that the fundamental right to relationship is not exclusive 'but declares that individual's entitlement to engage with others' (785). At the same time the object relations theory views individual integration as the end of nurture and education and so cannot advocate the merging of the individual within society: 'Differentiation is for object relations a medium for maintaining community' (786). This is where the parallels with Macmurray are most obvious and where his views might usefully supplement the developed theory.

Basing his account on Suttie's work, Gerson (781) describes the process of the infant moving out from exclusive concern with mother to fuller participation in the wider world in terms that rehearse Suttie's view 'that play, co-operation, competition and culture-interests generally are a substitute for the mutually caressing relationship of the child and mother. *By these substitutes we put the whole social environment in the place once occupied by mother*' (Suttie 1960: 16). Using Fairbairn, Winnicott and Bowlby, Gerson goes on to look at the question of social reform, welfare, law enforcement and education. He quotes Fairbairn (1952a: 85), noting that health for object relations theory is a 'matter of object relations within the social order' (2004a: 787). He notes the object relations arguments, that breaks in care, separation from attachment figures, parental neglect or abuse, poverty, war, etc. all prevent the emergence of healthy autonomous people; that 'failure in the family afflicts society' (787), as he puts it, and that stability and cohesion of the political order presupposes integrated citizens: 'The political framework that object relations theory shores up operates to secure conditions for attachment. From the individual's perspective society is charged with safeguarding his or her right to be held and cared for. From society's perspective, its own good depends on the presence of benevolent, sociable and autonomous individuals' (788).

This process of producing benevolent, sociable, autonomous individuals operates through two distinct levels of activity: one within the family structure is satisfied by a specialised caring agent – the primary caregiver who is usually the biological mother and who, in part, guarantees the appropriate attachment and development; the other, which Gerson says is argued less often in the object relations literature, is the explicit argument for particular forms of social welfare:

> Society is charged with fostering individuality, which can only emerge from a supporting environment.... The fluctuating and complex modern economy does not constitute a caring environment; unless balanced by other institutions, it invades the home to make parents anxious and undermine their capacity to hold their children. The market therefore needs the welfare apparatus to produce the agents who are capable of playing in the market. This involves active defence of the family through social measures such as allowances and professional services.
> (788)

This echoes the conclusions of people familiar with attachment theory and the necessary consequences for the social order of taking attachment theory seriously (Marris 1996; Kroemer and Roberts 1996). It seems to me that it is not just a matter of defending families from the worst predations of an unbridled market economy but of changing the basis of the society towards more decentralised power structures into locally based, participatory and communal forms.

In his conclusion Gerson summarises the argument he has put forward based upon his interpretation of the object relations view he has identified:

> Object relations perceives dependence as the fundamental condition all humans share. The sense of separation that classical liberalism ascribes to individuals is a product of early attention. In adulthood, separate individuality allows for communication with others through relation to the external world of material things, knowledge and culture. Accordingly, the right to relate and be cared for is the first right. Respect for separate individuality does not override the right to engage with others, but is instead an extension of that right. Politics focuses on maintaining the social unit where care is best given, a unit that the theory identifies with the family. Accordingly, the household is both supported by the broader society and exposed to its gaze through experts and officials. As the right to engage with others does not involve a notion of exclusive privacy in the way that Locke's concept of property does, there should be no objection to government's interest in the home. This active interest is meant, first, to protect the primary individual right, and second, to ensure that society's constituents would be autonomous agents capable of engagement with each other. No aspect of human life is seen as presocial, and no stage in life is seen as a break from the quest for company. Rather than being split into the private/natural and social/political spheres, the world as seen by object relations theory is concentric, extending from the infant's first cry to the broadest achievements and failures of civilization. A single set of principles pervades these expanding circles: Human individuality is driven and formed by relationships. Society and sociability are the premise, autonomous agency the end; it is the end, however, because in adult life individual autonomy is the means of healthy communication that is not aimed at dominating, ignoring, or incorporating others.
>
> (790)

Despite recognising and acknowledging in a number of places within the paper that significant contributions to this object relations theory pre-date the development of the welfare state in Britain after the Second World War, one criticism of the theory put forward by Gerson is that it *comes out of and reflects* 'The type of family and gender differentiation ... and the level of economic and social complexity ... the relatively consensual industrial society of the 1950s with its largely male workforce occupying steady jobs and entrusting many aspects of its life to government agencies and their scientific and social-scientific experts' (791). His warning is that anyone seeking to develop this theory 'should be aware of the extent to which the school's principles reflect the context in which they first appeared' (792).

Suttie's work was first published in the 1920s and 1930s, Fairbairn's mature theory was published initially during the Second World War, so it could be argued that rather than reflecting the development of the welfare state they were one of the many contributing factors towards its development. The later collection and publication of work by Suttie, Fairbairn, Bowlby and Macmurray in the 1950s can be seen as the further development of work completed before the welfare state was in existence and certainly before the 1950s as argued above. It may well be that this work was published because it was consistent with the development of the welfare state; but that would be a different argument.

There are two other main criticisms that Gerson develops, both of which depend upon his original argument. One relates to gender and family and the other to what he describes as an 'inability to perceive sharp disagreement as a normal social circumstance' (791). Regarding the second criticism, which Gerson expands upon as follows: 'Although it attempts to cut through assumptions of consensus back to a psychological core that precedes any context, object relations writes off hostility between social segments, competing value systems and alternative family structures as pathological symptoms' (791), I do not recognise Suttie, Fairbairn or Macmurray in this description. There is an existential aspect to both Fairbairn and Macmurray that sees the social order in which the infants find themselves as contingent. Suttie, who was fiercely critical of Freud and Adler for treating socially conditioned aspects of personality as if they were immutable instincts, argued that a matriarchal society would totally change the Oedipus situation since it would remove the need to give up mother and repress the tie to her that we all experience and value at some level. Fairbairn saw the Oedipus situation as a social situation that we constitute for ourselves based upon the prior development of the basic endopsychic structure, and influenced by our real experience of parents and others within the family. Macmurray was engaged in trying to think about and develop alternative communal forms of social organisation, and the logic of Fairbairn's concept of mature dependence is that even a liberal market-based economy, where attachment needs are protected, is a long way short of a society in which mature dependence would be the product: what Gerson calls 'benevolent, sociable and autonomous' individuals. If we consider attachment research and make a simplistic assumption that secure attachment is the same as mature dependence then we only have about 60 per cent securely attached people anyway.

The need for attachment, for care, is not dependent upon the form of the social order through which that care is provided. As has been argued, the provision of care during infancy is paramount but the exact type of family grouping is contingent. It may be that Bowlby and Winnicott were referring directly to the nuclear family they were experiencing in their daily life but that doesn't mean that their theory was restricted to that family form. The conditions for supporting infantile dependence and encouraging autonomy would remain constant across all social formations.

This takes us on to the objection to the theory on gender grounds. This follows from the assumption that this theory simply reflects the society of its supposed first appearance, something I have just argued against in relation to family form. Similarly I don't think there is anything in the need for some specialised mothering that requires women to revert to some old-fashioned, retrograde, subservient position if they want to be mothers. It depends upon the arrangements society makes to achieve its goal of specialised mothering. There are possibilities that the process of child bearing might be uncoupled from women and given to men or machines but this is for the most part science fiction and the reality is that, in general, the physical reproduction of the species is going to have to be carried out by women. But not women alone, or excluded, or underprivileged, as is sometimes the case today. One can easily imagine a society where the role of mother was a highly valued and responsible position that was economically rewarded. Less dramatically, the conditions surrounding birth and early care could be made considerably easier for everyone by allowing more maternity and paternity leave, better maternity pay, more flexibility in working hours, more work-based crèches, etc. One of Gerson's arguments which he expands upon in a paper criticising Winnicott (2004b) is that the 'specialist mother' is a second-class citizen because dependent upon another for economic support. This I think takes us into a consideration of Fairbairn's idea of mature dependence. Mature dependence as conceived by Fairbairn seems to me to have within it a radical concept of the social order in which equality, fraternity and reciprocity are of fundamental importance. This is what stops his view from simply reflecting 1950s Britain, as Gerson argues.

Mature dependence is Fairbairn's equivalent of the Freudian 'genital character'. But it is important to remind ourselves of the discussion in Chapter 3, that we are concerned primarily with self-enlargement here, to forms of social organisation consistent with the development of all of our powers to their fullest extent under our own direction. According to Fairbairn, mature dependence is characterised by the fact that all external objects are treated as differentiated others. There is an absence of the projection and introjection of internal objects. For Fairbairn this is an ideal and perhaps unattainable limit where the unconscious selves have disappeared, where everything can be thought about consciously and rationally. Here the internal object would be potentially conscious and represent a realistic reflection of outer reality: the ideal object would have become a realistic object. Relations would be with real external objects. If infantile dependence is the state of nature from which a political theory might be developed out of personal relations theory then what is the function of mature dependence in Fairbairn's theory and how might it add to this model?

First of all it would be critical of the elision between benevolent, secure and autonomous agents and abstract economic individuals. We never escape dependence; we are social through and through, however much we delude ourselves that we are totally independent. So mature dependence, if translated into economic terms, would need to find ways of making the specialised mother economically equivalent to the other potentially maturely dependent agents within society. This in itself already points towards a form of society we are unfamiliar with. If we look at mature dependence as an ideal end of a process that starts with infantile dependence and passes through the transitional stages to a maturity that is no longer characterised by splitting, but by a spirit of giving and a recognition of others uncontaminated by projection and introjection, then we have an ideal where liberty, equality and fraternity are constitutive of relationships in general. This image is immediately and obviously critical of the divided societies we live in and points towards the gulf between where we are and where we might be if we were to realise the path of development that personal relations theory describes. Secure attachments are a necessary and foundational aspect of mature dependency but are not sufficient to guarantee it. Achieving mature dependence by reducing splitting and promoting integration, within and amongst people, is a challenge to our imagination and resolve, and will not be possible without transforming the social order.

Notes

Introduction

1 Winnicott says this was first put forward at a 'Discussion at a Scientific Meeting of the British Psychoanalytic Society circa 1940' (1965: 39n).
2 At the inaugural Neuro-psychoanalysis Conference (London, 2000) Mark Solms reinforced the idea that Fairbairn was important, suggesting that it was he that 'lit the spark' for a neo-Freudian object relations psychoanalysis (personal communication).

1 Why Fairbairn?

1 Stephen Mitchell died unexpectedly at the tragically early age of 54 in December 2000. His major work, written jointly with Jay Greenberg, was responsible for bringing Fairbairn's work to the attention of many who might otherwise have forgotten him. He will be sadly missed.
2 Ellinor Fairbairn Birtles, personal communication.
3 See Young (1998), 'What is psychoanalytic studies?': 'Fairbairn believed that if you sorted out your psychoanalytic difficulties, you would have *no internal objects*, while Klein believed that the unconscious and perpetual conjuring with internal objects was the *sine qua non* of having a mind and of thinking. What are we to make of this apparent utter incompatibility?' I hope that this book will help answer that question.
4 During the early 1940s, which is when Fairbairn developed his own mature theory of object relations, there was a potentially catastrophic division within the British Psychoanalytic Society between the (Anna) Freudians and the Kleinians that led to what have been dubbed the 'controversial discussions'. These were a series of arguments about some fundamental concepts like phantasy and the status of child analysis. This was resolved by allowing for three distinctive threads to training within the Society – (contemporary) Freudian, Independent and Kleinian – which still exist today. This could be seen as a struggle for power, after the death of Freud, within the Society and within psychoanalysis itself, given that Freud and his daughter had come to Britain fleeing the Nazis. From the point of view of the tripartite model of the self that Fairbairn developed during the same period one could say that each of these strands was more concerned with the problems of one of the selves he identified: the contemporary Freudians with the central self and its ego-ideal, the Kleinians with the anti-libidinal self and aggressive and destructive phantasies, and the Independent group with the libidinal and creative possibilities of the libidinal self, but this would be 'wild analysis' (see King and Steiner 1991).

2 Fairbairn's model of mind

1 The emphasis on self-reflexive functioning and response to others capable of similar reflexivity links to both Bion's concept of the internalisation of maternal containment and metabolising and ultimately with self-analysis, and with the 'theory of mind' school and the digestive function of dreaming.
2 Margaret Mahler noted this ambi-tendency in the phase she termed 'rapprochement' but she did not elaborate the various specific anxieties and their manifestations. Similarly attachment theory notes the defensive responses of insecurely attached infants but not the underlying anxieties.

3 Fairbairn's theory and some philosophical interpretations of Freud

1 I would like to thank Mike Rustin for drawing my attention to the papers by Davidson and Rorty.

4 Internal objects and inner reality: Fairbairn and Klein

1 Quoting M. Klein, 'The emotional life and ego development of the infant with special reference to the depressive position' (1944), in P. King and R. Steiner (eds) (1991) *The Freud–Klein Controversies 1941–45*, London: Routledge.
2 'The (manifest) dream to which I refer consisted in a brief scene in which the dreamer saw the figure of herself being viciously attacked by a well-known actress in a venerable building which had belonged to her family for generations. Her husband was looking on; but he seemed quite helpless and quite incapable of protecting her. After delivering the attack the actress turned away and resumed playing a stage part, which, as seemed to be implied, she had momentarily set aside in order to deliver the attack by way of interlude. The dreamer then found herself gazing at the figure of herself lying bleeding on the floor; but, as she gazed, she noticed that this figure turned for an instant into that of a man. Thereafter the figure alternated between herself and this man until eventually she awoke in a state of acute anxiety' (Fairbairn 1952a: 95).

5 Fairbairn's theory of art in the light of his mature model of mind

1 John Carey, in his book *What Good Are the Arts*, published too recently to be included in these discussions, argues that 'A work of art is anything that anyone has ever considered a work of art, although it may be a work of art only for that one person', a view that is regarded as 'controversial' (Crompton 2005). I believe that this view is consistent with the view that Fairbairn is developing here. (See 'Do the arts matter' (2005); 'Wiping away the snobbish drips of the art world' (2005)).
2 I would like to thank both Professor Joan Raphael-Leff, for drawing Rosen's work to my attention, and Rosen's wife, Ruth, for allowing me access to some of his papers.
3 I have retained Kris's spelling of the term 'fantasy' throughout the following section for reasons of consistency.

6 The preconscious and psychic change in Fairbairn's model of mind

1 See Cavell (1998) for the importance of the triangular relationship. See also Wright's comments on the 'third' (1991), Britton's comments on the 'third position' (1989) and Ogden (1994a).

8 Fairbairn and Macmurray: psychoanalytic studies and critical realism

1 I would like to acknowledge that many of the parallels I see between Fairbairn and Macmurray were originally broached by Ellinor Fairbairn Birtles in conversations I had with her concerning her father's work and to thank her for her generosity in this regard. I can find no references to Macmurray's work in Fairbairn's work or vice versa. However, the parallels between the view of objects developed in Macmurray's 'Interpreting the Universe' and that developed in Fairbairn's book, published in 1952, are I hope demonstrable.
2 In a later section I will argue that the relationship between Macmurray and Fairbairn can be understood as that between phase one and phase two of this scheme.
3 In general I have tried to use gender-neutral constructions but where I am quoting I have retained whatever gender exists in the original. However, Fairbairn, in his 1952 book *Psychoanalytic Studies of the Personality*, was aware of the problem, as the following quote from p. 123 illustrates: 'in the preceding account the personal pronoun employed to indicate the child has been consistently masculine. This must not be taken to imply that the account applies only to the boy. It applies equally to the girl; and the masculine pronoun has been used only because the advantages of a personal pronoun of some kind appear to outweigh those of the impersonal pronoun, however non-committal this may be.'
4 This account of the origins of making a distinction between truth and falsity in early infancy could be usefully compared with the fundamental distinction between the transitive and the intransitive dimensions in critical realism, which has similarities to the distinction between epistemology and ontology. www.raggedclaws.com/criticalrealism/glossary/transitive_and_intransitive_dimension.html (last accessed 10 January 2006).

9 The politics of attachment theory and personal relations theory: Fairbairn, Suttie and Bowlby

1 Secretary of State for Health after the Cabinet reshuffle in 5 May 2005, when the UK Labour Party won an historic third term in office.
2 This close link between Bowlby's and Fairbairn's theories was noted by Greenberg and Mitchell in their now classic *Object Relations and Psychoanalytic Theory*.
3 If mature dependence was achieved this would be a situation in which the three different working models of mother would have become integrated into one realistic working model of mother or remain as three differently inflected but potentially conscious, as opposed to predominantly unconscious, working models of mother. That is they would be capable of being altered in relation to the current external reality being faced by the person (see Chapter 6).
4 This can also be seen as 'recognition' in Macmurray's terms: 'we may say that the first knowledge is the recognition of the Other as the person or agent in whom we live and move and have our being' (1956: 77).
5 In a collection of essays entitled *The New Egalitarianism*, published too recently to be included in this discussion, Patrick Diamond, 'a Downing Street adviser', John Edwards, 'a former US presidential candidate', and Anthony Giddens, 'the originator of the Third Way', argue strongly for the need to reduce inequality in the UK by taking effective redistributive measures: 'Britain is still a long way from significantly reducing inequalities of opportunity' (Hall 2005; Wintour 2005).

Bibliography

Ainsworth, M.D.S., Blehar, M.C., Waters, E., and Wall, S. (1978) *Patterns of Attachment: A Psychological Study of the Strange Situation*, Hillsdale, NJ: Erlbaum.
Balint, M. (1958) 'The three areas of the mind – theoretical considerations', *International Journal of Psychoanalysis*, 39: 328–40.
Bateson, G. (1973) *Steps to an Ecology of Mind*, London: Paladin.
Bevir, M., and O'Brien, D. (1999) 'The philosophy of John Macmurray', University of Newcastle. Online. Available HTTP: <http://www.psa.ac.uk/cps/1999/bevir2.pdf> (accessed 1999).
Bhaskar, R. (1978) *A Realist Theory of Science*, Hassocks, Sussex: Harvester Press.
Bhaskar, R. (1989) *The Possibility of Naturalism: A Philosophical Critique of the Contemporary Human Sciences*. London: Harvester Wheatsheaf.
Bhaskar, R. (2000) 'Introducing transcendental dialectical critical realism', *Alethia*, 3 (1): 18.
Bion, W.R. (1962) 'A theory of thinking', *International Journal of Psycho-Analysis*, 43: 306–10.
Bion, W.R. (1963) *Elements in Psycho-Analysis*, London: Maresfield Reprints.
Bowlby, J. (1969–1980) *Attachment and Loss*, 3 vols, London: Hogarth Press.
Bowlby, J. (1973) *Separation: Anxiety and Anger*, vol. II of *Attachment and Loss*, London: Hogarth Press.
Bowlby, J. (1988a) 'Foreword' to I.D. Suttie, *Origins of Love and Hate*, London: Free Association Books.
Bowlby, J. (1988b) *A Secure Base*, London: Routledge.
Brenner, C. (1996) '*Beyond the Ego and the Id* revisited'. Online. Available HTTP: http://users.rcn.com/brill/behond.html (accessed 1996).
Bretherton, I. (1987) 'New perspectives on attachment relations: security, communication and internal working models', in J. Osofsky (ed.), *Handbook of Infant Development*, New York: Wiley.
Bretherton, I. (1998) 'Attachment and psychoanalysis: a reunion in progress', *Social Development*, 7 (1): 132–6.
Britton, R. (1989) 'The missing link', in R. Britton, M. Feldman, E. O'Shaughnessy, and H. Segal (eds), *The Oedipus Complex To-day*, London: Karnac.
Carveth, D. (1996) 'Review essay', *Canadian Journal of Psychoanalysis*, 4 (2): 343–53.
Cassidy, J. (1998) 'Attachment and object relations theories and the concept of independent behavioural systems', *Social Development*, 7 (1): 120–6.

Cavell, M. (1998) 'Triangulation, one's own mind and objectivity', *International Journal of Psychoanalysis*, 79: 449–67.

Celani, D.P. (1998) 'Structural sources of resistance in battered women: a Fairbairnian analysis', in N.J. Skolnick and D.E. Scharff (eds) (1998) *Fairbairn, Then and Now*, London: The Analytic Press.

Civin, M., and Lombardi, K. (1990) 'The preconscious and potential space', *Psychoanalytical Review*, 77: 573–85.

Clarke, G. (1994) 'Notes towards an object relations view of cinema', *Free Associations*, 4 (3): 369–90.

Clarke, G. (1995) 'Dynamic structure, psychic growth and dramatic narrative', unpublished MA dissertation, University of East London: Tavistock Centre.

Clarke, G. (2003a) '*L.A. Confidential*: object relations and psychic growth', *British Journal of Psychotherapy* 19 (3): 379–85.

Clarke, G. (2003b) '*The Piano Teacher*: object relations and psychic disintegration', paper presented at the Culture and the Unconscious Conference, London, July 2003.

Clarke, G. (2005) 'Personal relations theory: Suttie, Fairbairn, Macmurray and Sutherland', in J.S. Scharff and D.E. Scharff (eds), *The Legacy of Fairbairn and Sutherland*, London: Routledge.

Collier, A. (1994) *Critical Realism*, London: Verso.

Collier, A. (1999) *Being and Worth*, London: Routledge.

Costello, J. E. (2002) *John Macmurray: A Biography*, London: Floris Books.

Crompton, S. (2005) 'The arts column', *The Telegraph*, 29 May. Online. Available HTTP: <http://www.arts.telegraph.co.uk/arts> (accessed 29 May 2005).

Damasio, A. (2000) *The Feeling of What Happens*, London: Heinemann.

Damasio, A. (2003) *Looking for Spinoza: Joy, Sorrow and the Feeling of Pain*, London: Harcourt.

Davidson, D. (1982) 'Paradoxes of irrationality', in R. Wollheim, and J. Hopkins (eds), *Philosophical Essays on Freud*, Cambridge, MA: Cambridge University Press.

'Do the arts matter' (2005) *The Observer*. Online. Available HTTP: <http://www.guardian.co.uk> (accessed 8 May 2005).

Edemariam, E. (2005) 'Diary', *The Guardian Review*, 14 May, 7.

Ehrenzweig, A. (1967) *The Hidden Order of Art*, London: Weidenfeld and Nicolson.

Fairbairn Birtles, E. (1997) 'From a Scottish perspective: Fairbairn's philosophical contribution', unpublished paper.

Fairbairn, W.R.D. (1936) 'The effect of a king's death upon patients under analysis', in Fairbairn (1952a) *Psychoanalytic Studies of the Personality*, London: Routledge.

Fairbairn, W.R.D. (1938a) 'Prolegomena to a psychology of art', *British Journal of Psychology*, 28: 288–303.

Fairbairn, W.R.D. (1938b) 'The ultimate basis of aesthetic experience', *British Journal of Psychology*, 29: 167–81.

Fairbairn, W.R.D. (1939) 'Is aggression an irreducible factor', in D.E. Scharff and E. Fairbairn Birtles (eds) (1994) *From Instinct to Self*, 2 vols, London: Jason Aronson.

Fairbairn, W.R.D. (1940) 'Schizoid factors in the personality', in his (1952a) *Psychoanalytic Studies of the Personality*, London: Routledge.

Fairbairn, W.R.D. (1941) 'A revised psychopathology of the psychoses and psychoneuroses', in his (1952a) *Psychoanalytic Studies of the Personality*, London: Routledge.

Fairbairn, W.R.D. (1943) 'The repression and return of bad objects', in his (1952a) *Psychoanalytic Studies of the Personality*, London: Routledge.

Fairbairn, W.R.D. (1944) 'Endopsychic structure considered in terms of object-relationships', in Fairbairn (1952a) *Psychoanalytic Studies of the Personality*, London: Routledge.

Fairbairn, W.R.D. (1950) 'Critical notice: on not being able to paint, Joanna Field (Marion Milner)', *British Journal of Medical Psychology*, 24: 69–72.

Fairbairn, W.R.D. (1952a) *Psychoanalytic Studies of the Personality*, London: Routledge.

Fairbairn, W.R.D. (1952b) 'Theoretical and experimental aspects of psychoanalysis', *British Journal of Medical Psychology*, 25: 122–7.

Fairbairn, W.R.D. (1953a) 'Psychoanalysis and art', in D. Scharff and E. Fairbairn Birtles (eds) (1994) *From Instinct to Self*, 2 vols, London: Jason Aronson, vol. II, 423–32.

Fairbairn, W.R.D. (1953b) 'Critical notice: psychoanalytic explorations in art', *British Journal of Medical Psychology*, 26: 164–9.

Fairbairn, W.R.D. (1954) 'Observations on the nature of hysterical states', *British Journal of Medical Psychology*, 27 (3): 105–25.

Fairbairn, W.R.D. (1956a) 'A critical evaluation of certain basic psycho-analytic conceptions', *British Journal for the Philosophy of Science*, 7 (25): 49–60.

Fairbairn, W.R.D. (1956b) 'Notes and comments: criticism of Fairbairn's generalisation about object relations', *British Journal for the Philosophy of Science*, 7 (28): 323–38.

Fairbairn, W.R.D. (1958) 'On the nature and aims of psychoanalytical treatment', *International Journal of Psychoanalysis*, 39 (5): 374–85.

Fairbairn, W.R.D. (1963) 'Synopsis of an object-relations theory of the personality', *International Journal of Psychoanalysis*, 44: 224–5.

Ferenczi, S. (1928) 'The elasticity of psycho-analytical technique', in his (1955) *Final Contributions to the Problems and Methods of Psycho-analysis*, London: Karnac Books.

Ferguson, D., and Dower, N. (eds) (2002) *John Macmurray: Critical Perspectives*, London: Peter Lang.

Freud, S. (1895) 'Project for a scientific psychology', in *Standard Edition* (SE), I: 281–397

Freud, S. (1914) 'On narcissism', in *Standard Edition* (SE), 14: 67–102.

Freud, S. (1915) 'The unconscious', in *Standard Edition* (SE), 14: 159–215.

Freud, S. (1917) 'A metapsychological supplement to the theory of dreams', in *Standard Edition* (SE), 14: 217–35.

Freud, S. (1921) 'Group psychology and the analysis of the ego', in *Standard Edition* (SE), 18: 65–144.

Freud, S. (1923) 'The Ego and the Id', *Standard Edition* (SE), 19: 3–66.

Freud, S. (1930) 'Civilization and its discontents', in *Standard Edition* (SE) 21: 57–146.

Freud, S. (1953–74) *The Standard Edition of the Complete Psychological Works of Sigmund Freud*, James Strachey (ed.), London : Hogarth Press and the Institute of Psycho-Analysis.

George, C., Kaplan, N., and Main, M. (1985) *The Berkeley Adult Attachment Interview*, unpublished manuscript, Department of Psychology, University of California at Berkeley.

Gergely, G., and Watson, J. (1996) 'The social biofeedback theory of parental affect-mirroring', *International Journal of Psycho-Analysis*, 77: 1181–212.
Gerson, G. (2004a) 'Object relations psychoanalysis as political theory', *Political Psychology*, 25 (5): 769–94.
Gerson, G. (2004b) 'Winnicott, participation and gender', *Feminism and Psychology*, 14: 561–81.
Greenberg, J. (1991) *Oedipus and Beyond*, London: Harvard University Press.
Greenberg, J.R., and Mitchell, S.A. (1983) *Object Relations in Psychoanalytic Theory*, London: Harvard University Press.
Grotstein, J.S. (1994a) 'Editor's Introduction' (with Donald B. Rinsley), in J.S. Grotstein and D.B. Rinsley (eds) *Fairbairn and the Origins of Object Relations*, London: Free Association Books.
Grotstein, J.S. (1994b) 'Endopsychic structure and the cartography of the internal world: six endopsychic characters in search of an author', in J.S. Grotstein and D.B. Rinsley (eds) *Fairbairn and the Origins of Object Relations*, London: Free Association Books.
Grotstein, J.S. (1994c) 'Notes on Fairbairn's metapsychology', in J.S. Grotstein and D.B. Rinsley (eds) *Fairbairn and the Origins of Object Relations*, London: Free Association Books.
Grotstein, J.S. (1998) 'A comparison of Fairbairn's endopsychic structure and Klein's internal world', in N.J. Skolnick and D.E. Scharff (eds) (1998) *Fairbairn, Then and Now*, London: The Analytic Press.
Grotstein, J.S., and Rinsley, D.B. (eds) (1994) *Fairbairn and the Origins of Object Relations*, London: Free Association Books.
Guntrip, H. (1961) *Personality Structure and Human Interaction: The Developing Synthesis of Psychodynamic Theory*, London: Hogarth Press.
Guntrip, H. (1968) *Schizoid Phenomena, Object-Relations and the Self*, London: Hogarth Press.
Hall, B. (2005) 'Blair adviser urges removing NI ceiling', *The Financial Times*, 25 May. Online. Available HTTP: <http://news.FT.com> (accessed 25 May 2005).
Harrow, A. (1998) 'The Scottish connection – Suttie – Fairbairn – Sutherland: the quiet revolution', in N.J. Skolnick and D.E. Scharff (eds) (1998) *Fairbairn Then and Now*, London: The Analytic Press.
Hesse, E., and Main, M. (2000) 'Disorganised infant, child and adult attachment: collapse in behavioural and attentional strategies', *Journal of the American Psychoanalytic Association*, 48 (4): 1097–128.
Hinshelwood, R.D. (1991) *A Dictionary of Kleinian Thought*, London: Free Association Books.
Hogg, J. (1992) *Confessions of a Justified Sinner*, London: Everyman's Library.
Holmes, J. (1993) *John Bowlby and Attachment Theory*, London: Routledge.
Holmes, J. (1996) 'Attachment theory: a secure base for policy?' in S. Kroemer and J. Roberts (eds) *The Politics of Attachment*, London: Free Association Books.
Hughes, J.M. (1989) *Reshaping the Psychoanalytic Domain*, London: University of California Press.
Kernberg, O.F. (1980) *Internal World and External Reality*, New York: Jason Aronson.
King, P., and Steiner, R. (eds) (1991) *The Freud–Klein Controversies 1941–1945*, London: Routledge.
Kirkwood, C. (2005) 'The persons-in-relation perspective: sources and synthesis',

in J.S. Scharff and D.E. Scharff (eds), *The Legacy of Fairbairn and Sutherland*, London: Routledge.
Klein, M. (1935) 'A contribution to the psychogenesis of manic depressive states', in Klein (1975) *Love, Guilt, and Reparation*, London: Hogarth Press.
Kohut, H. (1971) *The Analysis of the Self*, New York: International Universities Press.
Kris, E. (1950) 'On preconscious mental processes', *Psychoanalytic Quarterly* 19: 540–60.
Kris, E. (1953), *Psychoanalytic Explorations in Art*, London: G. Allen & Unwin.
Kroemer, S., and Roberts, J. (eds) (1996) *The Politics of Attachment*, London: Free Association Books.
Kuhn, T.S. (1964) *The Structure of Scientific Revolutions*, Chicago: University of Chicago Press.
Laborit, H. (1977) *Decoding the Human Message*, London: Allison and Busby.
Lacan, J. (1988) *The Seminar of Jacques Lacan, Book II*, London: W.W. Norton.
Laing, R.D. (1964) *Sanity, Madness and the Family*, London: Tavistock.
Laing, R.D. (1965) *The Divided Self: An Existential Study in Sanity and Madness*, Harmondsworth: Penguin.
Laing, R.D. (1967) *The Politics of Experience, and, The Bird of Paradise*, London: Penguin.
Likierman, M. (1995) 'Loss of the loved object: tragic and moral motifs in Melanie Klein's concept of the depressive position', *British Journal of Psychotherapy*, 12 (2): 147–59.
Lyons-Ruth, K. (1998) 'Lexicons, eyes and videotapes', *Social Development*, 7 (1): 128.
Macmurray, J. (1933) *Interpreting the Universe*, London: Humanities Press.
Macmurray, J. (1935) *Reason and Emotion*, London: Faber and Faber.
Macmurray, J. (1939) *Boundaries of Science*, London: Faber and Faber.
Macmurray, J. (1995a) *The Self as Agent*, vol. I of *The Form of the Personal*, London: Faber and Faber.
Macmurray, J. (1995b) *Persons in Relation*, vol. II of *The Form of the Personal*, London: Faber and Faber (first published 1961).
Macmurray, J. (1997) *Conditions of Freedom*, London: Humanities Press.
Main, M. (1991) 'Metacognitive knowledge, metacognitive modelling, and singular (coherent) vs multiple (incoherent) model of attachment: findings and directions', in C.M. Parkes, J. Stevenson-Hinde and P. Marris (eds), *Attachment Across the Life Cycle*, London: Routledge.
Marcuse, H. (1969) *Eros and Civilisation*, London: Sphere Books.
Marris, P. (1996) *The Politics of Uncertainty*, London: Routledge.
Milner, M. (1987) *The Suppressed Madness of Sane Men*, London: Routledge.
Mitchell, S.A. (1994) 'The origin and nature of the object in the theories of Klein and Fairbairn', in J.S. Grotstein and D.B. Rinsley (eds) (1994) *Fairbairn and the Origins of Object Relations*, London: Free Association Books.
Mitchell, S.A., and Greenberg, J.R. (1983) *Object-Relations in Psychoanalytic Theory*, London: Harvard University Press.
Monbiot, G. (2005) 'Sweden proves the neoliberals wrong about how to slash poverty', *The Guardian*, 11 January.
Money-Kyrle, R.E. (1955) 'Psycho-analysis and ethics', in M. Klein, P. Heimann, and R.E. Money-Kyrle (eds), *New Directions in Psycho-Analysis: The Significance of Infant Conflict in the Pattern of Adult Behaviour*, London: Karnac.

Ogden, T. (1994a) 'The analytic third: working with intersubjective clinical facts', *International Journal of Psychoanalysis*, 75: 3–20.

Ogden, T. (1994b) 'The concept of internal object relations', in J.S. Grotstein and D.B. Rinsley (eds) *Fairbairn and the Origins of Object Relations*, London: Free Association Books.

Padel, J. (1985) 'Ego in current thinking', *International Review of Psycho-Analysis*, 12: 273–83.

Padel, J. (1991) 'Fairbairn's thoughts on the relationship of inner and outer worlds', *Free Associations*, 2, Part 4 (24): 589–617.

Padel, J. (1994) ' "Narcissism" in Fairbairn's theory of personality structure', in J.S. Grotstein and D.B. Rinsley (eds), *Fairbairn and the Origins of Object Relations*, London: Free Association Books.

Phillips, A. (2005) *Going Sane*, London: Hamish Hamilton.

Povey, D. (ed.) (2005) *Crime in England and Wales 2003/2004: Supplementary Volume 1: Homicide and Gun Crime*, London: Home Office Statistical Bulletin.

Rey, R.J. (2005) 'From Fairbairn to a new systematisation of psychopathology: the intuitive position and the alienated and oscillating structures', in J.S. Scharff and D.E. Scharff (eds), *The Legacy of Fairbairn and Sutherland*, London: Routledge.

Rickman, J. (1950) 'The factor of number in individual and group dynamics', *Journal of Mental Science*, 96: 770–3; also in Rickman (1957) *Selected Contributions to Psycho-analysis*, London: Hogarth.

Rickman, J. (1951) 'Methodology and research in psycho-pathology', *British Journal of Medical Psychology*, 24: 1–7; also in Rickman (1957) *Selected Contributions to Psycho-analysis*, London: Hogarth.

Rickman, J. (1957) 'Number and the human sciences', in Rickman, *Selected Contributions to Psycho-analysis*, London: Hogarth.

Riviere, J. (1936) 'A contribution to the analysis of the negative therapeutic reaction', in A. Hughes (ed.) (1991) *The Inner World and Joan Riviere, Collected Papers 1920–1958*, London: Karnac Books.

Roheim, G. (1930) *Animism, Magic and the Divine King*, London: Kegan Paul, Trench, Trubner & Co.

Rorty, R. (1991) 'Freud and moral reflection', in R. Rorty, *Essays on Heidegger and Others*, Cambridge: Cambridge University Press.

Rosen, I. (1974) *Genesis: The Process of Creativity*, exhibition catalogue, London: Camden Arts Centre.

Rubens, R. (1984) 'The meaning of structure in Fairbairn', *International Review of Psychoanalysis*, 11: 428–40.

Rubens, R. (1994) 'Fairbairn's structural theory', in J.S. Grotstein and D.B. Rinsley (eds), *Fairbairn and the Origins of Object Relations*, London: Free Association Press.

Rubens, R. (1996) 'Review essay: the unique origins of Fairbairn's theories', *Psychoanalytic Dialogues*, 6: 413–35.

Rubens, R. (1998) 'Fairbairn's theory of depression', in N.J. Skolnick and D.E. Scharff (eds), *Fairbairn, Then and Now*, London: The Analytic Press.

Rustin, M. (1991) 'Psychoanalysis, philosophical realism and the new sociology of science', in Rustin, *The Good Society and the Inner World*, London: Verso.

Rustin, M. (1996) 'Attachment in context', in S. Kroemer and J. Roberts (eds), *The Politics of Attachment*, 212–28.

Rustin, M. (2001) *Reason and Unreason: Psychoanalysis, Science and Politics*, London: Continuum Interaction Publishing Group.
Sandler, J., Holder, A., Dare, C., and Dreher, A.U. (1997) *Freud's Models of the Mind*, London: Karnac.
Scharff, D.E. (1982) *The Sexual Relationship: An Object Relations View of Sex and the Family*, London: Routledge and Kegan Paul.
Scharff, D.E., and Fairbairn Birtles, E. (eds) (1994) *From Instinct to Self*, 2 vols, London: Jason Aronson.
Scharff, D.E., and Fairbairn Birtles, E. (1997) 'From instinct to self: the evolution and implications of W.R.D. Fairbairn's theory of object relations', *International Journal of Psychoanalysis*, 78 (6): 1085–103.
Segal, H. (1990) *Dream, Phantasy and Art*, London: Routledge.
Segal, H. (1996). 'Comments on Brenner's paper: the mind as conflict and compromise formation'. Online. Available HTTP: <http://users.rcn.com/brill/segal.html> (accessed 1996).
Shumar, W. (1999) 'Beyond anthropocentrism in ethics', *Alethia* 2 (2): 26–30.
Skolnick, N.J. (1998) 'The good, the bad and the ambivalent: Fairbairn's difficulty locating the good object in the endopsychic structure', in N.J. Skolnick and D.E. Scharff (eds), *Fairbairn, Then and Now*, London: The Analytic Press.
Skolnick, N.J., and Scharff, D.E. (eds) (1998) *Fairbairn, Then and Now*, London: The Analytic Press.
Slade, A. (2000) 'The development and organisation of attachment: implications for psychoanalysis', *Journal of the American Psychoanalytic Association*, 48 (4): 1147–74.
Steele, H., and Steele, M. (1998a) 'Attachment and psychoanalysis: time for a reunion', *Social Development*, 7 (1): 92–119.
Steele, H. and Steele, M. (1998b) 'Response to Cassidy, Lyons-Ruth and Bretherton: a return to exploration', *Social Development*, 7 (1): 137–41.
Stern, D. (1985) *The Interpersonal World of the Infant: A View from Psychoanalysis and Developmental Psychology*, New York: Basic Books.
Stevenson, R.L. (2004) *Dr Jekyll and Mr Hyde*, London: Penguin Books.
Sutherland, J.D. (1989) *Fairbairn's Journey into the Interior*, London: Free Association Books.
Sutherland, J.D. (1993) 'The autonomous self', *Bulletin of the Menninger Clinic*, 57 (1): 3–32.
Suttie, I.D. (1960) *The Origins of Love and Hate*, London: Pelican (first published 1935).
Symington, N. (1986) *The Analytic Experience: Lectures from the Tavistock*, London: Free Association Books.
Trevarthen, C. (2002) 'Proof of sympathy: the scientific evidence on the personality of the infant in Macmurray's mother and child', in D. Ferguson and N. Dower (eds), *John Macmurray: Critical Perspectives*, 77–117, London: Peter Lang.
Ward, L. (2005) 'Britain in top ten for closing gender gap', *The Guardian*, 17 May.
Will, D. (1980) 'Psychoanalysis as a human science', *British Journal of Medical Psychology*, 53: 201–11.
Will, D. (1986) 'Psychoanalysis and the new philosophy of science', *International Review of Psychoanalysis*, 13: 163–73.
Williams, R. (1977) *Marxism and Literature*, Oxford: Oxford University Press.

Winnicott, D.W. (1965) *The Maturational Processes and the Facilitating Environment; Studies in the Theory of Emotional Development*, London: Hogarth.

Winnicott, D.W. (1971) 'Mirror-role of mother and family in child development', in Winnicott (1971) *Playing and Reality*, London: Penguin.

Winnicott, D.W. (1989) 'D.W.W. on D.W.W', in C. Winnicott, R. Shepherd and M. Davis (eds), *Psychoanalytic Explorations*, Cambridge, MA: Harvard University Press.

Winnicott, D.W., and Khan, M.M.R. (1953) 'Review of *Psychoanalytic Studies of the Personality* by W. R. D. Fairbairn', *International Journal of Psychoanalysis*, 34: 329–33.

Wintour, P. (2005) 'Labour gurus call for a return to egalitarianism', *The Guardian*, 25th May. Online. Available HTTP: <http://society.guardian.co.uk> (accessed 25 May 2005).

'Wiping away the snobbish drips of the art world' (2005) 'Comment', 22 May. Online. Available HTTP: <http://www.timesonline.co.uk> (accessed 22 May 2005).

Wollheim, R., and Hopkins, J. (eds) (1982) *Philosophical Essays on Freud*, London: Cambridge University Press.

Wright, K. (1991) *Vision and separation*, London: Free Association Books.

Wright, K. (1995) 'Painting and the self: a psychoanalytic perspective on art', unpublished manuscript.

Young, R.M. (1998) 'What is psychoanalytic studies?' Online. Available HTTP: <http://www.human-nature.com/rmyoung/papers.> (accessed 1998).

Index

Page entries for main headings which have subheadings refer to general aspects of that topic.
Page entries for figures appear in *italics*. Page entries for tables appear in **bold**.

abuse, child 1, 149; *see also* maternal deprivation
action: approach based on 2, 144, 145–50, 168; primacy of 137–8, 141, 151, 154–5; *see also* critical realism
adaptations, infant 137–8
Adult Attachment Interview (AAI) 174, 179, 180
aesthetic experience/pleasure 92, 94–6; *see also* art, Fairbairn's theory of
aggression: basic/fundamental 15, 18, 85; between subselves 32, 33, 35–6, 46, 79, 89; infantile 149, 157–8, 161–5; secondary nature 149, 175; *see also* death instinct; destructive phantasies
Alvarez, Anne, depressive/paranoid-schizoid relationship 67
ambivalence: attachment pattern 172, 174, 178, 179; to original object 46–8, 81, 82, 86, 155; personal relations 16–17, 81, 82, 86, 155–6; *see also* disillusion, benign; withdrawal and return
The Analytic Experience, Neville Symington 19
anti-libidinal ego *see* libidinal/anti-libidinal ego
anxious attachment 178
anxiety, separation 28
art, Fairbairn's theory 13–14, 91, 105; appreciation 92; destruction–restitution thesis 93, 94, 96, 100, 101; and dream-work 92–3, 97; found objects 94, 95, 101; as fun 92, 94, 98,
99; and mature theory of dynamic structure 91, 97–8, 101–5; primary/secondary processes 97–8, 103–4; and repression 92–4, 103, 108–10; as solitary activity 100; as sublimation 93, 96, 103; symbolism 94–6, 99, 101; and unconscious needs 92–6, 101, 103, 106; *see also* creativity
artistic creativity theory 100–3, 105
Attachment and Loss, John Bowlby 175
attachment theory 3, 65, 142, 169; biological basis 175, 176; cultural/social expectations 177, 184; forms/patterns of attachment 169, 172, 174, 177–9, 184; internal working model of mother 172–4, *173*, 176, 177; and mature dependence 187; and object relations theory 171–6; proponents 169–71; and psychoanalysis 170–1; and psychology of dynamic structure 176–80; to significant others/more than one 176; and social welfare 169, 180–2, 185–6; *see also* science and psychoanalysis
avoidant attachment pattern 172, 174, 178, 179

bad: boy 161–2, 163, 164–5; objects 75, 77, 83
Balint, M., studying 143
basic fault 130–1
Being and Worth, Andrew Collier 135, 144, 150–3, 165–8

belief 166; *see also*
    rationality/irrationality; reason and
    emotion
benign disillusion *see* disillusion, benign
Bhaskar, Roy: *The Possibility of*
    Naturalism 144, 145–6, 168; *A Realist*
    Theory of Science 144
bio-social feedback 178
biology: and attachment behaviour 175,
    176; death instinct, objections to 140
Bion, W. R: depressive/paranoid-schizoid
    relationship 69; internal object 75
bizarre: behaviour 178, 179; objects 75
Black Sun, Julia Kristeva 79
Bowlby, John 138, 142, 169–70;
    Attachment and Loss 175; attachment
    theory 169–71; parallels with
    Fairbairn's theories 172, 174–5, 175–6;
    A Secure Base 172, 176; *Separation* 175

cave drawings 94
censorship, unconscious/preconscious
    122–3, 124, 127
central ego 36–9, 44, *51*, 67, 69, 128, 167;
    see also ideal object
change: avoiding 79, 80, 90;
    mother–infant relationship 163
child abuse 1, 149; *see also* maternal
    deprivation; mother-child relationship
circulating information 15
clinical settings, Fairbairn 20–1
closed system, depression as 79, 80, 90
Collier, Andrew: *Being and Worth* 135,
    144, 150–3, 165–8
Conditions of Freedom, John Macmurray
    153
Confessions of a Justified Sinner, James
    Hogg 4
conflict: manifestations of
    separation/union 52–5, **54**, 69;
    resolution 100
conscience *see* morality
contingency: detection 178; of object
    147–9
'Controversial Discussions' 14–15, 56,
    72, 143
conversion, hysterical *see* hysterical states
courses, psychoanalytic studies, UK 143
creation, book of Genesis 105–6
creativity: artistic creativity theory
    100–3, 105; elaborational 112;
    inspirational 112, 113–14; and
    personal relations theory 13, 14, 22,

37, 44/*45*; and preconscious mind
109, 114, 120–1, 122; regression
111–12; and splitting 2, 9, 37; stages
105–6; *see also* art; psychic
change/growth
critical realism 2, 144, 145–50, 168
cultural influences on self 10, 18, 140–1,
177, 184

da Vinci, Leonardo 102
Dali, Salvador: surrealist object 94;
    Visage Paranoiaque 95
Davidson, Donald: 'Paradoxes of
    irrationality' 12, 56–9, 61, 166–7, 172;
    partitions of the mind 13, 58, 59, 61,
    172
death instinct 18, 75, 84–5, 93, 151;
    biological objections 140; *see also*
    aggression; destructive phantasies
decency *see* morality
deconstructionism, studying 144
defensive mechanisms 11–12, 15, 79;
    internalisation 28–9, *30*, 81, 152, 155;
    splitting as 11–12, 155; *see also* manic
    defence; moral defence; repression
deficit theory 104
demoniacal possession 83; *see also* bad
    objects
denial, of loss 79, 80
dependence *see* infantile dependence;
    mature dependence; transition,
    infantile/mature
depression: and depressive position 87;
    Fairbairn on 68–9, 71, 78–80, 90
depressive position 34, 165; and art 101;
    and depressive illness 87; and Klein's
    model 21, 32, 39, 67–9, *68*, 70;
    Likierman's perspective 85–7;
    moral/tragic motif 85, 86, 88–90;
    Ruben's model 78–80, 89
deprivation, maternal *see* maternal
    deprivation; *see also* disillusion, benign
destruction–restitution thesis 93, 94, 96,
    100, 101
destructive phantasies 10, 11, 92, 93;
    disavowal/defences against 11, 15, 79;
    see also aggression; death instinct
development: first year of life 24–5;
    morality 159, 160, 161; stages 152, 153
devil, possession 83; *see also* bad objects
diagrams, models of mind 23, 34–6;
    central ego in control *51*; creativity *45*;
    depressive/paranoid-schizoid position

34; dreams/daydreams *41*, *42*; dynamics *36*; ego-ideal/superego *33*; endopsychic structure *26*, *32*, *33*, *48*; fusion to separation process *28*; fuzzy *35*; hysterical conversion *43*; incorporation, object *30*; mature dependence *51*; object relations origin *31*; Oedipus situation *49*, *50*; original model 118, *119*; original object *27*, *30*; psychic growth *42*, *45*; repression barrier *37*; similar strength sub-selves *50*; splitting, original object *30*, *31*
Dictionary of Kleinian Thought, R. D. Hinshelwood 76
differentiation of object 28/*28*; *see also* transition, infantile/mature dependence
disillusion, benign 139–40, 152, 155–60, 184; and dynamic structure 163–5; and fear 159, 160, 161, 164; and morality development 159, 160, 161; negative outcomes 139, 163; positive outcomes 160–2, 163, 164; rage 149, 157–8; relationship changes 163; and submissiveness/aggression 161–2, 163, 164–5; *see also* maternal deprivation; splitting; withdrawal and return
dissociation 11, 115; *see also* splitting
'Dissociation and Repression' MD thesis, W. R. D. Fairbairn 3, 11
distraction-soothing 179–80
The Divided Self, Ronald Laing 4
Dr Jekyll and Mr Hyde 4
dreams/daydreams 38, 39, 42–3, *41*, *42*; and art 92–3, 97; instinct derivatives 121; and preconscious mind 109, 111, 113, 125; and regression 19, 111–12, 125, 127; symbolism/interpretation 147–8
drive theory/model 128, 131, 171, 175; *see also* libido; motivation; pleasure principle; reality principle
dual-track hypothesis 20, 21, 70, 71, 87, 89
dynamic structures, internal objects as 23, 34, *36*, 69–71, 77; *see also* mature theory of endopsychic structure

ego 57; central 36–9, 44, *51*, 67, 69, 128, 167; original 15, 18, 68, 149, 152, 183; pristine 15, 18, 149, 152, 183; regression 111–12; *see also* ego-ideal; integration/synthesis; libidinal/anti-libidinal ego; original object; self
ego-ideal 29, 31, *33*, 63, 88; and preconscious mind 112, 113, 116–17, 121, 127; *see also* central ego; ideal object; original object
The Ego and the Id, Sigmund Freud 25
ego-structure(s): activity as unconscious phantasy 72; closed system relations between 79; and conscious self 63; and dreams 148; as dynamic structure 72; in Fairbairn's theory 24–5; and internal objects 19, 73; and preconscious 14; and primary process 62–3, 97–8, 104; and psychic growth/creativity 104–5; and secondary process 97–8, 104; and sublimation 97–8, 103; *see also* dynamics structures, endopsychic structure
elaborational creation 112
emergent self 100
emotion, and reason 153, 165–7; *see also* rationality/irrationality
emotional needs, unconscious *see* unconscious needs
endopsychic structures theory *see* mature theory of endopsychic structure
'Endopsychic structure considered in terms of object-relationships' 45–6, 115, 151
energy, psychic 116
enlightenment, Scottish 4, 136, 168
erotic imagination 10
Essays on Heidegger and others 61
Essex Institute for Psychoanalytic Studies 67
ethics *see* morality
evil, good and 93, 94, 96, 100, 101
exciting objects *see* libidinal/anti-libidinal ego
externalising internal objects 60, 152–3, 156

face, maternal, as protosymbol 102
Fairbairn, W. R. D. (Ronald) 2–5; comparison with Klein 74–5, 84–5; critique of Freud 4, 27–8, 57, 59, 151; critique of Klein 4, 29, 56, 73; Hinshelwood on 76–7; influence of Klein 11, 13, 71–4, 77, 99; on inner reality 149, 150, 157, 183; libido theory 70, 115, 154; links with attachment theory 169–70, 172–6; philosophical

training 20, 137; on preconscious mind 115, 116–21, 126; school of influence, failure to promote 4, 21, 136, 137; scientific approach to psychoanalysis 147; studying 143; on superego 117–18, 166; Sutherland on 99–100; on system unconscious 150, 153, 156; Will's critique of 147–50; writings *see below*; *see also* mature theory of endopsychic structure; personal relations theory

Fairbairn, W. R. D. (Ronald), publications by/about: 'A critical evaluation of certain basic psycho-analytical conceptions' 26–7; 'Dissociation and Repression' MD thesis 3, 11; 'Endopsychic structure considered in terms of object-relationships' 45–6, 115, 151; *From Instinct to Self* 3, 10; 'Observations on the nature of hysterical states' 23–5, 43, 60, 115, 148; 'Prolegoma to a Psychology of Art' 91; *Psychoanalytic Studies of the Personality* 3, 10, 91, 151; 'A revised psychopathology of the psychoses and psychoneuroses' 16, 52; 'Steps in the development of an object relations theory of the personality' 72; 'The ultimate basis of aesthetic experience' 94

Fairbairn Birtles, Ellinor and Scharff, David: *From Instinct to Self* 3, 10

false self 38

fantasy *see* phantasy

fear: and hatred 159, 175; and maternal disillusion 159, 160, 161, 164; personal relations theory 139, 140, 141, 149

feeling, structure of 5–6

feral children 1

Ferenczi, S. on superego 117–18

found objects 94; unconscious significance 95, 101; *see also* art

freedom *see* morality; rights

Freud, Sigmund 3, 14; critique by Fairbairn 4, 27–8, 57, 59, 151; on death drive 18, 75, 93, 151; on inner reality 148, 166; on libido/life drive 23, 26–7, 92–3; need for revision 70; object relations aspects of theories 60; structural theory 57, 59, 60; studying 143; on superego 32, *33*, 57, 166; on unconscious mind 61, 150; writings *see below*

Freud, Sigmund, publications by/about: *The Ego and the Id* 25; *Freud's Models of the Mind* 23; 'Freud and moral reflection' 56, 61, 62, 64–6; 'Mourning and Melancholia' 79; *Philosophical Essays on Freud* 57

fun, making things for 92, 94, 98, 99; *see also* art

fusion 47, **47**, 49, 69, 82

gender identification 49, 177
Genesis, book of 105–6
genital character 188
Gifford Lectures 145
God 20, 135–6
Going Sane, Adam Phillips 65
good: boy 161–2, 163, 164–5; -enough relationships 152; and evil, restitution/reparation phantasies 93, 94, 96, 100, 101; object *see* original object
good object: and Fairbairn 119; and Grotstein 87–9, 126; internalisation of 69, 80–3, 136; and Likierman 85–6, 88–90; and Mitchell 125; and moral defence 17; and psychic growth 17; and Rubens 126
Grotstein, J. S: interpretation of Likierman 87–90; mature theory, views 83–5, 87, 126, 128, 149
growth, psychic *see* psychic change/growth; *see also* developmental stages
guilt, absolution 112–13
Guntrip, Harry 5, 19–20; *Personality Structure and Human Interaction* 19; *Schizoid Phenomena, Object-Relations and the Self* 19

hallucination 108–9, 113
happiness, through relationships 1
hatred, and fear 159, 175
hedonism *see* pleasure principle
Hinshelwood, R. D. views on Fairbairn 76–7
Hogg, James: *Confessions of a Justified Sinner* 4
hypercathexis 129; *see also* psychic change/growth
hysterical states 23–5, 43–4/*43*, 53, **54**, 69; Fairbairn's 'Observations on the nature of ' 23–5, 43, 60, 115, 148

Index

id 57; redundancy of concept 70
ideal object 118, 121, 127; *see also* central ego; ego-ideal; original object
identification: parental 47–8; projective 15–16, 18, 39–41, 70
imagination, erotic 10; *see also* dreams/daydreams; unconscious needs
impingement concept 161–2
incorporation, object *see* internalisation
indirect repression: in Fairbairn's theory 24–5; and Oedipus situation 46; and preconscious 108; and two-person relationship 130; *see also* repression
individuality 2
infant: adaptations 137–8; development process, first year of life 24–5; research 141; *see also* mother–child relationship
infantile dependence 16, 22, 50, 152; abandoning 28, 52; rage 149, 157–8; *see also* transition, infantile/mature
information structures 15
inner reality: Davidson on 57–9; Fairbairn's conception 147, 149, 150, 157, 183; Freud's conception 148, 166; and Kleinian concept of phantasy 72; splitting 59, 148; truthful representation 100
insecure-ambivalent attachment 172, 174, 178, 179
insecure-avoidant attachment 172, 174, 178, 179
inspirational creation 112, 113–14
From Instinct to Self, David Scharff and Ellinor Fairbairn Birtles 3, 10
instinct derivatives 121; *see also* libido
integration/synthesis, ego 12, 60, 63–4, 110, 122–4, 129, 174; transformation of repressed contents 39, 44, 125, 127–8, 140; *see also* psychic change/growth; mature dependence; transition
internal objects 56, 58, 59, 73–6; dynamic structures 23, 70; externalising 60, 152–3, 156; model of mother 172–4, *173*, 176, 177; superego as 72, 166; *see also* internalisation
internalisation, good object 39, 69, 80–3, 88–90, 119; defensive role 28–9, *30*, 81, 152, 155; inevitability 152, 155, 156; structuring/non-structuring 13; *see also* internal objects
Interpreting the Universe, John Macmurray 153

introjection 72–3; *see also* internalisation
intuitive position 37

jealousy: and fear 159; Oedipal 47
Jung, C. G. studying 143

Klein, Melanie 2; aggressive/dark basis of self 15, 18; comparison with Fairbairn 74–5, 84–5; concept of phantasy 72; critique, by Fairbairn 4, 29, 56, 73; death instinct 18, 75, 151; depressive position 21, 32, 39, 67–9, *68*, 70; influence on Fairbairn 11, 13, 71–4, 77, 99; introjection 72–3; libido/instinct emphasis 72, 77; phantasy 15, 56, 67; projective identification 15, 70; studying 143; *see also* Kleinian model of mind; paranoid-schizoid position
Kleinian model of mind 34, *34*, 137; comparison, endopsychic model 67, 68, 69, 70; reconciliation with endopsychic model 71, 88, 128; unconscious 15, 56, 67, 73
Kris, Ernst: *Psychoanalytic Explorations in Art* 91, 97–9, 120
Kristeva, Julia: *Black Sun* 79

Lacan, J: studying 143–4; subject 68; Will's views 150
Laing, Ronald: *The Divided Self* 4
layering 47/**47**, 49, 69, 82
Leonardo da Vinci 102
libidinal/anti-libidinal ego 24–5, 31–2, *31*, 36–9, 47–8, 83–4; resistance to therapy 69, 90; *see also* sub-selves; splitting
libido 16–17, 114, 156; Fairbairn's views 70, 115, 154; Freudian theory 23, 26–7, 92–3; Kleinian theory 72, 77; *see also* drive theory/model; motivation; pleasure principle; reality principle
life drive/principle *see* libido
Likierman, Meira: depressive position 85–7; Grotstein's interpretation 87–90
Locke, John, state of nature theories 183, 184
loss: attachment figures 170; denial of, and depression 79, 80; good object 85–6
love 149, 175; murder of those we love 1; unconditional 168; *see also* libido

Macmurray, John 2, 135; contribution to attachment theory 169–70; disillusion 139–40; and Fairbairn, parallels/influences 135, 144, 150–3, 153–6; infant adaptations 137–8; primacy of action 137–8, 141, 151, 154–5; rationality/irrationality 135; religious dimension 135; self in relation concept 138; and Suttie 135; writings *see below*; *see also* personal relations theory

Macmurray, John, publications: *Conditions of Freedom* 153; Gifford Lectures 145; *Interpreting the Universe* 153; *Persons in Relation* 5, 20, 145, 151, 175; *Reason and Emotion* 151, 153; 'The rhythm of withdrawal and return' 157–62; *The Self as Agent* 145

manic: defence 37, 120; womb 114, 132

masochistic states 53, **54**, 69

maternal deprivation 75, 79, 84–5, 138, 149, 170; *see also* child abuse; disillusion, benign

maternal face, as protosymbol 102

matriarchy 140–1, 187

mature dependence 16, 17, 22, *51*, 56–7; externalising internal objects 60, 152–3, 156; and genital character 188; as goal state/ideal 59, 188–9; and morality 156; realistic objects 51; Rorty on 59–60; and secure attachment 177, 187; *see also* integration/synthesis; psychic growth/change

mature theory of endopsychic structure 2, 3, 9, 10, 13, 15; and art 91, 97–8, 103–5; and attachment theory 176–80; cultural dependence 18; and Freud's structural theory 71; Grotstein's views 83–5, 87, 126, 128, 149; importance of dynamics in 23, 34, *36*, 67, 69–71, 77; integration of split selves 12; and Klein's model of mind 34, 67–71, 88, 128; model 23, 36–7, 118, *119*; modifications/criticisms 115, 125–6, *129*; object relations basis 70; as open system 71, 89; and phantasy 72; and preconscious 115, 120; and psychic energy 116; topographical categories 127–8, 132; and unconscious 115; *Weltanschauungen* 84; *see also* diagrams; personal relations theory; psychic change/growth

Milner, Marion: *On Not Being Able to Paint* 91, 96–7

mind: mechanisation of 60, 61, 65, 66; partitions 13, 58, 59, 61, 172; as society of minds 58, 59, 61–2, 172; *see also* splitting; sub-selves

minimal works of art 94

mirroring: affect 178–9; mother–infant 183; paintings as mirrors 102–3

Mitchell, S. A.: Klein/Fairbairn comparison 74–5

models, of mind diagrams *see* diagrams, models of mind

models, of mother, internal working 172–4, *173*, 176, 177; *see also* original object

Money-Kyrle, Roger: 'Psycho-analysis and ethics' 61

moral: defence 13, 17, 161; motif, depressive position 85, 86, 88, 89, 90

morality 22, 60–3; development 159–61; and mature dependence 156; public/private 64

mother: internal working model 172–4, *173*, 176, 177; specialist 188, 189; *see also* original object

mother–child relationship 101–2, 138; changes 163; maternal face as protosymbol 102; mirroring 183; phantasy in absence of mother 157; substitutes for 185; *see also* disillusion, benign; maternal deprivation; withdrawal and return

mother–infant dyad 1; *see also* mother–child relationship

motivation, object-seeking 23, 27, 99, 147, 149, 151, 171, 183; *see also* drive-theory; libido; pleasure principle; reality principle

multiple self model 91, 142, 172; *see also* mature theory of endopsychic structure; splitting; sub-selves

murder, of those we love 1

narcissism 152

neurological perspective 12

neurosis 152

Nietzsche, F. W. on self-enlargement 64

nursing couple 1; *see also* mother–child relationship

object: bad 75, 77, 83; bizarre 75; contingency of 147–9; ideal 118;

pre-linguistic 10; realistic 51; *see also* internal object/internalisation; libidinal/anti-libidinal ego; original object
object relations psychoanalysis 144, 151; and attachment theory 171, 175; proponents 182–3, 187; state of nature theories 183–4; *see also* personal relations theory; politics
object relations theory of personality 2, 3–4, 60, 62; and art 98, 101; as basis of other psychoanalytic theories 9, 10, *31*, 60, 70; synopsis 25–33; *see also* personal relations theory
object-seeking motivation 23, 27, 99, 147, 149, 151, 171, 183; *see also* drive-theory; libido; pleasure principle; reality principle
obsessional states 53, **54**, 69
Oedipus situation, Fairbairn's conception 46–9, *48*, *49*, 187; ambivalence 46, 47, 48; conflict/resolution *49*, *50*; fusion 47, **47**, 49, 69, 82; jealousy 46–7; layering 47–8/**47**, 49, 69, 82; parental identification 48; primal scene 46–7; two/three-person relationships 129–31
Ogden, Thomas, views on internal object 75–6
On Not Being Able to Paint, Marion Milner 91, 96–7
open systems 71, 89, 148
original ego 15, 18, 68, 149, 152, 183
original object *27*, *30*, 118; ambivalence towards 46–8, 81, 82, 86, 155; and art 102, 104–5; incorporation into individual 28, 29, *30*, 39, 69; loss 85–6; and repression 81–2; restoration 100; return to consciousness 82; unconscious/preconscious 81, 89; *see also* mother-child relationship; transition, infantile/mature dependence; splitting; withdrawal and return
original sin 15, 18, 152, 183
The Origins of Love and Hate 5, 136, 169–70
overcoming process 18, 87
over-symbolisation 95–6, 99

Padel, John 10, 12–14; on psychic change/growth 12–13, 37–41, 60, 89, 104–5, 125, 167; process 127, 128, 140

paintings as mirrors 102
'Paradoxes of Irrationality', Donald Davidson 12, 56, 57, 161, 166–7; and inner reality 57–9; mind as society of minds 58, 59, 61, 172
paranoid-schizoid position *34*, 39, 67–70, *68*, 77, 87, 165; *see also* schizoid phenomena/position
paranoid states 53–4, **54**, 69
parental identification, exciting/rejecting objects 48
partitions of the mind 13, 58, 59, 61, 172; *see also* splitting; sub-selves
pathology 17–18, 38, 152, 168; degree relative to degree of splitting 177; infant 149; source, Klein/Fairbairn comparison 75, 84–5; structure as 88, 126, 127; *see also* maternal deprivation; system unconscious
patriarchy 140–1
perception, role of projective identification 18
personal relations theory 2, 4, 5–6, 135, 141, 168; fear 139, 140, 141, 149; primacy of action 137–8, 141, 151, 154–5; reality-orientation 141; social nature, innate 1–2, 141; *see also* mature theory of endopsychic structure; politics
personal relationships, central role 1–2, 141
personality, object relations theory of *see* object relations theory of personality; *see also* personal relations theory
Personality Structure and Human Interaction, Harry Guntrip 19
Persons in Relation, John Macmurray 5, 20, 145, 151, 175
persons-in-relation perspective 2; *see also* object relations theory of personality; personal relations theory
phenomenological approach 21
phantasy 15, 56, 67, 72; in absence of mother 157; Fairbairn critique 73; regression 111–12; restitution/reparation 93, 94, 96, 100, 101; unconscious 114
Philosophical Essays on Freud 57
phobic states 52, **54**, 69
play 109, 114; *see also* art; creativity
pleasure principle 23, 26–7, 92, 99, 123, 147; *see also* drive theory/model;

libido; motivation; reality principle
politics of attachment 3, 169, 180–2; and object relations psychoanalysis 183–9; social order, radical concept 188–9; and social welfare 169, 181, 185–8; and women's rights 188–9
The Politics of Attachment 169, 170, 180–1
The Politics of Uncertainty 169
The Possibility of Naturalism, Roy Bhaskar 144, 145–6, 168
postmodernism 144
poststructuralism 144
potential space concept 131–2
preconscious: and access to consciousness 82; and bodily self 150; and early self 38; and ego-ideal 81; and Grotstein 87–8; importance of 13, 14, 15, 21–2; and the manic 37; and mature dependence 153; psychic change 115–32; and psychic growth 39; as repository of good objects 89; and Rosen 106; structured 38; vs system unconscious 17; *see also* preconscious mental processes
preconscious mental processes 106, 107–14; censorship 122–3, 124, 127; centrality 128–31; contents 122; creativity/play 109, 112–14, 120–1, 122; definition 121; dreaming 109, 111, 113, 125; ego-ideal 112, 113, 116–17, 121, 127; ego integration/synthesis 110, 122, 124, 129; ego regression 111–12; Fairbairn's conception 115, 116–21, 126; and good object 81, 89; guilt, absolution 112–13; hallucination 108–9, 113; libido 114; making conscious 109, 111, 113, 125, 174; mature theory of endopsychic structure 115, 120; mediating role 127; nature of 121–4; phantasy 114; in absence of mother 157; psychic energy 107–8, 111, 113, 114; reactions to reaching consciousness 112; reality principle 123; repression/disguised material 108–10; role 14, 17, 21–2; structured 128, 129; and superego 112, 117–18; verbal 122, 123; *see also* integration/synthesis
pre-natal existence 19
primal scene 46–7
primary processes 62, 97–8, 103–4; repression 24, 62

pristine ego 15, 18, 149, 152, 183
projective identification 15–16, 18, 39–41, 70
psychic energy 106–8, 114, 116; discharge 111, 113
psychic growth/change 17, 20, 44; and art 91, 104–5; and benign disillusion 160, 164; diagrams *42*, *45*; failure 160–2; Fairbairn's conception 56–7, 64, 167; integration/synthesis, ego 110, 124, 129; mature theory 38, 39–40, 115; Padel's conception 12–13, 37–41, 89, 104–5, 125, 167; process 125, 127, 128, 140, 167–8; Rorty on 60; Ruben's conception 36–7; transformation of repressed contents 39, 44, 125, 127–8, 140; *see also* integration/synthesis; mature dependence
'Psycho-analysis and ethics', Roger Money-Kyrle 61
psychoanalysis: objections to 11; resistance to 69, 90
'Psychoanalysis as a human science', David Will 147
'Psychoanalysis and the new philosophy of science', David Will 147
Psychoanalytic Explorations in Art, Ernst Kris 91, 97–9, 120
psychoanalytic studies: academic/clinical approaches 144, 151; courses, UK 143; schools of influence 4, 21, 136, 137, 143
psychopathy *see* pathology
psychosis 152
psychosomatic illness 43, *43*; *see also* hysterical states

rage, infantile 149, 157–8
rationality/irrationality 135; *see also* reason and emotion
realism, critical 2, 144, 145–50, 168
A Realist Theory of Science, Roy Bhaskar 144
reality, inner *see* inner reality
reality-orientation, personal relations theory 1–2, 141
reality principle 27, 92, 123, 155; *see also* drive theory/model; motivation; pleasure principle
Reason and Emotion, John Macmurray 151, 153
reason and emotion 153, 165–7; *see also* rationality/irrationality

reductionism 149
reflective functioning 169
regression: during sleep 19, 111–12, 125, 127; to primary process level 97–8, 103–4
rejecting objects *see* libidinal/anti-libidinal ego
relational model 131; see also mature theory; object relations; object-seeking; pleasure principle
relationships: good enough 152; and happiness 1; therapeutic 21, 147; transference 21, 39–40, 147; two/three-person 129–31; *see also* mother–child relationship; object relations theory; personal relations theory
relativism studying 144
religion 20, 135–6
reparation 90; phantasies, and art 93, 94, 96, 100, 101
repetition compulsion 151
repression 11, 59, 61; and artistic expression 92–4, 103, 108–10; failure 68, 69; internal object 24, 81–2; overcoming barrier 36, *37*, 39, 40; primary/secondary 24, 62; recognition/recall 109–10; and resistance to therapy 69, 90
'Repression, Dissociation and' MD thesis, W. R. D. Fairbairn 3, 11
restitution 90; phantasies, and art 93, 94, 96, 100, 101
'The rhythm of withdrawal and return', John Macmurray 157–62
rights: individual 184, 185, 186; women's 188–9
Rorty, Richard: on Davidson 61; *Essays on Heidegger and others* 61; 'Freud and moral reflection' 56, 61, 62, 64–6; maturity/mature dependence 59–60, 63–5; mechanisation of mind 60, 61, 65, 66; mind as society of minds 62; morality 60–3; narratives, social/intellectual 65–6; and object relations model 60, 62; psychic change 60; self-knowledge 63; on unconscious 62, 63
Rosen, Ismond: creativity, stages 105–6; preconscious 106
Rubens, R: depressive position 78–80, 89; pathology and structure 126, 127

sadistic states 53, **54**, 69

sadness, and depression 79, 80, 89
Scharff, David and Birtles, Ellinor Fairbairn: *From Instinct to Self* 3, 10
Schizoid Phenomena, Object-Relations and the Self, Harry Guntrip 19
schizoid phenomena/position 32, 76–9, 87, 90, 115, 132; *see also* paranoid-schizoid position
schizophrenia 87
schools of influence, psychoanalytic 4, 21, 136, 137, 143
science/scientific: approach to psychoanalysis 141–2, 144, 145–50, **146**, 147; biological basis of attachment 175, 176; objectivity 18; reductionism 149; three-phase scheme of scientific activity 163; *see also* attachment theory
Scottish: culture 156; enlightenment 4, 136, 168
secondary processes 24, 62, 97–8, 103–4, 123
secure attachment 177, 187; *see also* attachment theory
A Secure Base, John Bowlby 172, 176
Segal, Hanna: interpretation of Klein 70, 100, 101, 105
The Self as Agent, John Macmurray 145
self: Fairbairn's conceptualisation 9, 36–9, 44; multiple self model 91, 142, 172; need for comprehensive theory 135; as open system 71, 89, 148; in relation concept 138 *see also* ego; splitting; sub-selves
self-enlargement/self-expansion 13, 64, 103, 188; *see also* integration/synthesis; mature dependence; psychic growth/change
self integration *see* integration/synthesis; mature dependence; psychic growth/change
self-knowledge 63; *see also* integration/synthesis; mature dependence; psychic growth/change
self–other distinction 158
'Sensations' exhibition, Royal Academy 96
Separation, John Bowlby 175
separation anxiety 28
sex *see* libido/love
sharing/commonality 153–4
Skolnick, N. J. Fairbairn/Klein comparison 80–3, 89, 90

sleep *see* dreams/daydreams
social nature, innate 1–2, 141
social order, radical concept 188–9
social welfare 169, 181, 185–8
society of minds 58, 59, 61–2, 172; *see also* splitting; sub-selves
sociocultural influences *see* cultural influences
soothing-distraction 179–80
specialist mothers 188, 189
Spinoza, B. reason and emotion 153, 166
splitting 13, 29–30, *30–1*, 58, 156, 172; and creativity 2, 9, 37; as defensive mechanism 11–12, 155; degrees of 177, 178; and illness/death 2, 9; inevitability 150, 152, 155; inner reality 59, 148; making conscious 174; pathological 168; rejecting/exciting objects 24–5, 31–2, *31*, 36–9, 48, 83–4; and resistance to therapy 69, 90; as two-way process 127; unconscious 59, 61; *see also* integration/synthesis; sub-selves
state of nature theories 183–4
Strange Situation 177, 178, 180
structural theory 21, 166–7; Freudian 57, 59, 60, 71; *see also* mature theory of endopsychic structure
structure: as pathology 88, 126, 127; preconscious mind 128, 129
sublimation 93, 96, 103, 121
submissiveness 161–5
sub-selves 58–62, 91, 142, 172; aggressive relations between 32, 35–6, 46, 79, 89; conscious/unconscious 126, 128, 140, 174; disruption/repressive failure 68, 69; repression 59, 61; similar strength *50*; *see also* integration/synthesis; splitting
superego 23, 25, 115; and art 104; Fairbairn's conception 117–18, 166; Ferenczi on 117–18; Freud's conception 32, *33*, 57, 166; as internal object 72, 166; need for revision/importance of concept 70; and preconscious 112, 117–18
surrealist object 94
Sutherland, J. D.: on Fairbairn's art theory 99–100; on infant research 141
Suttie, Ian D. 2, 5, 135–6; contribution to attachment theory 169–70; sociocultural influences on self 140–1; *see also* personal relations theory

symbol/symbolism: art 94, 95, 101; contingency of 147; dreams 147–8; maternal face as protosymbol 102; over/under-symbolisation 95–6, 99
Symington, Neville: *The Analytic Experience* 19
symptoms, neurotic 43, *43*, 121
synthesis, ego *see* integration/synthesis
system unconscious 15, 17, 18, 22, 119, 150; Fairbairn's conception 150, 153, 156

tension, relief through art 92–4
terrorist attack, World Trade Center 1
therapeutic relationship 21, 147
three-phase scheme of scientific activity 163
topographical categories 14, 21, 115, 124–5, 127–8, 132
tragic motif 85, 86, 88–90
transference relationship 21, 40, 147
transformation *see* integration/synthesis; psychic growth/change
transition, infantile/mature dependence 16, 22, 28/*28*, 39–40, 50–1, 152, 176; separation/union conflict manifestations 52–5, **54**, 69; stages 52–3; transitional techniques 52–5, 140; *see also* integration/synthesis; psychic growth/change

unconscious: accessing through dreams 109, 111, 113, 125; contents, censorship 122–3, 124, 127; and dynamic structures 71; Fairbairn's conception 150, 153, 156; Freud's conception 61, 150; good object 81, 89; Kleinian view 15, 56, 67, 73; making conscious 174; mature theory of endopsychic structure 115; motives, obligation to explore 60–3; needs 94, 95, 96, 106; phantasy 14–15, 71, 114; Rorty on 62, 63; significance, found objects 95, 101; social/cultural nature 18; sub-selves 126, 128, 140, 174; system unconscious 15, 17, 18, 22, 119, 150; *see also* preconscious mind
unsatisfying relationship: and badness 75; and Fairbairn's theory 24; and good and bad objects 29; and Grotstein 87–8, 126; and introjection 152, 155; and Macmurray 161; and original object 28, 155, 163; and

origins of endopsychic structure 37, 139; and pre-ambivalent object 16; and preconscious ego-ideal 81; and splitting 149; as substitute for real relations 74; and transitional technique 54–5

Visage Paranoiaque, Salvador Dali 95

war neuroses 3, 12
Weltanschauungen 84
Will, David 145–50; 'Psychoanalysis as a human science' 147; 'Psychoanalysis and the new philosophy of science' 147
Winnicott, D. W. 1, 19, 100, 101, 137; impingement concept 161–2; potential space concept 131–2; studying 143

wisdom 61
wish fulfillment 94, 95; *see also* phantasy; unconscious needs
wishful thinking 59
withdrawal and return, mother 157–62; and fear 159, 160, 161; and morality development 159, 160, 161; phantasy in absence of mother 157; and psychic growth 160; rage at absence 157–8; submissiveness/aggression 161–2; *see also* disillusion, benign
women's rights 188–9
World Trade Center, terrorist attack 1
Wright, Ken, artistic creativity theory 100–3, 105

95 Artistic creation. Object fulfilling emotional needs. A tautology? unless we can specify the needs. Can we always? Perhaps art is most complete when we can't. Fairbairn' theory reductionist

107 The San Marco fallacy?

195 Rangy well beyond of analysis?